CONTRIBUTORS

George Archibald
Department of Psychiatry
University of Nebraska Medical Center
Omaha, Nebraska 68105

Jane Crowley
Department of Psychiatry
University of Nebraska Medical Center
Omaha, Nebraska 68105

Charles Golden
Department of Psychiatry
University of Nebraska Medical Center
Omaha, Nebraska 68105

Jeffrey Katz
Department of Psychiatry
University of Nebraska Medical Center
Omaha, Nebraska 68105

Iris Rucker
Department of Psychiatry
University of Nebraska Medical Center
Omaha, Nebraska 68105

Elizabeth Teegarden
Department of Psychiatry
University of Nebraska Medical Center
Omaha, Nebraska 68105

Forensic Neuropsychology

Edited by

Charles J. Golden

and

Mary Ann Strider

University of Nebraska
Omaha, Nebraska

PLENUM PRESS • NEW YORK AND LONDON

Library of Congress Cataloging in Publication Data

Luria–Nebraska Symposium on Neuropsychology (3rd: 1985: University of Nebraska
  Medical Center)
  Forensic neuropsychology.

  (Nebraska neuropsychology symposia series; v. 1)
  "Proceedings of the 1985 Luria-Nebraska Symposium on Neuropsychology, held May 6–
11, 1985, at the University of Nebraska Medical Center, Omaha, Nebraska"–T.p. verso.
  Includes bibliographies and index.
  1. Forensic neuropsychology–Congresses. 2. Luria–Nebraska Neuropsychological Bat-
tery–Congresses. I. Golden, Charles J., 1949–   . II. Strider, Mary Ann. III. Title. IV.
Series. [DNLM: 1. Expert Testimony–congresses. 2. Forensic Psychiatry–congresses.
3. Neuropsychological Tests–congresses. W3 LU974 3rd 1985/W740 L967 1985f]
RA1147.5.L87   1985   614′.1   86-21176
ISBN 0-306-42394-4

Proceedings of the 1985 Luria–Nebraska Symposium on Neuropsychology,
held May 6–11, 1985, at the University of Nebraska Medical Center,
Omaha, Nebraska

© 1986 Plenum Press, New York
A Division of Plenum Publishing Corporation
233 Spring Street, New York, N.Y. 10013

PREFACE

Neuropsychology has become an increasingly active participant
in forensic issues over the past decade. This has been the
result of increased recognition by psychologists of the potential
role they can play in evaluating patients involved in lawsuits
and the increasing sophistication of lawyers who have recognized
that damages can go beyond claims of physical and motoric
impairment.

However, this increase in involvement has not always been
matched by a more sophisticated recognition of how the client
(whether plaintiff or defendant) can best be served by the
neuropsychologist. I have personally seen or reviewed many cases
in which the psychologists involved did not effectively present
their case. This partially occurred because they failed to
recognize the difference in presentations aimed at clinical
audiences and those aimed at a legal proceeding. It also
occurred because they failed to recognize that the standard of
proof necessary is very different in a hospital and in a
courtroom. Finally, it occurred because they rarely recognized
what the unique role of the psychologist can be in either
countering or supporting the testimony of medical specialists.

The purpose of this volume is to bring some light on these
questions. The presentations here are write-ups of the work
presented at the Third Annual Conference on the Luria-Nebraska
Neuropsychological Battery held in Omaha during May, 1985. All
of the papers emphasize the role of the Luria-Nebraska but the
ideas can be used with almost any test.

The first paper in the volume is a detailed consideration
of some of the issues which face the neuropsychologist
testifying in court. This is followed by a series of papers
examining specific cases which raise important legal issues.
Two additional papers give an example of a deposition/testimony
in a case and the kind of psychometric information needed to
defend a procedure in court. The final paper gives a brief
introduction to the Nebraska Neuropsychological Evaluation, a
new test with which many of the readers of this volume are
unlikely to be familiar.

This volume is not a "how to" book on what to wear to
court, how to impress a judge, or how the legal system works.
Rather, we have attempted to deal with the issues of the kind of

information that can be presented by the neuropsychologist, how that information is ideally presented and investigated, and the issues one should be aware of in presenting testimony. In conjunction with other books which examine the more general areas omitted here, it is hoped that the volume will give the practitioner ideas and approaches which will be effective on a day to day basis.

This book is the first in a series of specific topics important to neuropsychology and the Luria-Nebraska. The second volume, scheduled for 1987, is to be on the topic of psychiatric uses.

Charles Golden
Omaha, Nebraska
May 15, 1986

CONTENTS

FORENSIC NEUROPSYCHOLOGY:

INTRODUCTION AND OVERVIEW

Charles J. Golden

Department of Psychiatry
University of Nebraska Medical Center
Omaha, Nebraska

One of the strong factors in the growth of clinical neuropsychology has been the use of such evaluations for legal evaluations. These cases have ranged from cases of social security disability to multi-million dollar lawsuits involving accidents and medical malpractice. Moreover, neuropsychology "defenses" have become more common in the litigation of murder cases both in terms of establishing guilt and innocence and as considerations in deciding on punishment.

Forensic cases have demanded an increasing sophistication on the part of the neuropsychologist beyond those issues encountered with other types of psychological testimony. These issues touch on the actual nature of neuropsychological testing, the ways in which such testing is conducted and interpreted, the relative strength of neuropsychological versus neurological examinations and the capacity of the neuropsychologist to testify in areas many lawyers (on the other side) see as essentially "medical" matters. The latter issue brings us to the difficult question of where the line is drawn between the expertise of the M.D. and the expertise of the Ph.D. neuropsychologist.

The following material is drawn from a symposium on Forensic Issues given at the Third Annual Conference on the Luria-Nebraska Neuropsychological Battery in May, 1985. While some of the issues discussed are of general relevance to areas other than neuropsychology, most were chosen because of their unique relevance to this area. However, almost all the issues are applicable to a broader range of instruments other than the LNNB and its related tests. Examples chosen to illustrate the points, however, are largely chosen from cases with the LNNB but could have been chosen from cases with other tests as well.

The material here does not purport to cover all of forensic psychology. The reader is cautioned to examine more general literature in the area if he or she wishes to be familiar with all of the pitfalls and advantages of testifying in court.

CHOOSING A NEUROPSYCHOLOGICAL TEST BATTERY

The choice of what tests to give a patient for a case destined to go to court may differ considerably from what is necessary in a routine clinical case. For example, in the clinical case many facts may be "obvious" or established by someone else without one's opinions being questioned. In court, however, the expert is often asked to discuss a wide range of issues in which independent confirmation of information is often essential.

It is usually inadequate to simply state that it wasn't necessary to look at something to rule it out. In the legal case, one must rule out all the alternatives so that the (hopefully) correct answer stands out as the most likely possibility. Thus, to state that it is obvious that the patient has no higher order speech deficits is much less adequate than providing testing showing that such disorders do or do not exist. As a result, cases must be investigated much more thoroughly, often involving extensive time periods beyond what is needed in a routine clinical case.

This issue shows up in court in two major ways. First, if an area is not tested because it is obviously impaired, the other side may argue that the level of impairment is not established and is only a guess on the clinicians part. They may get someone else to present testing showing that the level of impairment estimated without evaluation is wrong. Even when the error is only slight this can be used to impeach the witness' credibility.

Such an attack, while it may seem silly and insubstantial to the witness, can bias the jury towards rejecting all of the witness' testimony even if the error itself is really minor. The witness must remember that in the end all one has is credibility. The correctness of one's views or the demands of justice are irrelevant if the other witness (the one with the wrong opinions) is more credible. Invariably, completeness of testing allows one to back up one's views more effectively, allows you to refrain from relying solely on your reputation and insight, and adds to the picture of the careful expert who makes no assumptions and takes nothing for granted.

The same problem can arise when one omits testing supposedly strong areas which are intact. The other side may argue that the witness was simply attempting to prove a conclusion they reached even before seeing the patient, such as the presence of memory problems. If only memory testing was done, how does the clinician know (not believe) that factors like malingering or anxiety did not account for the results? Since etiology is invariably important in establishing liability, perhaps there are other untested deficits which would support another etiology. Again, the speculation may be silly but it goes again to the heart of the issues of credibility and the openness of the expert to all the possibilities. That is, are you making a fair and neutral evaluation or are you simply trying to make one side look good because they paid you.

This can be an especially effective tool when used simply to catalog all the areas and things one did not look at. It is difficult to recover from this approach since one is usually forced to argue that one's expertise somehow exempts one from having to do this extra work. It goes without saying that such omissions are disastrous if actual testing shows or suggests losses in the "normal" areas.

INDIVIDUAL VERSUS STANDARDIZED TESTING BATTERIES

If we work from the assumption that a test battery of some kind is necessary, we come face to face with one of the more divisive debates in neuropsychology today: the individualized versus standardized battery and the related debate of quantitative versus standardized testing.

Quantitative Versus Qualitative

The latter question is more easily dealt with. The one factor that discriminates the neuropsychological examination from the examination of the neurologist or psychiatrist is the presence of standardized test results. While neurologists do evaluate higher cognitive processes in a manner ranging from cursory to extensive, the evidence is based generally on their qualitative, intuitive analysis of the results in most cases. While this is fine for more obvious cases and for the needs of neurologists in medical treatment, it is ineffective for the more subtle cases which are likely to end up in court. (As a rule, insurance companies and other liable parties are much more likely to settle out of court in obvious cases.)

For the psychologist to depend on similar opinions and testimony is quite dangerous. First, there is no reason to suspect that a psychologist should be better at doing what a neurologist does than the neurologist. If the psychologist and neurologist do the same thing, then it is likely that the jury will trust the neurologist more if all other factors are equal. Standardized testing offers the psychologist a whole new area of information which the neurologist cannot counteract.

The physician may denigrate psychological testing but there is an impressive body of research which makes this quite difficult to do. There is not a similar body of research which supports the use of intuitive opinion based on qualitative factors. Indeed, there is a useful body of research which suggests that different clinicians will reach quite different results when given the same facts. In the final analysis, the psychologist is much better off emphasizing that which is uniquely the province and strength of psychology rather than pretending to be an oddly (and poorly trained) neurologist.

Thus, standardized quantitative testing must be seen as preferable to qualitative impressions. This is not to say that qualitative information should be ignored or omitted. Rather, the combination of both together provides by far the strongest approach for the psychologist.

Then one can argue that the psychologist not only does what the neurologist does in terms of observation but in addition, adds the extra accuracy and power of standardized testing. When the two are integrated effectively, complimenting one another so one can explain both how the neurologist reached her/his conclusion and why one is disagreeing, this provides a powerful

3

impression. Juries are especially impressed since such integrative testimony helps give the juror a logical reason why the experts disagree. Thus, the juror need not choose one expert over another but rather can, in effect, "agree" with both while accepting the psychologist's conclusions.

A simple example of this comes in the case of motor functions. In previous cases, I have had neurologists testify that a patient had no motor problems which could be observed. We repeated that essential examination and agreed that those were proper conclusions from that point of view. However, more detailed psychometric testing revealed a distinct and unusual left/right body side difference which was subtle but real, as well as difficulty with complex tasks which required kinesthetic feedback, a modality important to the kind of work that the individual did.

The deficit explained effectively the individuals inability to return to his former job, and the testimony itself took care of the competing opinion by demonstrating where the deficit came from and why. On rebuttal, the neurologist was forced to admit that testing had not been done of more complex kinesthetic feedback skills, nor had he employed any techniques able to pick up the kind of difficulty suggested by the psychological testing. The neurologist's final statement on the stand was an admission that he did not know about those things, although he would not change his opinion because there was more data available (which made him look quite rigid as well as biased.)

Individual Test Evaluation

Once we have decided to use standardized psychological testing, we must examine the criteria on which we judge tests. More importantly perhaps, one must recognize the criteria on which jurors and judges will eventually judge the test. We must constantly keep in mind that the purpose of doing the testing in an adversarial system is to present evidence which will be clear and convincing proof that the opinion of the expert witness is more likely to be true than any other contradictory opinions which will invariably be stated at the trial.

The reader will note that this could be seen as being at odds with the idea that the expert witness is supposed to be neutral. This is not the case at all. The expert should be neutral in examining the facts and rendering an opinion but once one has rendered the opinion that one believes to be true within the limits of our science, one is not to be neutral in presenting it to the jury but rather is responsible along with the lawyer for making the most effective presentation of the case. This does not mean that one will shade facts, lie, misrepresent or say something simply because one is working for a given client but rather that each side in the adversarial relationship is ethically bound to present their client's strongest case within the limits of professional ethics and legal demands. A lackluster examination or presentation of the facts, or use of instruments or procedures which one knows will be successfully challenged, is a violation of one's responsibilities in the legal system.

Thus, in choosing tests one must be cognizant of what questions are likely to arise about the test. The first questions are the most obvious: is the test adequately standardized? Many tests that are out there are in fact administered in inconsistent ways, invalidating the normative data, and making interpretation impossible. For example, we used the testimony of one "expert" to show that she had not administered the test in the way required by the test norms she used, invalidating her interpretation which she had presented as focal to her whole case. (Obviously, it is always better to attack the focal points of an argument if one can do so.)

In another case, an expert was ridiculed because one test he used was standardized solely on 10 Italian undergraduates, another used tests norms which were guessed at by estimating from a different but similar test, a third test was normed only on 12 year olds, and the final test was normed on 17 American psychology graduate students (the latter group likely being representative of nothing in the real world). Whether the expert was right or not in his opinions was completely lost in his inability to show awareness of these facts or their importance.

The appropriateness of the norms, as illustrated by the above, is always an issue. Many neuropsychological tests, even those used commonly, have very poor normative basis. In some cases the data is substantially out of date (from the 1940's or even earlier), in others the norms are inappropriate (using norms from the original French version of the test in an English translation), and in still others the populations are inadequate (30 or less subjects). In all these cases the meaning of the data can be substantially questioned.

Even if a test is adequately normed, there remain other problems. These involve issues of reliability and validity. Reliability is probably the weakest area for most tests. There are several important kinds of reliability. First, intra-test reliability measures the consistency of the items in the test as to whether they all measure the same thing. For most tests, this has been assessed on the basis of someone saying that the items look like they all measure the same thing (a weak defense at best). In many tests, no one has even tried to investigate the reliability of the test scores, while in others the actual published data is quite poor. The use of such tests is problematical, especially against an opponent able to argue these issues in a manner which the jury and judge can understand. (It should also be clear that one can always get away with something if the opposition does not question it. In such circumstances, you can use almost any test you like.)

Another important form of reliability is test-retest reliability. Simply put, can you get the same scores from a patient twice? Again, for many tests, such reliability data is not even published. For others, it is very poor. This is a very serious problem since if the other side does retest and gets different scores with the same test, they can and do argue that the test score are meaningless. This in turn means that any opinions based on the score are meaningless. Poor test-retest reliability can simply be argued to indicate that a test is meaningless. The lack of reliability data can be used to suggest that a test is poorly researched and of questionable meaning.

More important than reliability data is validity data. In neuropsychology validity data generally consists of three forms: face (intuitive) validity, the ability to separate groups of brain injured patients, correlations with other psychological tests and substantiation of theoretical predictions. Face validity is simultaneously the most common type argued, as well as the weakest. Basically, the argument goes that Test A measures Skill B because it seems to measure Skill B.

This is a very weak argument for several reasons. Most obviously, someone else can always argue that the test seems to measure something other than what you are saying it measures. In such cases the argument then boils down to whoever seems the most credible to the judge and jury. Such an outcome is more often based on personality and style and physical appearance than it is on any neuropsychological issues.

Moreover, the concept of functional systems argues that every test measures more than one skill. As proposed by Luria, a functional system represents all the brain areas which must be involved in order to complete a given task. All tasks, according to Luria, require multiple brain areas and multiple skills, a supposition well supported by the literature. Thus, any test may measure a wide variety of skills in any given situation and one can always argue that it was missed for different reasons other than those which may be most obvious. This is true for any test but is especially true for those highly complex tests which are popular in neuropsychology. In general, this is less of a problem for a test which is simpler but there is, in fact, no test the author can recall that cannot be criticized in this manner.

How does one get out of this problem? The primary method is not to rely on face valid interpretations of single tests but rather on empirically derived patterns of test scores which have been shown to relate to specific neuropsychological disorders. Such an approach allows one to use the research to establish a given idea. At that point, face valid arguments may be used to communicate the meaning of the research finding. In such cases, the face valid approach cannot be challenged since one can also drop back to rely on the empirical data. Lawyers will quickly learn not to challenge any statement if they fear they will be hit by an avalanche of impressive statistical data. Indeed, the author has seen lawyers become so gun shy in such a circumstance that they fail to challenge those points which are not so easily defended. Thus, such an approach tends to add credibility and gives a "halo effect" which increases the acceptance of all of one's testimony.

The research basis for such an approach comes from the other three types of validity which are commonly seen in neuropsychology. The first of these is the comparison among brain injured and normal patients. In its most primitive form, such research simply shows that there are differences between brain injured and normal subjects. Such studies are available for almost every test. Indeed they are almost considered absolutely necessary if one wants to develop and prove an instrument useful and effective. Despite this, however, such studies are largely meaningless.

One reason for this is that almost any test will

discriminate between some group of normals and some group of brain injured patients. The research may be easily manipulated: if I select as my brain injured group patients with severe left hemisphere middle cerebral artery strokes, I will find many significant differences, especially if the patients are more acutely injured. As they become chronic, the deficits and differences will lessen. However, if I pick a group of patients with Transient Ischemic Attacks, I may find nothing since such individuals typically return to normal within a short period of time (lasting from minutes to days).

If I select normals with high IQs who are highly cooperative, I will get more discrimination than if I pick hospitalized patients from an internal medicine ward or patients with significant personality disorders or (as in some studies) frankly psychotic patients. One study the author read used medical interns as the normal controls! Other studies will use college undergraduates or executives of large companies, groups whose generality is questionable. It is, unfortunately, often difficult to tell from reading many studies what kind of manipulation if any takes place. Comparing a hit rate in one study against another is generally more a comparison of apples and oranges than it is a fair evaluation of test effectiveness.

More important studies look at comparisons of groups of brain injured patients either with specific etiologies or specific types of deficits. The clearer the groups involved, the more useful and interpretable the studies. It should be noted that in this regard the studies are not used to find out whether a test is good or bad but rather to enlighten us as to how to interpret a test. If an aphasia test cannot separate out two groups of patients with only nonlanguage disorders, this does not make the aphasia test bad: it simply gives us information as to what we can say and not say on the basis of that test. In many trials, "experts" (and I sometimes must use that word advisedly) attempt to turn such studies into assessments of the adequacy of a test. Such arguments can easily be countered since such studies fail to speak to such questions at all.

The most common type of comparison is between patients with injuries in different parts of the brain. Of these, comparisons between right and left hemisphere patients are the most frequent but again the least meaningful. This is because there is quite a difference in performance among left and right hemisphere patients. Indeed, left hemisphere patients without language disorders typically look more like right hemisphere than left hemisphere patients. In such studies, the degree and incidence of language disorder influences greatly the results of any study. Studies which make comparisons among specific injuries, such as right versus left parietal injuries, are much more useful and meaningful. These studies must be carefully read as well; the ability to discriminate right parietal from left parietal does not mean one is able, with a test, to tell right parietal from left frontal or even from normals.

Another common form of validity is the correlation with other tests. In this type of study, we are interested in whether two tests which claim to measure the same thing correlate highly with one another. Whether they do or not, such studies again yield insight into the interpretation of a given test score and thus are quite valuable. Again, there are several cautions with such studies. Correlations may not be the same in all populations: restriction of the range of scores can yield low estimates of the real population correlation, while expansion of the range with an unusual number of extreme cases can elevate and overestimate the correlation.

Such studies again do not judge a test's usefulness but rather effect its interpretation. Interpretive issues are often clarified by this kind of work, but require an understanding of both tests before the study can be used meaningfully. Thus, the meaning of the study in practical terms is effected by how much we know about the test we are using to correlate the test under question. If we correlate two unknown tests, we know the correlation between them but not what that means for interpretation. Because of the difficulty in getting groups of brain injured patients with specific disorders this type of validity research is generally more common.

The last type of validity research involves the confirmation of theoretical predictions. For example, it is generally accepted that in a pure case of Korsakoff's disorder there is a delayed memory deficit because of the inability to form new long term memories, however, short term (immediate) memory should generally be intact. Thus, if we had tests which measured these skills, we would expect better performance on the test of short term memory and increasingly worse performance on tests which measure new long term memories (but good performance on the measure of old long term memories). If we were to find such a result, the findings would suggest that the tests do indeed measure what they claim to measure.

This type of research is the most sophisticated of all the forms of validity research. It requires both a theoretical understanding of specific neuropsychological disorders, as well as intimate understanding of the tests involved. Such predictions are more difficult and hence more impressive when they discuss the performance of a variety of tests to rule out alternate explanations. For example, a person may miss any tests if they are malingering or unable to cooperate. Thus, the ability to show that a similar but different test is normal while a predicted test is impaired is a much stronger argument than showing that only a given test is impaired or not impaired.

Similarly, the more different comparisons that are made the more difficult the predictions. It is one thing to show a difference between right and left parietal patients (just about any language test will do this) but much more impressive to show differences among normals, left and right parietal, and left and right frontal and to be able to predict the patterns of results which would accomplish this. Such predictions are sometimes made on the basis of past research alone, as well, but the procedure is more useful to our understanding of the tests and the brain when there is a theoretical model to explain the "why" of the pattern of test results.

For many tests in use, there is surprisingly little validity research. What there is may be poorly done, using only one or two subjects or failing to make appropriate comparisons which allow one to rule out alternate explanations of the results. Using a criteria, such as the presence of 20 useful validity and reliability studies, for a test would rule out more than 90% of the tests used in the field. This is a somewhat ironic result when one listens to the people praising neuropsychology because it is more scientific than other areas of psychology. The truth lies in the statement that it is potentially much more scientific and research based but the label "neuropsychology" on a test does not automatically confer the status of "research based" on the test.

Whatever test one chooses to use, one should be very familiar with the research on the test. It is extremely embarrassing to be unaware of a major study related to your testimony that the other side knows about. While it is also embarrassing to not know about minor studies, no one can know everything. However, the major generally available work must be mastered before one can be considered well prepared. Again, we must emphasize that one need not always be well prepared to win a case as that is the product of many factors, including most importantly, the competence of the other side. Being prepared is more the responsibility of the expert because of one's ethical and professional responsibilities to one's clients. Psychologists have been protected in the past by lawyers' lack of knowledge of how to get at neuropsychological testimony (other than the common statement that one is not an MD) but this protection will lessen as lawyers become increasingly sophisticated and begin to hire real experts to help them.

In selecting a battery of tests using the above criteria, another important question arises: how to compare the tests to one another. There are two types of test batteries, which can be combined together into a third type. The major types are individual batteries, which reflect different combinations of tests for different individuals and problems, and predetermined batteries in which the tests used are already set regardless of the patients problems. We will discuss the advantages and disadvantages of each in the forensic setting.

Individualized Test Batteries

It is argued that individualized test batteries are superior since tests can be chosen appropriate for the individuals problems and circumstances. Thus, if the major problems are said to be memory problems, then we can include more memory testing in the battery and slight unimportant areas to the case. In this way more testing of important functions may be accomplished in the same amount of time. The fallacy of this argument lies in allowing oneself to slight a given area: this can be used by the other side in impeaching the testimony. Thus, it is actually necessary to emphasize an area not by slighting another but by increasing the overall time for evaluation.

If this were the only problem with such a battery, this would not be an overwhelming difficulty. However, there looms a much more serious problem: our ability to compare test performances. To discuss this issue, we must go back a little bit into how individual neuropsychological tests are interpreted.

For most neuropsychological tests, performance by the subject is divided into "unimpaired" versus "impaired" with most tests indicating varying degrees of impairment. Whether a performance is impaired is generally based on either a cutoff point or because performance is a certain number of standard deviations from the mean performance of normal individuals. Each of these methods needs to be discussed separately.

Cutoff points are the result of determining which score, when chosen as the cutoff point, will maximize the correct diagnosis of brain injured and normal patients. A typical cutoff would be a score above which patients would be classified as brain damaged and below which patients would be classified as normal. The cutoff can be chosen in several different ways. One can try to maximize the correct diagnosis of brain injured patients with less regard to the accurate diagnosis of normal individuals. In such cases, a cutoff may be chosen which has an accuracy rate of 90% with brain injured patients, 60% with normal patients, and an overall rate of 75%.

Alternately, one could choose to maximize correct identification of normals, yielding perhaps a 85% rate in the normals and 55% in the brain injured. One can also choose to get a cutoff designed to yield equal hit rates in both groups. Such a cutoff might result in 68% accuracies in both groups. Finally, one can simply choose the cutoff which maximizes the sum of the hit rates in the two groups, or a hit rate which maximizes the number of people classified accurately. If the groups are equally sized in the research, then the latter will yield the same results as the former. However, if one group is larger the results will be distorted depending on the relative sizes of the groups. These latter two techniques can yield unpredictable results in terms of the exact hit rates in both groups, although the latter technique will most generally favor the larger group, while the former tends to favor the smaller group.

The final method – looking for scores two standard deviations above the normal mean – always seeks to minimize the number of diagnostic errors in the normal group. In such cases, the number of errors in the normal group will range from 2% to 10% or so depending on how close the curve is really a normal curve. In such cases, the accuracy in identifying brain injured individuals depends upon how much the score distributions of the two groups overlap. The number of performances in the brain injured group may range from 100% to 50% or less. The latter accuracy is unpredictable and obviously varies considerably from test to test.

The question we must address now is what is the effect of the use of differing cutoff methods. This can be seen by illustration with some hypothetical tests. Test A's cutoff is chosen so that almost no normals are identified as brain damaged and only 50% of brain injured patients are so identified. It is claimed by the tests author to be a test of "parietal" function. Test B is supposedly a test of frontal function which correctly identified 90% of the brain injured patients as injured and 45% of normals as brain injured. If we gave this test to a normal patient, 45% of the patients might do poorly on the frontal test and well on the parietal test because of the way cutoffs were chosen. We would then conclude each of these patients had frontal damage.

In the case of brain injured patients, almost all would do poorly on the frontal test, while half of these would do poorly on the parietal test. We would then conclude that almost all the patients had frontal damage, half had frontal and parietal (diffuse?) damage, while almost none had only parietal damage. These conclusions would be reached regardless of the actual location of the brain damage: it would simply be a function of the tests themselves and the way in which their cutoffs were determined.

While such an example may be seen as extreme, such cases have been seen in court by the author. While it is easy to rebut such testimony, the occurrence of such errors casts doubts on the competence of psychologists as a whole. Rarely does one see a clinician concerned with the fact that different tests have different underlying accuracies. Rather it appears that once tests are chosen there is an automatic assumption that they are somehow all comparable to one another.

Moreover, the problem does not stop here. As noted in the earlier section, there will be substantial differences in the underlying normative and brain injured populations used to establish the cutoffs. Thus, even when the same approach to cutoffs is used, different answers will still be found depending on whether we use a group of mild or severe brain injured patients or whether our normals come from a low educated or Harvard trained population. In reality, these differences among normal groups interact with the cutoff method chosen to produce often unpredictable results.

It should be noted that none of the methods employed here are right or wrong. Each can be justified for specific circumstances and for specific goals. But when these tests are compared to one another looking for patterns indicating brain damage, such issues cloud both interpretations and conclusions. This is made more difficult by the fact that it is not clear how cutoff points were chosen or how a given normative group relates to another. Even more frighteningly, cutoff points today are being increasingly chosen by computers. Some of the programs which do these have decidedly unusual quirks: we found one program whose results could be manipulated widely simply by adding or dropping one subject. There was no way to determine what was the correct or incorrect answer, just the obvious conclusion that little could be trusted.

Despite these problems it is not impossible to compare these individual tests to one another. In some rare cases there is actually research on how two tests relate to one another and their relative diagnostic quirks. However, such comparisons are few and far between and rarely paid attention. In most cases, statements that two scores differ significantly from one another are simply opinion with no basis in actual fact.

Thus, while it is possible to correct for these errors it is rarely done. Because of the lack of data and information on many of the tests, it is in those cases actually impossible to do so. In all such cases the clinicians fall upon fallible clinical intuition to decide on an answer, a questionable procedure in cases where extensive amounts of money or even someone's life or freedom may hinge on the need of the jury to understand what a patient's real condition may be. Reliance on such techniques alone is (in the author's opinion) questionable except in the clearest of cases.

It is useful to note here that these techniques did evolve specifically for very clear cases of brain injury. These were situations where patients suffered massive strokes, dementing illnesses, and other disorders which are easily diagnosed, in many cases, simply by inspection and a conversation with a patient. In such clear cases the role of these factors is overwhelmed by the brain injury itself. These techniques become questionable when they are taken from such evaluations to the more subtle and difficult forensic evaluations where all this information is neither so striking nor so clear.

Standardized Test Batteries

If we ignore the old joke that batteries are found in cars and flashlights (at least the ones that work), the standardized test battery is made up of a series of tests or procedures which ideally are standardized and normed on the same population. In addition, cutoff points are chosen in similar manners and data is made available on test intercorrelations and the size of score differences necessary to find a significant difference between scores. Ideally, scores will be expressed in similar units such as t-scores, although they may be expressed only in raw scores. The latter unfortunately makes score comparisons more difficult. A true battery should be as comprehensive as possible.

In reality, there are few test batteries around by this definition. The Halstead-Reitan Neuropsychological Battery (see Appendix II) does consist of a core of tests normed on the same population but also includes a number of additional tests whose norming and cutoff points reflect different methods and populations. The Luria-Nebraska Neuropsychological Battery (see Chapter IV) does meet the criteria set out above, as do several more limited batteries designed for the evaluation of only language disorders. There is neither at present (nor likely to be) a battery which covers everything possible in any case. This latter problem is probably the greatest theoretical weakness of test batteries in general, no matter how well normed they may be.

Standardized test batteries do have the great advantage of handling almost all the criticism listed in comparing individual batteries. We would still have the same problem, however, in comparing batteries to one another. For example, the Halstead-Reitan is much more likely to call a normal patient brain damaged than the Luria-Nebraska (LNNB), while the LNNB is more likely to call a mild brain injured case normal or borderline. A disagreement between the two batteries is much more likely to be due to the differences in how the batteries choose cutoff points than in any real difference in patient performance.

The only real problem with the standardized battery lies in the fact that it may not sufficiently emphasize an area of importance in a given situation. Thus, the Halstead-Reitan is weak in its coverage of memory while the LNNB slights some complex visual-spatial skills. In some cases, these omissions can be serious.

The answer to this dilemma actually furnishes us with a third method of putting together a collection of tests for the forensic evaluation. In this method, we use a standardized battery as the centerpiece of our evaluation but augment it with tests in specific areas as suggested by the test results and the history. In these cases, the standardized tests are used to provide the research/data based facts and to structure the case with the fine points being delineated by the additional tests. This relieves the selected additional tests of any of the burdens imposed by the considerations listed above and relieves the need for the standardized test battery to represent all things to all people.

Such a method also frees one up in testimony as well. In some cases, knowledgeable lawyers on the other side will take the position that whichever of the two major techniques you used, you used the wrong one. This combination method allows you to use both and thus foil such an approach. One can also then more easily agree with lawyer's criticisms. ("Yes, you are right, the Halstead-Reitan covers memory inadequately so I added the Randt memory test.") Such an approach makes one look knowledgeable and open minded, traits generally found admirable by judge and jury (unless one is also pompous and smug). In our own cases, we almost invariably use this joint method except in very extreme and clear cut cases which we find rarely go to court.

One final point is the usefulness of redundancy. Any test can be criticized on some level, so it behooves one not to be too dependent on any one test method. As much as possible, design augmenting tests so that there is more than one test measuring the factors that are of key interest to the case and to your arguments. Such preparation is, again, impressive to a jury and it is helpful in protecting oneself against cross-examination. The more pillars on which a conclusion can be based, the more solid the case.

QUALITATIVE AND CLINICAL FACTORS

From the discussion up until now, one might get the impression that the ideal neuropsychological examination is one which is entirely objective and research based. This is not true. Quantitative information is not sufficient by itself. There is no quantitative system which can yield 100% accuracy. It is the role of the clinician to provide the additional accuracy to bring the overall assessment into higher levels of accuracy. The information used by the clinician is of three varieties: (1) qualitative data on how the patient performed tests and observations of the specific errors made; (2) consideration of historical factors; (3) integration of the data with known facts from neuropsychology in general.

Qualitative data can play a large role in many cases. It is one thing to say that a patient has difficulty with memory. It is much more useful and specific to say the patient can recall material but cannot do it in a way that allows him or her to organize the data into sequential or spatial relationships, or to say that the patient has the memory but is unable to recall it on demand. Qualitative information comes from two sources: (1) examination of how the patient performs the items and the types of errors made; (2) comparisons of how the patients' performances change in similar but different tasks. That is, how differences in input modality, response demand, or cognitive task changes the patient's behavior in otherwise similar tasks. Such information is an invaluable augment to the conclusions reached from the standardized data. In such cases the qualitative data is no longer simply an opinion but rather additional information which can clarify and be supported by the standardized data.

The second role for the clinician is obtaining a history. Histories are absolutely essential in forensic neuropsychological work. Testing data can tell us what the patient's problems are or are not but it cannot tell us whether it is directly related to a specific accident or event. The purpose of the history is to first pinpoint as closely as possible when the onset of the symptoms occurred. The need for this is obvious: if the patient had an accident in May 1984, then the symptoms should have begun in May 1984. If they began in December 1984 or December 1983, there can be significant questions about the role of the accident.

In one case seen by the author, a women claimed that she was caused a brain injury by an accident in April, 1982. However, a careful history showed she was functioning at a high level of skills until the following November when there was a precipitous drop in function. This drop was not related to the accident as claimed. The jury ignored the testimony of the psychologist who claimed substantial deficits but was surprised by the revelations of the history he had failed to elicit. Getting a history is not always simple. In the case above, the patient actually had a stake in hiding or forgetting certain aspects of her history. We first discovered this obvious contradiction only after seeking out and interviewing the employer, a task which the other psychologist had failed to do. Interviews with family and friends and school may also be important. In many cases, it becomes necessary to establish early functioning levels of adults. This may entail getting old high school and college records, armed forces records, employment records, test scores (such as the SAT) and so on. One may also need birth records, hospital records, previous samples of writing and spelling, and other factors which will point to a change or lack of change due to some specific event.

A good history can involve multitudinous details of all accidents and diseases which could affect brain function. Indeed, it doesn't hurt to have information, as well, on things which do not affect brain function. Several times I have had lawyers, who were unable to attack my testimony, try to establish that I did not know all there was to know about the patient. In one trial I waited expectantly to be asked the patient's shoe size.

In another I was asked "Are you aware that the patient was unconscious for 48 hours in an accident only three weeks before the events discussed in the trial?" I was forced to say no. I later learned there had been no such event. He was trying to get me to say I knew, so that he could then impeach me. Alternately, if I said I knew he could use it as evidence that the second accident was irrelevant. One is much more confident about saying no if one has done a detailed job of investigating everything. While I would have said no regardless of the work I had done on the case (it is insane to even contemplate lying), I feel much better when I know that the other lawyer is unlikely to know something I don't.

History is routinely integrated with the neuropsychological results to make sure the two match. If the deficits seen and the history do not match, there is a need to explain and discover why. In such cases there are often factors no one is aware of which make the case much easier to analyze. Failure to match may also identify errors in the testing, errors which need to be discovered before you testify or are deposed, not after.

The final role of the clinician is to integrate all the data: quantitative, qualitative and historical. This may require one to understand in detail the injury or other cause of the deficit along with the testing. Expertise as a neuropsychologist routinely requires understanding of neurology, internal medicine, pediatrics, obstetrics and psychiatry. If your case involves such factors, then it is necessary to understand their role. Forensic work places a much greater demand on the clinician to understand all aspects of the case.

FORENSIC REPORTS

There are many different theories as to the proper manner of writing a forensic report in psychology or neuropsychology. Reports are quite important in most forensic situations. They represent the basic statement of the case which will be closely gone over by both sides for "ammunition" both for and against the positions suggested by the psychologist. Thus, the report must be prepared with extreme care. One must always remember that the other side in a case has a positive reason to misinterpret anything you write, or at least take it out of context and misuse it. Rather than tell one how to write a report, we will focus on the types of errors that are made and what to avoid.

Most easily, read the report carefully for errors in dates, spelling, grammar, accuracy and so on. It may seem trivial to you that you wrote the accident happened on 2/6/75 rather than 6/2/75 but someone will make something out of it. A misspelling may be trivial to you but offer opportunity to someone trying to discredit or humiliate you. (This is often done simply to get you angry, so that you lose your evenhandedness and control.)

Secondly, be careful about ascribing your conclusions to single pieces of data. For example, one report I saw said "The Category Test proved the patient was brain damaged" and went on to base almost all the conclusions on this fact. This allowed the lawyer to attack the Category Test, to bring up many reasons why it could be done poorly for reasons other than brain damage (in this case, low IQ was a prominent problem), and to force the psychologist to retreat and state that he didn't base his conclusion just on the Category Test. This unfortunately contradicted his report (which was pointed out) and made the expert look quite foolish. In most cases, this error is made unintentionally because what is actually written has not been carefully examined.

Whenever possible, stay away from issues of localization.

Rather, reports should concentrate on the patient's deficits, problems, and possible treatments. Lesion localization, especially in the kinds of cases which show up in court, is difficult at best and sometimes impossible. Effects of a lesion are rarely textbook and any absolute statement that a patient has a single given lesion is almost always open to attack by a clever opponent, even when they may have to concede the deficits the patient has. By distracting judge and jury to the more doubtful issue of localization, a lawyer may again cast doubt on otherwise sound testimony.

As an example, I was called into a case that was badly floundering because the psychologist, who had done a perfectly adequate examination and description of the patients deficits, had been attacked mercilessly by the opposing attorney and psychologist because he insisted on localizing each and every deficit. I needed to come into the case during rebuttal, showing that while the localization was overdone the description of the patient and the fact that the patients problems were caused by the accident were the important issues. The case was won but my testimony should have been unnecessary and could have been avoided.

Another common problem is relying too much on unverified information. While it is necessary to work from history in regard to etiology and the like, I omit statements of that kind from my reports unless everything has been verified. To make a positive statement that turns out to rest on incorrect data makes one look biased and perhaps too quick to reach a judgment. If a statement on etiology or other similar area is absolutely necessary, I will say something like "Although we are gathering additional data, based on the evidence to date, we would have to conclude that X was the cause of the injury." If I am really concerned I might add "These opinions are subject to change when the full investigation is completed." This has the advantage of protecting you from information which cannot be verified, as well as firmly showing that you are open to alternate conclusions.

Saying too much is a common problem. When writing something out, keep it as short as possible and still reach your goal. If the goal is only to give an attorney information as to damages in general, a short report is generally more than adequate. If the report is to rebut another report or interpretation, a longer report may be necessary. A longer report may also be necessary in cases where a report may be used to force a settlement before trial. In such cases, a forceful detailed report will often have more impact. However, no report which trails into unnecessary trivia is impressive; it simply either confuses or convinces people one doesn't know what one is doing. One report I read trailed off into the authors discussion of her own sexual habits. Such comments are rarely necessary (although in this case it did provide some bizarre titillation.)

Never commit yourself to unnecessary opinions or to things you are not sure of. It is far better to leave things out and add them later in a supplementary report than to have to change your mind. What is committed to paper is generally regarded as written in stone. Do so at your own risk and with the full knowledge of how it can backfire. Never over-interpret data to

make a lawyer happy or go beyond your expertise. If you have to
rely on someone else's authority or statements, then you had
better check with that person first before making the statement.
I have had the unfortunate experience of having to tell workshop
attendees that they have misquoted me and made serious errors in
their forensic reports. Always assume you know less than you
do. It is much safer and encourages you to double check and
make sure.

When writing your report, remember that you are a
neuropsychologist, not a lawyer, liability expert, gun master,
or anything else. When writing the report, you should be trying
to answer specific questions from the lawyer which you and he
have agreed are possible to answer from your data. You should
never comment on liability if it is not directly relevant to the
psychological examination, on insurance companies (one report
told of a psychologist's hatred of the insurance company which
was being sued), on purely medical matters, on the adequacy of
medical treatment or any other side issues. Such comments
should be reserved for oral communication to the lawyers as they
are not part of your expertise.

In writing any report, it is necessary to assume that
everything one writes is going to be seen and dissected by the
other side. The purpose of their investigation will be to
ferret out errors of any kind to identify your weaknesses and
strengths. Thus, the more you write the more one chances an
error which will be used to ridicule or embarrass you in court.
It is best to have someone else read the report critically to
see what they read into it that you may not have seen.

The present author prefers to keep reports short,
emphasizing conclusions but not how they are reached. This
allows me the freedom to explain such factors when I am deposed
or testify in trial. Longer reports are dangerous because they
commit you to a specific line of thinking which you may
reasonably change later when retesting is done or when more
information comes to light. Even if you don't change your mind
but simply sharpen your thinking, the opposition may try to show
this to be a recant or sign of indecisiveness. When I oppose
someone else, I enjoy a long report since it gives me, as a
rule, all the ammunition I need to see the flaws in their test
usage, logic or understanding of brain function.

I might emphasize that these rules apply whether or not you
care if you are embarrassed in court or deposition. While some
people handle such circumstances better, if you fail it is not
you who loses but the client. One must always recognize that
one's ethical duty is to the client and then act in ways most
helpful to the client. When in doubt about this, discuss
anything with the lawyer and client before writing it down. We
routinely have such discussions in person or over the phone to
make sure we haven't misinterpreted what is wanted or what is
known. Such last checks have saved us from problems several
times.

TESTIMONY

There are actually two kinds of testimony involved in
cases: testimony at a deposition which acts as a fact finding

forum for the lawyers or testimony in court before judge and/or jury. One handles oneself somewhat differently in these situations. Depositions are less formal (you don't need to be as dressed up), you need not attend to the needs of the jury, the rules allow more flexibility to questions and areas in which questions are asked, you can be a little more argumentative, and you can do anything you like with the tone of your voice unless the deposition is videotaped. (It is truly impressive what one can say with tone rather than words.)

The lawyers on the other side may use a deposition to see if you can be made angry, made to contradict yourself, or whether certain tactics can cause you to "lose your cool." On the other hand, you can use the deposition to overwhelm the other side in data, make the lawyer lose his cool, or frighten them into settling by appearing in complete command of the case and the data. The deposition can represent a feeling out which allows everyone to know where he or she stands.

It can, however, also be used to bamboozle you. The lawyer may be very kind in deposition to lull you into thinking you are in command when, in fact, many surprises await you at trial. On the other hand, an aggressive lawyer in the deposition may be very nice at trial if you convince her or him that you can't be pressured. Lawyers dislike a confident, cool but not arrogant opposing witness. You must remember in either case not to get overconfident or show fear, or worse yet confusion. One must always remember, however, that anything said at deposition can be repeated to you in trial if things get that far.

I have discovered that lawyers I work with feel more comfortable with differing styles from me at deposition. Some want the other side to know everything so they encourage long detailed answers which give away all information as an aid in pushing for a settlement. (In one case we managed to go 12 hours in a deposition, forcing me to stay in Honolulu an extra day.) Others prefer the other side to get exactly what they ask. No elaboration or extra data unless one is asked (the Joe Friday school of answering for you Dragnet fans). Such depositions may go quickly, especially if the other side has no real conception of the case.

In testifying, it is best to stay cool and in control but not aloof to the judge or the jury. Frequent eye contact with the jury is important but it should not be blatant. Long technical answers should be directed to the jury with some attention paid to keeping their interest; if they look puzzled, go back and repeat or explain yourself. Models of the brain or pictures can be helpful, as can explanations of how the brain works. Other witnesses should be discussed with respect due to an expert but one should not be afraid to show why and how differences of opinion exist. There is a need to be sensitive to the desire of the judge; some will allow long answers with minimal prompting by the lawyer, while others are annoyed with any kind of elaboration unless specifically asked for in the question to the witness.

However, always define technical terms, or better yet, say what you want to say in English rather than jargon. It is just as easy to say "front of the brain" as it is to say "anterior superior cerebrum." Listen closely to questions and never get angry or upset. Ask the lawyer to repeat questions if you don't hear them or don't understand them. If the lawyer asks more than one question at a time, ask him or her which one to answer first. Don't be afraid to ask for clarification of a question or to admit you don't know something. Never lie; all you have going for yourself is your credibility and integrity. Dress neatly but not more ostentatiously than the lawyers (a trial is not a fashion show). Think your answers through and talk slow enough so someone can write it all down. If you don't know an answer, say so. Testimony is not the time to do a comedy routine, although jokes may be OK if the judge is receptive and they arise naturally. These tips are all really common sense as are most suggestions about court behavior. Much more can be read in the plethora of books written for physicians and others who have to testify in court frequently.

CREDENTIALS

The issue of credentials is becoming an increasingly complex question as courts begin to recognize that there is a difference between a psychologist and a neuropsychologist. Before one claims to be a neuropsychologist, then, it is necessary to review what the qualifications are in this area at present, although it must be recognized that such criteria are at the discretion of the presiding judge at any trial since there is not at present a large body of precedent determining what a neuropsychologist is.

At present, the most emphasis is being made on having board certification as a neuropsychologist. This is for several reasons. First, in medicine, board certification has long been accepted as the way of establishing authority within a subspecialty. Consequently, since the creation of boards within neuropsychology, this has become a natural way to establish such credentials.

Because of the importance of credibility in testifying, it is strongly suggested that anyone who wishes to testify as a neuropsychologist get board certification. In some cases, this may require extra training or supervision. However, it is believed that these issues will become increasingly critical as lawyers become more sophisticated about the differences among psychologists and as neuropsychology becomes involved in increasingly larger suits. We refer the reader to the excellent chapter by Meiers in Foundations of Clinical Neuropsychology published by Plenum (1983).

CHILDREN: SPECIAL CONSIDERATIONS

Working with child neuropsychological cases presents some special problems due to the issues which arise with children and not with adults. The most frequent error seen is assuming that children are simply little adults. In the following sections, we shall examine some of what we know about child neuropsychology which must be understood when reaching conclusions in child cases. However, before we can examine the nuances of working with children in this area, we need to examine some of the basic assumptions about how the brain works.

Such assumptions are quite important when working in the forensic arena, since most of our conclusions about the relationship of behavior and brain function stem from these ideas. If one is not clearly aware of what assumptions underlie one's tests, this can be a source of possible attack on one's testimony. This is especially true in child neuropsychology where the facts are hazier and the analysis much more difficult. Thus, we will start with an examination of these basic ideas and then see how they apply to the analysis of children.

THEORIES OF BRAIN FUNCTION

It was not until the 1800's and the work of Gall, that modern neuropsychological theory began to develop (Krech, 1962). Gall postulated that the brain consisted of numerous individual organs, referring to what are today viewed simply as specific cortical areas. Each organ, he stated, has specific psychological function such as reading, writing, arithmetic, walking, talking and friendliness. Furthermore, the size of a given organ determined the amount of skill a person had in a given area.

For instance, a person who was good at reading was assumed to have a large reading organ. Brain injury caused deficits in specific skills by interfering with those organs which controlled a given function. If an organ was intact, the skill was intact. This belief about the significance of organ size led to the study of skull configuration because it was postulated that if an underlying organ was large, the skull over that area would be pushed out forming a "bump" and if an organ was small, there would be a valley in the skull. These postulates led to the study of the skull and the clinical diagnosis of personality and intellectual skill on the basis of skull configuration, the field of phrenology.

Gall's theories, of course, served as the forerunner of the localizationist doctrine, suggesting that all areas of the brain have a specific function which is exercised in isolation from skills in the rest of the brain. This assumption met great resistance in many scientific circles of the time. Of Gall's opponents, one of the most influential and persuasive was Flourens. Flourens did not believe localizationist doctrine and set out to do a series of experiments disproving such theories. Using pigeons and chickens, Flourens selectively removed parts of their brains. On the basis of these experiments, Flourens found little support for Gall's localizationist doctrine. He found that the area of the chicken or animal brain that was removed made little difference in the nature of the symptoms shown by the chicken or hen. The only thing that seemed to make a difference was the mass of the lesion; large lesions seemed to cause much more impairment than small lesions.

Based on these results, Flourens postulated the assumptions that underlie the equipotential theory of brain function. He stated that all areas of the brain are equipotential; there is no differentiation of brain tissue for psychological behavior as suggested by the localizationists. It is from this assumption that the term equipotentalism comes, with the name indicating that all brain tissue is equivalent in terms of what it does or can do. A second, related assumption is the postulate of mass action. Since all brain tissue is equal, the effects of brain injury are determined by the size of the injury rather than its location. Another well-known proponent of the equipotential approach to the understanding of brain behavior relationships was Lashley.

These two theories, with minor changes, have essentially remained the same since the time of these first studies. Localizationists have become more precise in defining specific skills and have rejected the assumptions underlying phrenology. However, they continue to publish maps of the skull showing the function associated with each area of the brain. Equipotentialists have limited their theories to higher cortical functions, generally acknowledging the localization of basic skills such as motor functions, auditory reception and visual reception.

These two approaches have generally dominated American psychology and education. Most theories of brain function, rehabilitation and assessment utilize the assumptions of one of these approaches in their formulations, though these underlying theoretical beliefs have not always been recognized or stated by the individuals formulating these theories. For example, the classic description of "the brain-damaged child" includes attentional deficits, emotional lability, coordination difficulties and poor academic functioning as being characteristic of such children. Though never stated, such a description implies that all brain damaged children are alike, regardless of the localization of their injury and that the brain is homogeneous in terms of function, e.g., reflects equipotential thinking.

Despite this, neither the equipotentiality nor the localizationist approach has enjoyed universal acceptance. Many modern theorists have begun to question the assumptions underlying both of them. For example, localizationist theory has been criticized since many clinical and experimental cases have been observed with lesions in a specific area which are not accompanied by the symptoms predicted by localizationist theory. In other cases, a specific area may be intact but the patient still shows symptoms associated with that area. The equipotentiality theory has similar problems. Some small lesions result in extensive deficits, whereas some large lesions produce relatively few problems in comparison. For example, Halstead was unable to find any support for the doctrine of mass action in his extensive studies of brain injured patients.

LURIA'S ALTERNATIVE

The evidence in regard to the inadequacies of both the localizationist and equipotential approach to brain behavior relationships has resulted in a growing exploration of alternatives to these basic theories. Probably the most comprehensive and well known alternative was postulated by the Soviet neuropsychologist, A.R. Luria. Luria, in his extensive publications noted that any alternative theory must do three things: (1) explain the data that fit the localizationist hypothesis; (2) explain the data that support the equipotential hypothesis; and (3) explain the data inconsistent with one or both theories.

To do this, Luria has developed a set of alternative hypotheses to describe brain function. The most basic and important concept in this theory is that of the <u>functional system</u>. A functional system is probably best explained by first looking at the operation of the rest of the human body. The theory suggests that the function of a brain system is similar to the function of other systems, such as the digestive system. For example, if we were to remove the stomach from a person, we would find that digestion had stopped in that person. Using the same techniques as employed by localizationist research, we would then conclude that the stomach is the digestion center of the body. (Indeed, the same methodology was used to identify the function of various areas of the brain.)

It is clear that the assignment of digestion to the stomach alone is a fallacious assumption. Although the stomach plays a specific role in digestion, it is not solely responsible for that process. If the rest of the digestive system were removed, the stomach would not be able to carry on digestion by itself. The brain, Luria suggests, operates in a similar manner. Each area of the brain can operate only in conjunction with other areas of the brain to produce a behavior. No area of the brain is singly responsible for any voluntary human behavior. However, just as the stomach plays a specific role in the digestive system, each area of the brain plays a specific role in given behaviors. The assumption that functional systems produce behavior is consistent, to some degree, with both the equipotential and localization theories. Like the equipotential theory, Luria regards behavior as the result of an interaction of many areas of the brain. Like the localizationist theory, Luria assigns a specific role to each area of the brain.

However, Luria's theory has clear disagreements with both the localization and the equipotentiality approaches. Luria assumed that only specific parts, not all parts of the brain, combine to form a behavior. Furthermore, there is no equipotentiality of brain tissue. Brain tissue is conceptualized as being specialized both psychologically and physiologically. Localizationist assumptions of centers for specific observable behaviors are in contradiction to this theory. Behavior is conceived of as being a function of systems of brain areas rather than unitary specific areas. A given behavior will be impaired when any part of the functional system responsible for the behavior is impaired. Thus, for example, some individuals without injury to the "reading center" still are unable to learn to read if there is damage to any of the number of parts of the functional system for reading.

Some additional assumptions need to be made to account for all observations. The most important of these is the concept of <u>alternative</u> functional systems. This concept suggests that a given behavior may be produced by more than one functional system. In more colloquial terms, there is more than one way to skin a cat and more than one way to engage in most behaviors. This principle both accounts for the lack of expected deficits in some patients and explains many cases of spontaneous recovery of behavior despite permanent damage to the brain. (Cases of recovery after temporary damage need not be explained by this assumption.) This recovery can take place in several ways. In some cases, higher level brain skills can compensate for lower

level skills. For example, adults with a partial deficit in
auditory discrimination may compensate by using lip reading to
supplement his/her ability to decode spoken language and use the
context of the talk to decipher further words or phrases which
were not understood. Under informal conditions, it may be
impossible to notice any deficit in such individuals.

Recovery can be enhanced by using lower skills for higher
level skills. For example, a person may lose the ability to
generate problem solving strategies after certain injuries. By
teaching this person a concrete approach to problems that
requires no independent generation of a problem-solving
strategy, this deficit can be minimized. Finally, the role of
the injured area may be assumed by other areas of the brain.
The brain, under the right conditions, is indeed plastic and the
normal organization of skills is not absolute. In addition, by
changing the nature of the task (e.g., by changing to
composition of the functional system used to complete a task),
we can change where in the brain the information is processed.
This might involve using another input or output modality, or
changing the verbal or nonverbal emphasis of the information
transmitted to the patient.

Luria's theory, based on these assumptions, is attractive
in that it can explain nearly all the observations which have
been made of brain-injured patients, regardless of the approach
used to generate that information. However, we should recognize
that it remains a theoretical structure that while consistent
with current data, is not more necessarily fully correct than
were the former models. There still remains much we do not
understand about the operation of the brain. Indeed, despite
our growing sophistication, we remain relatively primitive in
our analysis of brain-behavior relationships. This theory does,
however, fit the data currently available and provides, as we
shall see, a strong theoretical basis for understanding
neuropsychology.

Structure of Functional Systems

To understand fully the applications of Luria's theories,
we need to understand how functional systems work. As noted
above, Luria assigns specific functions to each of the areas of
the brain, with this assignment based both on physiological data
and psychological observations. Each area in turn participates
in functional systems. An area can be involved in any number of
functional systems, depending on the importance to the person's
behavior of the discrete skill mediated by that area. The
multiple functional role of each area of the brain is referred
to as pluripotentiality. This distinguishes it from
equipotentiality (or the localizationist theory). An area can
then be involved in relatively few or many behaviors.

The specific areas involved in a behavior depend upon how
the behavior has been taught (Luria, 1980). The person taught a
phonetic approach to reading does not use the same functional
systems for reading as the sight reader. As a consequence, we
can never assume that because overt behaviors are similar that
the underlying functional systems are the same. Indeed, such
assumptions about equivalence of underlying functional systems
are a major error even in many theories that outwardly agree
with Luria's basic conceptions. Thus, a test administered to a

child as a measure of specific neuropsychological skills may not, in fact, measure what we assume it does. This can lead to significant misunderstandings about the neuropsychological basis of a behavior and to inappropriate treatment or rehabilitative programs.

To understand further functional systems, we must have some recognition of the basic skills which go into any given functional system. It is not within the scope of this chapter to describe Luria's entire theory, so an attempt will be made only to give a general description of these skills. Luria divides the brain into three basic units. In addition, two of these units are further subdivided into more distinctive areas. Each of these units is involved in all behavior without exception, although the relative contribution of each unit will vary with the behavior. The three units can be described as (a) Unit I: Arousal and Attention Processes; (b) Unit II: Sensory Reception and Integration; and (c) Unit III: Motor Execution, Planning, and Evaluation.

First Unit. The Arousal Unit (Unit 1) consists of those parts of the brain identified as the Reticular Activating System (RAS). This system is a collection of diffuse intertwined structures which act to raise or lower cortical arousal. The structure itself extends from the pons and medulla through the thalamus to the cortex. The system is absolutely necessary for survival and behavior, since without arousal the cortex is unable to respond to incoming stimuli. Disorders of the RAS can vary in the extreme, from narcolepsy (chronic, pathological sleep) to insomnia.

In addition to its role in arousal, the RAS is also responsible for the filtering of input, especially from those senses which are always "on" (tactile/kinesthetic, auditory). This prevents the cortex from being flooded with constant, irrelevant stimuli which can interfere with cognitive processing. Thus, this system plays an important role in focusing attention, concentration and other similar tasks.

Second Unit. The second unit is the sensory reception and integration unit. This unit is responsible for most early life learning skills, as well as for many of the abilities tapped by tests of intelligence for young children.

The second unit can be subdivided into three types of areas: primary, secondary and tertiary. The primary areas act as sensory reception areas. Of all the areas of the cortex, this area is the most "hard wired", meaning that the functions of the primary areas and the connections within the area are largely predetermined by genetics. In the primary areas, input is received on a general "point to point" basis from the appropriate sensory organs. It is at this stage, as well, that initial cortical integration of the material occurs. In the second unit there are three primary areas, each devoted to a specific sense. The auditory primary area is in the temporal lobe; the visual primary area is in the occipital lobe; the tactile/kinesthetic primary area is in the parietal lobe. There is little difference in the primary areas of the two hemispheres. One can be injured very early in life with only minor effects. Destruction of both primary areas for a given modality results in such conditions as cortical blindness or cortical deafness.

There is a secondary area corresponding to each of the primary areas of the second unit. It is the role of the secondary area to analyze and integrate the information received at the primary areas. Thus, the acoustic secondary area (in the temporal lobe) is responsible for analyzing sounds, organizing them into phonemes, pitch, tone, rhythm, and so on. The secondary visual area (in the occipital lobe) does the analogous task for vision, differentiating foreground from background, detecting movement, analyzing color, shape, form and so on. The secondary tactile area (in the parietal lobe) will analyze direction, strength, localization of touch, movement of muscles and joints and so on.

The secondary areas of the second unit process information sequentially. This allows us to be aware of stimulus changes (e.g., detect movement) and to link events temporally. This is an important function. For example, in the case of speech, phonemes must be sequentially linked in order to form words and sentences. Injuries to the secondary area generally will first affect the sequential nature of the analysis. For example, a person may be able to understand two but not three phonemes in a row after a partial injury to the auditory secondary area. An individual may only be able to examine one object at a time, or one word (or letter) at a time in injuries to the secondary visual area. Injuries to the secondary parietal area will not impair sensation but may inhibit two point discrimination, detection of direction of movement, or recognition of shapes or letters traced on the skin.

At the secondary level, there is a greater differentiation of function between the parts of the second unit in the left and right hemispheres. The left hemisphere (in most individuals) predominates in the analysis of verbal, overlearned material while the right hemisphere predominates in the analysis of nonverbal material, especially spatial relationships and musical skills. However, it should be recognized that both hemispheres play a role in most behaviors. Thus, there are linguistic skills mediated by the right hemisphere, as in the recognition of long, complex words, and the perception and retention of consonant sounds, and the left hemisphere is capable of some spatial analysis (as in recognition of familiar figures). Indeed, for many behaviors, there is an interaction between the hemispheres that is necessary for efficient behavior. Physiologically, there are large tracts in the brain (chiefly the corpus callosum), the purpose of which is the integration and coordination behavior between the hemispheres.

Another way of looking at the right-left hemisphere differences is in terms of how overlearned material may be processed. In the case of music for example, primary musical interpretation is usually localized in the right hemisphere, however, in accomplished musicians such skills may be localized more in the left hemisphere. Similarly, verbal skills, when not overlearned, require extensive right hemisphere input to analyze unfamiliar sounds (when first learning speech or in learning a foreign language later in life), to analyze squiggles which eventually become overlearned letters and numbers, and to analyze the spatial movements necessary to write which begins as a simple right hemisphere copying task. Thus, the stage at which one is learning a given type of material may strongly influence the brain areas across the hemispheres that are primarily involved in those behaviors.

This differentiation of hemispheric function is also similar to the concept of specific analysis of more familiar material, whereas more overall, integrated analysis occurs in the right hemisphere. Indeed, there are physiological differences between the hemispheres that promote this differentiation. The left hemisphere functions as a discrete analyzer and is more attuned to material in which there is a standard method of analysis. The right hemisphere is more diffusely organized, with structures emphasizing interconnections between areas and deemphasizing localization of function. This allows the right hemisphere to function in a more holistic or gestalt manner, a skill necessary when facing new material. All of these approaches to functions of the hemispheres are obviously similar and represent different attempts to describe roughly the same observations. It should be noted, however, that as a result of these considerations, the specific localization where a behavior is processed will differ depending upon level of experience, method of attacking the task and general environmental feedback, as well as the intactness of each of these area. In most cases, behaviors involve both hemispheres rather than being processed by only one. These differences between hemispheres extend to the other areas of the second and third units of the brain that will be discussed below.

The tertiary level of the second unit, located primarily in the parietal lobe of the two hemispheres, is responsible for cross-modal integration and simultaneous (as opposed to sequential) analysis of input from the sensory modalities. This simultaneous integration across sense modalities complements the sequential analysis of the secondary units. However, these areas are also capable of sequential analysis of material that is initially integrated.

The tertiary parietal areas play a primary role in many of the tasks commonly subsumed under "intelligence". Auditory-visual integration is necessary for reading, whereas auditory-tactile integration is necessary for writing. Arithmetic, as well as body location in space and visual-spatial skills, depends upon visual-tactile integration. Grammatical skills, syntax, abstractions, logical analysis, understanding of prepositions, spatial rotation, angle determination and stereognosis are just a few of the skills mediated by the tertiary parietal area. Indeed, with only a few exceptions, all of the skills measured on the WISC-R are mediated by the tertiary area of the second unit.

There is increasing hemispheric differentiation of tasks at the tertiary level of the second unit. The left hemisphere is largely responsible for reading, writing and the understanding of arithmetical symbols and processes. Grammar, syntax and other language related skills are generally left hemisphere. The left tertiary area also is involved in the reproduction of complex figures, especially in the reproduction of details (rather than major outlines). The right hemisphere is responsible for visual-spatial relationship of parts, the spatial nature of arithmetic (such as borrowing or carrying over), verbal-spatial skills, facial recognition, recognition of emotional (nonverbal) facial and postural reactions, and the analysis of unusual or unknown pictures.

Third Unit. The primary area of the third unit is the motor output area of the brain. Commands are sent from this area (through the motor tracts of the brain) to the specific muscles needed to perform any given behavioral act (including speech functions). The secondary area of the third unit is responsible for organizing the sequence of motor acts. Whereas the primary areas send individual commands, the secondary areas must organize and sequence the temporal pattern of movement.

These two areas do not function independently. In order for motor movements to take place, there must be adequate information available on muscle and joint status (kinesthetic and proprioceptive feedback). To allow for this, there are multiple connections between the motor and tactile primary areas, and between the motor and tactile secondary areas. In addition, 10% of the cells in the primary motor area are tactile cells and 20% of the cells in the primary tactile area are motor cells. Thus, these areas interact on a behavioral level. Developmentally, these areas also tend to develop in tandem (i.e., the two primary areas and the two secondary areas develop in about the same time, in the absence of injury). Coordination with both the visual and auditory-sensory areas is also necessary for accurate motor movement.

The functions of the tertiary area of the third unit, most commonly called the prefrontal lobes, are in many ways dramatically different from the functions of the primary and secondary areas. The tertiary area of the third unit of the brain represents the highest level of development of the mammalian brain. The major tasks of this area can be described as follows: planning (decision making), evaluation, temporal continuity, impulse and emotional control (delay of gratification), focusing of attention, and flexibility (creativity).

The planning function is unquestionably central to human behavior. The prefrontal lobes receive information from the tertiary area of the second (sensory) unit, as well as from the emotional (limbic) system and the first unit. It proceeds to analyze this information and then plans behavioral reactions. This function allows one to respond rationally to environmental changes and demands according to sensory input and past experience. This function is especially important for long range planning, rather than the short term "reactions" which dominate behavior in most animals as well as children. This ability is closely related to the skill of delaying gratification (without external reward or restraint) and impulse control (again, without external restraint or reward), two more important functions of the prefrontal lobes.

As the prefrontal lobes develop, they assume dominance over the first unit of the brain (RAS). The prefrontal tertiary areas thereafter direct attentional focus and have direct connections with the subcortical areas, so that the level of arousal may be consciously modulated.

Another major function of the frontal lobes is evaluative

skills. The frontal lobes must evaluate whether a person's behavior is consistent with long term goals and plans, much as the secondary (premotor) area monitors behavior to ensure that short term motor goals are accomplished (e.g., walking across a room or communicating specific information). Evaluative skills, when intact in injured people, can be a source of depression. These individuals continue to exercise the capacity to recognize when they are unable to formulate or put long term plans into action.

Since many of the skills mediated by the tertiary frontal lobe area can be subsumed under the word "maturity", it is difficult to be sure if one is seeing a frontal lobe deficit or immaturity due to environmental training in children and adolescents. Thus, it may be late adolescence or young adulthood before the behavioral pattern of such a deficit is clearly discriminable from childishness, juvenile delinquency or psychiatric disorders common to the adolescent period.

DEVELOPMENTAL SEQUENCING

In adult neuropsychology, all the units of the brain are theoretically fully functioning before the onset of a given disorder. Thus, all one has to do is identify deficits in order to identify brain injury (assuming a normal environment). However, child neuropsychology presents a unique difficulty because the child is developing and changing. All skills do not exist at any given age. Thus, it is of no concern to anyone that a six-month old does not speak. Such an infant is not expected to talk. The major problem that developmental change causes in neuropsychological evaluation is the need to be able to identify, for a given child, what skills should exist. This is further complicated by the fact that children develop neurologically at different rates, making dubious any set list of expected skills. At any given age, lack of some skills might be considered sure signs of brain damage, lack of other skills might be considered normal, whereas still others may be seen as perhaps indicating dysfunction. To complicate matters even further, this neurological growth must interact with an appropriate environment; if one is raised only by monks who never speak, one will never learn to speak.

Given this situation, it is absolutely critical for anyone wishing to understand child neuropsychology to be aware of the developmental sequences likely to be reflected in children. In general, there are two major types of theories to describe neurodevelopmental processes. The first assumes that the child's brain is the equal of the adult's brain -- it is capable of all skills and skill levels but must develop sequentially, with quantitative gains being made as the child grows older. Thus, at 3 years a child can fingertap 12 times, at 4 years 16 times and so on, until one reaches adult speeds. Similarly, the young child is viewed as having all essential problem solving skills. Only the complexity, speed and other related dimensions with which the child can successfully cope change with age.

Other theories assume that there are distinct neurodevelopmental periods in which qualitative rather than just quantitative changes in skills occur. Thus, one is not able to use certain problem strategies appropriately until a certain stage is reached. This type of theory is very similar to developmental theories advocated by Piaget, Vygotsky and others.

It is this latter type of theory on which the following discussion is based. It is assumed that certain skills are more developmentally advanced than others and that the child cannot learn them until that neurological stage is reached. Thus, if frontal lobe skills do not develop until age 12, it is senseless to include a test of frontal lobe abilities in a battery designed for the 8 year old. Although the child may give an answer, its correctness or incorrectness will not measure frontal lobe activity because that area is not contributing to the child's behavioral processing at that age.

In the present context, neurological development is seen as the end product of several factors: myelinization, dendritic growth, growth of cell bodies, establishment of pathways among neurons and other related physical and biochemical events. All of these processes are necessary for complete neurological development but none alone is sufficient. Thus, there is at present no known one-to-one relationship between periods of physical growth in the brain (such as myelinization) and psychological maturation. Any such relationship that exists remains poorly understood. As a result, times for various developmental periods given here are based on behavioral rather than physiological observations. As such, they are subject to change as our understanding increases and are not to be seen as rigid or essential to the basic theory.

In addition to the necessary physiological substrate, there is also an environmental requirement before behavior emerges. Thus, at any level above the basic primary sensory and motor skills, physiological maturation serves only as a potential basis for the emergence of skills mediated by that area. Without the appropriate experience, the abilities will not develop. Thus, although the secondary visual area (and the eye itself) can differentiate red from blue, one will not give import to these differences unless one is taught to see them. This is true of all the skills that are mediated by secondary or tertiary levels of the brain. In the following discussion, for the sake of simplicity, normal environmental experience will be assumed.

Finally, it needs to be recognized that as a child passes through developmental stages, the nature of the functional system underlying a behavior changes. Even though the child may have the same behavior at five that the adolescent has at 19, the way in which the brain processes the information for that behavior and executes the behavior is quite likely to be different. If we were to give the same test to both the 5 and the 19 year old, we cannot assume that we are measuring the same skills or the same underlying processes. Nor can we test the child at age 5 to predict a skill that does not develop until age 8 or 13. Since the child has not passed through the developmental stage required for the emergence of the more sophisticated behavior, our "information" on the skill at age 5 is essentially meaningless. This phenomenon, for example, particularly explains why IQs for adolescents cannot be predicted reliably at early ages; the areas necessary for that later "IQ" are not yet developed in the young child. The predictive potential of any task is dependent upon the developmental pattern normally associated with that task. We must be careful at each stage to be aware of the limitations on the child's ability that are defined by the developmental stage the child has reached and the constraints this places upon our possible conclusions.

Five Stages of Development.

For our purposes, we can divide brain development into five stages. (1) Development of Unit 1; (2) Development of the primary motor and sensory areas; (3) Development of secondary motor and sensory areas; (4) Development of the tertiary areas of the Second Unit (parietal lobe); and (5) Development of the tertiary areas of the Third Unit (prefrontal lobes). Each of these stages will be discussed individually.

Stage 1. The most basic part of the brain clearly lies in the RAS and related structures. This system is, in general, developed by birth and certainly fully operative by twelve months after conception. The neuropsychologist, in working with infants, should be clearly aware that the development of this unit depends upon time since conception, not since birth. We cannot expect a premature infant, born at six months after conception, to show behavior that we see in a full term baby. Before development of this system, we would expect the child to show disorders of arousal and attention relative to the full term baby, although such deficits need not be permanent if the problem is developmental and not related to brain dysfunction.

The RAS is particularly sensitive to damage during the time it is being formed. While we need not concern ourselves with more severe disorders (which often lead to death or severe retardation), disorders of attention/filtering appear to be much more likely in injuries prior to 12 months after conception. Indeed, Rutter and his associates have found that head injuries in childhood after this period produce no unusual attention deficits. Later hyperactivity may then be related to emotional environmental factors rather than to brain damage. This idea would suggest that children with acquired brain damage, contrary to clinical lore, should not necessarily be more active or have greater difficulty with concentration than their normal peers.

After this initial period, injuries to the RAS appear to result more often in disorders of consciousness (coma, stupor, etc.) rather than disorders of attention (the direction of conscious activity towards specific and appropriate stimuli). Injuries to the nearby limbic system may cause emotional disorders which simulate hyperactivity to some degree. These disturbances are qualitatively different from true attention disorders and are more stress and anxiety related. (Later, similar behavior can be created by frontal lobe dysfunction, but not until Stage 5.)

Stage 2. Stage 2 of neurological development proceeds concurrently with Stage 1 development. Stage 2 involves the primary areas of the brain in the second unit and the third unit. Unlike the secondary and tertiary areas, the "wiring" of the primary areas is built in, not the result of environmental interaction. Generally, this area is fully operational by twelve months after conception similar to the timing in Unit 1.

During the early part of life, cortical response to the outside world is "dominated" by these primary areas. Built into these areas are basic motor behaviors - for example, crying, grasping, - and basic sensory behaviors - depth discrimination, recognition of high pitched voices, etc. All of these behaviors are genetically "built-in" and all appear to have (or have had-- such as the Moro response) some definite survival function. In general, these behaviors last only as long as the primary areas dominate cortical functioning. As secondary areas take over, these more primitive behaviors become quiescent. For example, a baby may be able to make a differential response to certain sounds as an infant but if not taught the differential response on a secondary level, will be unable to make the discrimination at age 3.

Depending upon the age and extent of injury, children respond differently to damage to the primary areas of the cortex. If the injury occurs early - before birth or shortly thereafter - the complete destruction of the sensory primary area can be compensated for by the primary area in the opposite hemisphere. This, of course, only applies to unilateral injuries. For example, a child might be born partially paralyzed on one side of the body due to primary level injuries. But if the child is seen at age 5, there may be no residual behavioral sequelae -- the child has apparently normal motor and sensory function. If the injury occurs early enough no deficit may be seen even at birth. One child seen by this author was born without a right hemisphere, yet showed no motor, tactile, visual or auditory deficits of any kind. Caution should be taken in applying these results, however. Injuries must be of a certain size (severity) and must include certain areas for this takeover to occur. Secondly, many motor deficits and sensory deficits arise from injuries to places other than the four primary areas.

Injuries after this period are more serious but many can be compensated for by the brain. Thus, loss of a primary auditory area on one side will result in a higher threshold of hearing but otherwise not interfere with day to day life. Loss of the primary visual areas will cause the loss of half the eye fields, which can be compensated partially by eye movement. Motor loss can cause hemiplegia but with proper therapy and exercise some control can be regained. Bilateral injuries are much more serious. These can cause deafness, blindness or paralysis. Partial injuries produce some fraction of the above results depending upon their seriousness.

Stage 3. This stage begins concomitant with the first two stages but extends through about age 5. Secondary level discriminations begin to develop as soon as the adequate attentional focus of Stage 1 and the capacity to relay information from the primary areas to secondary levels is adequate. Such behaviors as fear of strangers mark the emergence of significant secondary visual discriminations, whereas such behaviors as differential responses to a particular woman's voice
as opposed to other female voices mark auditory development. Eye-hand coordination, crawling, early walking and so on, mark secondary motor milestones.

The secondary areas are highly related to the concept of

dominance. It is at this level of the brain that we see the first significant differentiation of the brain into "verbal" and "nonverbal" hemispheres. However, the brain is not committed to the left hemisphere as verbal (as it is in 93% of the population) until the development of the secondary areas is markedly advanced. This occurs at about age 2, or more precisely, when the child develops consistent verbal skills. Injuries prior to this time to the left hemisphere will result in much less deficit than injuries after this time. In general, injuries prior to 2 years will result in switch of dominance for verbal skills to the right hemisphere. The earlier this occurs the better and more complete the transfer. After age 2, some transfer may occur but this is usually minimal. The results of injuries incurred subsequent to two years of age begin to resemble the results of adult injuries more and more. Thus, there appears to be a critical period in which these unilateral injuries are minimized; thereafter, they are much more serious. Such "plasticity" mechanisms do not apply when the injury is diffuse.

This plasticity of the brain also does not occur with small injuries - only when there is significant injury to these secondary areas. As a consequence, we have the paradox that a small injury at birth may produce no less deficit than larger injuries and in some cases have greater effects on later behavior.

During the first five years of life, the secondary areas are the primary sites of learning in the human cortex. This age limit, like others in this chapter, is only approximate. There are extensive individual differences. During this period, the child's primary and most important learning occurs within single modalities rather than between them. Crossmodality learning at this stage does not represent integrative learning but rather rote memory. The child learning to read at this level must memorize the letter or word-sound combinations. The visual symbol for a word lacks meaning for the young child except through its association with the spoken word. Thus, the child must say the word to understand it or repeat the phonemes in an attempt to integrate the sounds and recognize the word. It is not surprising that countries, such as the Soviet Union, which emphasize early reading, teach rote repetition until the lesson is learned. It is not until Stage 4 that the child is capable of true integrative cross-modality learning.

Stage 4. Stage 4 is primarily concerned with the tertiary area of the second unit, located primarily in the parietal lobe. This area, along with the prefrontal lobes of Stage 5, represents the most advanced parts of the human brain. More of the human brain is devoted to tertiary, integrative areas than is the brain of any other animal.

The parietal tertiary area is responsible for efficient performance in most major educational skills: reading, writing, arithmetic, grammar, syntax, drawing, logic, analogies, naming, categorizing, dimensionality and other similar skills. Not surprisingly, most major IQ tests tap skills related to this tertiary unit.

The tertiary parietal area is not psychologically active until about age 5 through 8. As a result, the effect of earlier injuries to the tertiary area may not be observable until ages 8 to 12. Therefore, if a child has an injury limited to this area at age 2, one might conclude at age 3 that the child is normal and unharmed only to discover at age 10 that the child has serious learning impairments. This consideration is extremely important in legal cases or situations in which one is asked to predict future behavior. It is essentially impossible to do better than actuarial data in predicting whether a 4 year old will later have tertiary level problems (except, of course, in cases where brain damage in other areas is already obvious). Neither a young normal child nor a young child with a discrete tertiary parietal injury will be able to complete tasks requiring development of this area. Failure to successfully perform such tasks subsequent to brain damage is meaningless, for the normal child will fail as well. In cases where the injury is limited to the tertiary injuries, real prediction is impossible at the earlier ages.

Stage 5. During this final stage of brain development, the prefrontal (tertiary) areas of the third unit develop. In general, this development does not begin until the 10-12 year age range and may continue into the earlier twenties. The age of onset of development in this period varies significantly across children. Initiation of development is often related to the onset of puberty but may precede or lag behind this event.

During this stage, many of the behaviors we associate with maturity begin to develop. Individuals with injuries to these areas do not necessarily show any decrease on intelligence tests which focus on skills in the second unit and the primary and secondary areas of the third unit. During this stage such skills as inhibition of impulses, inhibition of response to outside distractors, inhibition of emotional impulses, and organization and planning for the future take place. The ability to fully evaluate one's behavior is developed, as is the ability to develop higher levels of moral and ethical control. Sophistication in the interpretation of complex and abstract events is increased, especially in the areas of analyzing emotional cues and interpersonal interactions. Without these areas, as we shall see, severe behavioral disorders may develop.

Perhaps the best method for recognizing the implications of this material is an examination of specific case material which illustrates how the theoretical information affects actual case interpretation. The following cases are drawn from Golden (1984) "Clinical Implication of Neuropsychological Assessment of Children".

Case 1 is a child seen at 18 months of age by a psychologist about 25 years ago. The child at that time showed motor retardation, lack of speech, little walking behavior, poor coordination and so on. The child scored an estimated IQ of 50 on an infant development test. On the basis of this obtained IQ, the child was placed in the state home for the mentally retarded and stayed there until the age of 25.

When the child was 25, the institution was engaged in a "deinstitutionalization" campaign, the intent of which was to place retarded children as much as possible in community placements. The patient was evaluated at this time to determine which community placement would be appropriate. He was given

the Luria-Nebraska Neuropsychological Battery. His results
indicated motor and tactile problems and problems in writing and
arithmetic. He also shows a slight receptive speech deficit.
He has problems with tasks requiring motor speed, especially
those requiring bilateral coordination, and tasks involving
tactile and kinesthetic feedback. He had difficulty with
sensation (an inspection of the individual items shows that this
difficulty increases with the complexity of the stimulus, as he
is capable of basic perception of touch but poor at integrating
multiple stimuli), understanding complex grammar but no problems
in basic areas, and some spelling, arithmetic, and complex
reading problems. General intelligence is a low score
indicating few errors. One can infer from this pattern of
performance that the patient indeed has had a form of brain
damage but that it was quite limited and did not involve the
cognitive parts of the brain to any great extent.

The patient was also given the Wechsler Adult Intelligence
Scale. Verbal IQ was 101, very close to that estimated by the
Luria-Nebraska. Other testing--including the Halstead-Reitan,
aphasia tests and so on--essentially agreed with these results.
The patient had significant sensory motor problems but no
cognitive problems. That he managed an average IQ in an
institutional environment suggests that his IQ should have been
higher. It is unclear how he managed to achieve such an IQ
level and even more importantly, how no one who saw him from day
to day noticed his intelligence.

Clearly, this case is an extreme version of the tendency to
overgeneralize from test results. In recent years,
psychologists have become more sensitive to this problem but
similar mistakes are not unusual to see in a clinical practice.
Extrapolation of results from one developmental state to another
must be made cautiously, for extrapolation assumes that the
skills lacking in the current stage are indispensable to the
development of later skills. If these skills are not
indispensable, predictions will be weak. The potential for
error also exists if an alternative "functional system" is
available. Basically, this concept implies that there is more
than one way to complete most tasks. Thus, the
neuropsychologist must not only consider how a task is normally
completed but also other ways in which it can be completed. The
brain-injured child who cannot learn to read by phonetics may
still be able to learn to sight-read. Such alternatives,
indeed, form the heart of any rehabilitation system.

While predictions of future behavior cannot be made with
complete accuracy for a deficient patient, predictions can be
made with limited accuracy if the results are used properly.
Specifically, the neuropsychologist must make sure that the
skills being measured are indeed the skills necessary for the
behavior being predicted, which raises the question of what a
test measures. Luria, in his theoretical discussion of the
brain, has suggested that the skills responsible for a given
behavior may change as the child passes through different
developmental stages. Thus, if the same test is given to a 6
and a 15 year old, it may not be measuring the same skills in
the two children.

For example, a 6 year old child may get a normal or
superior scale score on the Similarities subtest of the WISC-R

by giving highly concrete, nonabstract answers that earn one point each. A 15 year old child must provide better answers to achieve the same scale score because more raw score points are necessary. Obviously, it is wrong to suggest that the two children, even though they have the same scale score, function on the same level. It is equally wrong to suggest that the difference between them is simply quantitative. Such a difference is qualitative because the way in which a child approaches and processes a similarity problem is very different at age 6 than at age 15. Score differences reflect qualitative differences as often as they do quantitative differences. Without this realization, predictions can be very poor.

So far, the problem of using current test deficits to predict later problems has been discussed. However, there is also a parallel problem with children who demonstrate good performance on tests. In the adult, the assumption is likely to be made that if a person can do a test today, barring further injury he/she will do the same or perhaps better on the test in the future. If the person displays a skill on the test necessary for success in a job, the prediction would be made that the person is probably capable of succeeding at that job. But, as illustrated dramatically in Case 2, this type of prediction may not be true with children.

Case 2 was an A student in the first and second grades. She had an estimated IQ, according to teachers, of about 120, consistent with the IQ of her parents. She was friendly, outgoing and normal in every respect in which she could be evaluated. During the third grade, she was in an automobile accident and very briefly unconscious. She was bruised and was thought to have internal injuries but these injuries could not be substantiated later as the symptoms disappeared. Leaving the hospital after several days of observation, she returned to school. Because the parents and school were concerned about the effects of possible head trauma, she was evaluated upon return by a school psychologist.

On a WISC-R she received a Verbal IQ of 123 and a Performance IQ of 117, well into the normal range and highly consistent with what would be expected of her on the basis of her previous performance and her parents. She took a Bender-Gestalt and it was also normal. A Peabody Individual Achievement Test showed grade level achievements between one and two years ahead of her actual grade level. The psychologist concluded that she apparently had suffered no ill effects from the accident and that she could return to class without fear of any problems. This conclusion was communicated to the child, the parents and the teachers. All were happy and the insurance company paid off for the accident and closed the case.

While she continued to do all right in school for the next several months, a transformation, largely ignored at the time, began to take place. The child started to play less and less with friends and began spending more time at home alone in her room. She became frustrated more easily and although not a behavior problem, appeared somewhat depressed. Her superior grades continued but she stopped enjoying school. Because this change happened relatively slowly (according to the reports of adults), it was largely ignored for a year until it became more noticeable, at which time another psychological evaluation was

suggested. The child was given a WISC-R, a Bender-Gestalt, a
Rorschach and a Draw-a-Person Test, the latter two tests given
primarily to evaluate her depressive state. Her Verbal IQ
declined from 123 to 113 and her performance IQ dropped from 117
to 108. These declines were attributed by the tester to the
normal variation in the WISC-R and to anxiety, as the score with
the most obvious decline was Coding, a section highly sensitive
to anxiety.

The raw scores on the WISC-R subtests are of more interest
than the scale scores. The child's raw scores either stayed
essentially the same or declined between the two testings, which
were eight months apart. Her Similarities score improved by 1
point, as did Picture Completion and Object Assembly. Generally
she showed an essential stagnation between the two testings,
rather than some improvement as might be expected. However, as
the psychologist noted, declines in IQ towards the "mean" in
high functioning children are not unusual, nor are declines
uncommon in children who are depressed, anxious or both. And,
indeed, the child's Draw-a-Person and Rorschach were interpreted
as indicating depression and anxiety. These emotional factors,
it was concluded, were the cause of her problems and family
therapy was suggested and initiated.

Family therapy did little good. The child's problems
continued to get worse and began to affect her school grades,
which went from As to Bs. The child became increasingly more
isolated from her parents and other children, more withdrawn,
more anxious and more negative about school, despite the fact
that her study time actually seemed to increase. She began to
have temper tantrums, which were rare but triggered by seemingly
unimportant events. Therapy was increased, more tests of
emotional function were administered and a psychiatrist
prescribed several different medications, all to little avail.
Finally, some two years after she was injured, the child visited
a neuropsychologist.

By the time the child and parents were evaluated by a
neuropsychologist, 26 months after the accident, the child had a
chronological age of 10 years 7 months. In light of the fact
that two previous WISC-Rs had been administered, another WISC-R,
along with the Luria-Nebraska Children's Battery, was
administered. Again, her original raw score performance
remained essentially stable. Her scale scores, however, done
since the normative data had changed, reflected her increased
age. Her Verbal IQ fell to 105 and her Performance IQ was 100.
Clearly, compared to her first testing, the expected cognitive
improvements that should accompany maturation were not
occurring. The child was essentially running in place. At the
same time, if the results of the WISC-R are viewed in isolation,
there is nothing all that alarming. She obtained scale scores
from 8 to 12 with the lowest score being Coding, again
consistent with a little girl who places a great deal of
pressure on herself to perform (as could be seen from the
intense manner in which she took the test) and who also is
apparently depressed. Her IQ is in the normal range and it is
unlikely that a "blind" evaluator would see her as brain
damaged.

In addition to the WISC-R, however, the experimental
version of the Luria-Nebraska Children's Battery, a modification

of the adult battery designed to trace deficits in 8-12 year old children, was administered. The results clearly demonstrated that the child's profile was elevated over the cutoff score. The cutoff score indicates the highest score a normal child her age should obtain. In fact, a normal child should have scores substantially below this level by up to 20 to 30 points, obviously not the case with the current child. She has seven scales of the eleven above the cutoff (Motor, Rhythm, Visual, Receptive Language, Expressive Language, Reading, Memory). The Intelligence Scale at a t-score of 50 reflects an average performance, consistent with the WISC-R results although not with the history. Overall, this profile indicated the presence of brain damage; to understand the nature and extent of that damage, one must evaluate the specific item patterns within the scales.

On the Motor Scale, the child was slow on items requiring speed. She generally had borderline performances on items requiring motor speed alone and items requiring drawing, although the quality of her drawings was quite normal. She had significantly more difficulty with bilateral coordination tasks. She also had some difficulty in changing set (alternating behavior according to instructions on a timely basis). She was able to copy movements, although she showed a tendency to mirror image, which she could correct spontaneously when told to do so.

On the Rhythm scale, she showed no difficulties in hearing the items or discerning that they were different but had trouble describing how they were different. She had problems with more complex series of beeps, tending to miss some when they were presented quickly.

On the Visual Scale, she showed no problems in naming familiar objects whose pictures were presented but experienced difficulties when the pictures overlapped one another or when they were out of focus or incomplete. She had no difficulty telling time but had trouble placing the hands on a clock correctly on command. She was slow with some items from Raven's matrices and had difficulty rotating items in her head and imagining three dimensions.

On the Receptive Language Scale, she had no problems in basic understanding of phonemes, words or sentences, however, when complex grammatical phrasing was used, such as "point to the pencil with the key", the child made numerous reversal errors and showed confusion regarding the actual meaning of the sentences. Thus, complex grammar and syntax, along with statements involving spatial relationships, showed deficits beyond what would be expected from a bright or even average 10 year old.

On the Expressive Language Scale, she had difficulty pronouncing complex words and repeating sentences--the memory component apparently interfered with her ability to express herself. She also had difficulty reversing sequences, such as saying the days of the week backward and she was slow in spontaneous expressive speech but she had no trouble with naming.

On the Reading Scale, she was comfortable with letters and short words but showed difficulty when dealing with unfamiliar words and had problems integrating separate syllables. She was slow in reading a paragraph and tended to skip from one line to another, suggesting some kind of spatial problem.

Finally, on the Memory Scale, she showed the ability to memorize words by rote but took more trials than would be expected. She also set very high standards for herself, consistently expecting herself to do better than she actually did. She also had considerable difficulty when interference was present between learning and recall; she did not forget entirely but clearly showed more of a handicap from such a procedure than expected.

Overall, these results are consistent with a child who had difficulty learning and retaining new information, in addition to difficulty in coordinating bilateral activity and other tasks requiring the cooperation of the two hemispheres. This pattern clearly is not the result of a single focal deficit but a combination of deficits reflecting sporadic injuries throughout the brain. Signs of right hemisphere injury are evident in her poor ability to decode complex spatial stimuli--especially those which are novel, in her difficulty in coordinating bilateral activity and in other tasks requiring the cooperation of the two hemispheres. Her sequencing deficits also suggest a right hemisphere involvement, as may the spatial reading errors. In the same way, left hemisphere problems are signaled by her difficulties with grammar and syntax, her pronunciation problems and her inability to integrate phonemes. Her slowness at reading, right-sided and bilateral motor signs, impairment in verbal memory and the historical decline in verbal intelligence all further point to left hemisphere damage.

Clearly, these are problems which can lead to serious difficulties. The child has a much harder time reading, due both to her spatial and verbal deficits and a harder time decoding and understanding statements with complex syntactical or grammatical forms than would be expected from one with her intellectual abilities. She can understand these tasks only if given enough time and only if she works very hard. Such work, though, is more difficult for her now than before her accident. Moreover, as the demands placed upon these skills increase as she moves from grade to grade, she is finding herself less and less able to compensate in an adequate fashion. Thus, her grades are slowly declining and she is finding herself under more and more pressure to study harder, causing more stress, depression, withdrawal and a sense of hopelessness as each day looks harder than the day before.

Apparently, the injury did not affect her previously learned abilities to any great degree but did impair future growth and development. Thus, early testing following the accident indicated there was nothing wrong. However, that assessment was based on the assumption--which is true in most children--that if development proceeds normally up until a certain point, then development will continue to proceed in a normal fashion. While true for the normal child, it is not necessarily true for the child with an injury. Such a child, indeed, may look normal at one point after an accident only to fail to show normal development thereafter.

One can argue that most children with an injury such as

suffered by Case 2 would have shown problems with preexisting skills had the proper test been employed. That, of course, is impossible to know in hindsight.

At the age of 3, Case 3 was involved in a car accident. After the accident he was unconscious for a period of two weeks and after regaining consciousness, showed weakness greater on the right side than on the left side. At that time he displayed signs of aphasia as well as confusion, drawing problems and a number of very obvious neuropsychological deficits. Over the next year he received physical and speech therapies. By the age of 5 no deficits were found. The child entered school where his performance was consistent with his IQ level of about 100. All went well until adolescence. Somewhere in the 12-15 age range, teachers and parents began to observe that he suddenly appeared more immature, impulsive and less controlled than other children his age. Of course, the problem was not that he was becoming less mature but that other children were becoming more mature. Also, as the demand for higher intellectual skills increased, his grades began to slide. He got involved with the "wrong crowd" and at the age of 16 was picked up for a robbery planned by one of his friends in which he took all the risks. He was, however, easily caught as he had no idea how to carry off the robbery when things did not go as planned nor did he have a clear idea of how to escape. He was placed first in a juvenile detention center and then in a state institution. His condition slowly grew worse as he continued to fail to mature. He was eventually admitted to a psychiatric hospital during what was diagnosed as a schizophrenic crisis.

During this admission, he was seen for neuropsychological testing. His Luria-Nebraska profile was quite classic. The profile of deficits is highly consistent with a frontal lobe injury that is anterior enough not to have caused significant motor deficits.

An analysis of the patient's performance across the test indicates deficits in bilateral motor control, deficits in using verbal schemes to alter behavior and change sets quickly, some slowness in drawing, difficulty in abstracting, problems interpreting complex grammatical structures and problems with spontaneous speech and sequential skills. Mild memory problems with interference also were seen. This pattern of deficits is highly consistent with the left frontal focus indicated by the scale patterns.

To further study this patient, a CAT-scan was requested. While a scan is not confirmatory in every case, inasmuch as injuries of this kind may not show on the CAT-scan (although they may show on PET-scans or regional cerebral blood flow when these are available), the scan in this case did show clear sulcal enlargement in the left frontal area, suggesting atrophy of this area. Such atrophy was interpreted as reflecting an old injury, specifically the injury received by the patient at the age of 3. No other instances of head trauma or neurological disease were recorded in the patient's history.

The above case again illustrates the limitations of prediction in such situations. Although the child improved on all measures given, he still had a serious brain injury. It should be noted that probably no test given when the child was 5 could have predicted the later effects of the injury since the skills in which the deficits were later found are not even expected of a normal 5 year old. Thus, the people who assessed this child made no error in their assessment, only an error in how they interpreted their data and in their understanding of how the brain develops over time. They also erred in assuming that if the areas of the brain that were accessible to their testing were normal, then all areas were normal. Statistically, such an assumption would have a high accuracy rate. However, clinical reports must be based on an understanding of all the possible probabilities and guidelines, not certainty.

Is the Brain Necessary?

Another issue in this area is the clear question of whether the brain is even necessary. Of course, this issue is exaggerated; no one believes that one can do without a brain or at least believes that such a condition would not constitute a handicap. However, it is obviously true that a brain injury in the child may not lead to brain dysfunction in the same way that it does in the adult. Examples in the literature are frequent of children who have lost hemispheres without serious impairment. For example, Smith reported a child with only one hemisphere who had an IQ of 126.

Another example of this phenomenon is Case 4, who was seen as a teenager. The boy was born completely without a right hemisphere. On the CAT-scan, the right hemisphere was replaced by hugh ventricles. Yet, the Luria-Nebraska revealed no deficits whatsoever. In order to verify that no deficits were overlooked, the Halstead-Reitan, which included the Wechsler Adult Intelligence Scale, was also administered and the boy again performed normally; indeed, his Verbal IQ was 130 and his Performance IQ was 128. He was given a number of other tests, including an intensive motor battery devised by Matthews and his colleagues, additional cognitive tests such as the Stroop Color and Word Test, Bender-Gestalt, Benton Visual Retention Test, Token Test and others. He received a full neurological examination and detailed visual field and hearing tests. No abnormalities appeared on any of these tests. An MMPI did suggest a psychopathic personality disorder which could not be confirmed by history nor would it have been possible to establish a connection to the missing hemisphere had this diagnosis been supported.

On the other hand, brain injuries of much less or similar severity can produce extensive deficit in children. A child who had a large tumor removed at about 2 years of age from the left temporal-parietal area showed extensive deficits in all verbal-mediated skills with little understanding of instructions even on a simple level. There were significant motor and sensory problems on the right side of the body, as well as restrictions of the right visual fields. The child was operating at an IQ level of about 63.

Case 5 is a junior high school cheerleader who did a somersault at a basketball game and landed with her head on the corner of the scorer's table. The corner of the table pierced her skull and entered the brain, disrupting the middle cerebral artery on the right side. She demonstrated extensive deficits on left-sided motor and sensory skills, construction dyspraxia,

inability to understand or process tones and rhythms, visual
spatial impairment, memory disruption, sequencing problems,
intellectual impairment in interpreting pictures, trouble
understanding sentences with complex grammar or syntax and
difficulty with arithmetic.

Clearly, then, when assessing a brain-injured child, the
primary consideration is not simply whether a child has been
injured or even where or how badly. Some injuries may be
totally silent--so that the child is diagnosed as normal and is
able to function as normal--whereas other injuries can create
severe deficits. In some cases, the functional effects of the
injury may exceed those caused by the same injury in adults. As
a consequence, in order to make clinical predictions about the
child, it is necessary to understand which parameters of injury
determine which outcome is likely or expected.

The more closely one reads the literature on brain injury
in children, the more obvious it becomes that there are numerous
variables involved in this process and it is their interaction,
rather than their summative effect, that is important. As a
consequence, only some of the major conclusions can be reached
from this work and they must be considered tentative hypotheses.

Hypothesis 1. The effects of diffuse injuries--defined as
those involving the entire brain--appear to be much worse when
the injury occurs early in life. One reason for this outcome
could be that the other child has achieved some repertoire of
behavior before the injury and these behaviors can be at least
partially maintained after the injury. In the very young child,
no such behaviors exist and the effects of the damage are
consequently much greater.

Hypothesis 2. The effects of medium size injuries appear
to depend on their location as well as the time of injury.
Specifically, there appears to be greater recovery the earlier
the injury, for injuries before age 2 located in the temporal-
parietal-occipital area. This outcome appears to be due to the
ability of the unaffected hemisphere to take over the operation
of the injured hemisphere, which is, of course, dependent on the
biological integrity of the unaffected hemisphere. The fewest
deficits are seen in children whose injuries were prenatal or
occurred at or shortly after birth. The later the injury
occurs, the more deficits seen. Somewhere between ages 1 and 3,
the ability of the brain to "shift functions" diminishes rapidly
causing more severe deficits as the child gets older and
reaching a peak of severity somewhere in the 2-3 year age range.
Thereafter, as the child gains experience and past learning, the
effects decline in intensity, eventually to match the same
effects seen in adults.

Hypothesis 3. Small injuries in the same areas of the
brain do not seem to call in this "rehabilitative" mechanism.
Apparently, some critical size for the injury or some similar
variable is necessary before this occurs. As a result, small
injuries may cause much the same impairment that they do in
adults. It has been suggested that such injuries may be
responsible for some forms of permanent learning disabilities.
Whether this is so is debatable and research is currently being
devised to answer this question.

Hypothesis 4. Injuries to the frontal lobes take on a very different look from injuries elsewhere, especially when the nonmotor areas, often called the prefrontal lobes, are considered. These areas have always been of interest to neuropsychology because researchers have hypothesized that they are responsible for the higher cognitive behaviors such as planning into the future, evaluation of behavior, flexibility, creativity and impulse control--many of the behaviors collected under the word "maturity". Thus, it is hypothesized, these areas show considerable development in and around adolescence, perhaps until 16 years of age, some suggesting for even longer. As a consequence, injuries to this area occurring during childhood and adolescence can lead to the failure of this area to develop properly or to develop further.

Thus, injuries during adolescence should show different symptoms than in adults with the same injury and indeed, this seems to be the case. Injuries before age 12 or so, depending on the child, have little effect on the child if the injury is fully localized to this area and does not affect subcortical areas or any other area of the cortex. However, after age 12 these children apparently fail to mature in a normal manner and develop a wide variety of disorders, in some cases similar to the boy described earlier (Case 3). Sometimes these children are diagnosed as schizophrenic or become criminals, in whom there is a surprisingly high incidence of such disorders. (For example, in a sample of child molesters, four of six had definite evidence of brain damage on neurological and neuropsychological tests; in the two cases that were absolutely confirmed, the brain injury was in the frontal areas of the brain.)

These ideas and information should be applied carefully but they are of definite use in forensic situations where we strive to find the most likely explanation, given the present state of knowledge in the field. It is incumbent upon the expert to keep up to date with new data and major advances in the field, of course, but the lack of certainty does not prevent the testimony of the expert from being influential, nor should it, as despite this lack of certainty the well trained expert can help the court in making as fair a decision as possible.

ETIOLOGY

As noted earlier, neuropsychologists can be much more secure when speaking of the types of deficits patients have. It is a much more complex issue to speak of the etiology of the disorders. In many cases, it is sufficient to demonstrate that the symptoms identified by the test began at the same time of the accident or other event of interest and that the symptoms did not exist in the same intensity before.

This latter point needs to be emphasized. In the case of many subtle brain injuries, we are faced not with outright aphasias or paralysis (those cases generally settle out of court) but rather with changes in personality and in complex cognitive functions. On the surface the individuals look and seem to act within "normal" limits. The basic problem is that the behavior is different from prior to the accident. The symptoms include intolerance of stress, difficulty in dealing with novel situations, exacerbation of preexisting personality characteristics, apathy and a general diffuse background of problems which are often difficult to pinpoint. These symptoms are the result of injuries to the tertiary frontal lobes which are especially sensitive to the effects of trauma as well as many toxins and poisons.

On the other hand, frontal patients may have little difficulty with well learned tasks, conversational speech, motor control and other typical daily tasks. The problems arise only when elements of novelty or stress become involved and may be explained away as psychiatric symptoms. This is common because many of the symptoms seem to be exacerbations of preexisting tendencies. This, in turn, results from frontal injuries loosening inhibitions and general controls over emotional impulses. What arises then is the expression of the emotional symptoms that were always there in many of us that are now more openly expressed due to the loss of inhibitions.

In such cases, one must carefully document the differences in the patients behavior before and after, to degree as well as to kind of behavior. One must also note what types of situations could be handled by the patient before but cannot be handled now. One must also document that stressors in general are affecting the patient's behavior, not just a specific stressor. The latter information helps discriminate between a psychiatric reaction to an event or accident versus a neurological injury causing brain dysfunction. In the former case, the response is to more specific stressors; in the case of brain damage, we are seeing a general loss of stress handling and inhibitory skills. Thus, the symptoms will involve many disparate aspects of the patient's life, not just one.

One must also document the cognitive symptoms characteristic of frontal damage as well. These will be difficult, again, in dealing with novel tests and situations while such factors as psychometric intelligence will be preserved. It is the perseveration of basic, well learned skills along with the loss of simple skills which requires flexibility and the ability to handle novelty that most definitely point to the frontal disorder of this kind.

In other cases, questions of etiology will arise in which one must identify which of alternate events have caused specific symptoms. For example, we have frequently seen trauma cases of older individuals in which it is contended that their symptoms are not due to trauma but a degenerative disorder of aging such as Alzheimer's. This is complicated by the fact that both disorders have common memory problems. However, the major differences lie in that the Alzheimer's disorder will get worse over time, while the head trauma will not. In addition, head trauma results in a much more sudden and obvious onset of symptoms. One must rely in such cases on the report of family, friends, co-workers and others in such cases, as well as on being familiar with the literature about the disorders involved so as to make the often subtle distinctions necessary in such important discriminations.

When relying on the testimony of family, friends, co-workers and so on, one must be very sensitive to the fact that such individuals may be biased (both pro and con) and that such individuals are not neuropsychologists. I might note here similarly that the family doctor is also not a neuropsychologist nor are many neurologists. A fifteen minute or even hour long medical examination will not identify changes in personality or the ability to think correctly if the person is not looking for it in an appropriate manner.

In all cases, information should be gathered not on what they concluded but what they actually saw. The emphasis must be on what information they have, not statements like "He was OK" or "He had lots of problems". In addition, all information must be double checked and confirmed by independent sources. I remember one case where a friend stated on the stand that the plaintiff had memory problems. When asked how the friend knew, he replied that the patient had told him he had memory problems. Such testimony is not the kind one wishes to base one's case upon.

HYPOTHETICALS

In many cases, it is difficult if not impossible to establish for oneself the specific facts necessary to make a definitive diagnosis. As noted earlier, it is not necessary in most courts for you to be absolutely certain of your conclusion or even 80% certain: fifty-one percent is adequate. However, there will be cases in which one simply cannot clearly establish some basic facts necessary to reach any conclusion.

In such cases, the hypothetical comes in very useful. One may answer questions about etiology and recovery by assuming certain facts such as "Assuming this patient has no history of any neurological problems and was normal prior to May 3, 1984, do you have an opinion on whether the events of May 4, 1984, could have resulted in the plaintiff's current deficits?" In such cases it is not your responsibility to argue about the previous history but rather the responsibility of the opposing lawyers to convince the jury as to what the patient's life was like prior to the accident.

This allows one to reach conclusions in cases where one might otherwise be held back by lack of information. In all such cases, of course, one must be honest enough to admit that if one makes different assumptions, that the final conclusion can be changed.

Hypotheticals can be used by the other side as well. They can say, "Assuming this child was born prematurely with Apgar scores of 1 and 2, can you conclude that his deficits are all due to the accident of May 3?" My personal favorite hypothetical from an opposing attorney came when I was asked after several hours of testimony "Doctor, assuming that the patient has none of the problems you have discussed, is there any evidence for brain damage present in this case?" My answer was "Assuming that the patient has no symptoms of brain damage, then there is no evidence to suggest brain damage." Such questions arise from a desire to confuse the jury or occasionally out of the total confusion and frustration of the cross-examining lawyer.

CRIMINAL LAW

The use of neuropsychological testing in criminal law is not nearly as well developed as the use in civil law. While neuropsychology is not relevant to many aspects of criminal law, it can be used in place of more traditional methods in the determination of competency and motivation. In the determination of competency, neuropsychological measures can be employed in the description of individuals who appear to posess normal intelligence and judgment but who, in fact, are impaired due to frontal injuries. In the case of motivation, neuropsychological deficits may be used to explain the reasoning of an individual in reaching a given conclusion which can be used in determining the intent of the individual.

In competency cases, the use of a "frontal lobe" syndrome argument is both controversial as well as yet uncertain. In these cases, the argument usually is that while the person does well on formal tests of judgment and intelligence as well as traditional tests of competency which ask such questions as "what is the role of the judge and jury", that the individual, in fact, has an inability to understand these things except by rote and does not appreciate the consequences of their knowledge nor the impact of their decisions and behavior. Luria described this in part as a breakdown between behavior and verbal statements. While the person may articulate an idea or a fact, the information does not influence behavior because of the disconnection caused by the brain injury.

Thus in such cases, a patient may understand the role of a defense attorney but will still believe without understanding the consequences that they can be a better defense attorney than any lawyer. In one case with significant frontal damage, a judge allowed such a patient to defend himself in a capital trial for first degree murder because his intelligence was in the normal range and he was thus "competent". (The case is currently under appeal based on the above concepts.) Frontal patients may refuse to cooperate with their lawyers or engage in maneuvers such as lying, outbursts or otherwise which they feel helps their case despite warnings and cautions.

Such patients in my care have given confessions to crimes they did not commit because they are easily convinced that the District Attorney and police are fighting for them. (In one case we successfully had such a confession thrown out of court.) Such individuals may end up as accomplices to crimes because they are convinced by more intact associates that what they are doing is "OK". (It is my personal belief that of criminals who are easily caught, there is a substantial overrepresentation of such people.)

In arguing such a case, it is important to detail the brain injury in such a manner that there can be little question as to the interpretation of the data. This usually involves "overtesting" as previously described. Second, the effects of the injury must be described as concretely as possible (with examples) to illustrate the nature of the deficits and why the patient can do some things normally or do adequately on an IQ test. The other side on the case is most likely to argue that the person is OK because the IQ tests and traditional competency tests are normal. They may also try to attack the testing, or failing that, cause as much confusion about the nature of the deficits as possible. Finally, they may insist on the voluntariness of the behavior in that the frontal lobe patient is not "compelled" to do what they do.

The latter argument must be countered with the argument that the voluntary behavior is not under the control of the patient and/or the patient is not aware of the meaning of the behavior. This is further complicated by the interaction between frontal lobe disorders and alcohol or drugs. As a rule, frontal patients are much more impaired by drugs or alcohol than are normal individuals as their compromised brains overreact to the disinhibiting effects of the substance involved. Further, because of their injury such patients are unlikely to understand the need to abstain or acknowledge the effects on their behavior. State laws vary as to whether patients are responsible for their behavior while under the influence of such substances and these variations can effect the impact or meaning of this defense.

In cases where motivation and intent are issues, the frontal lobe/brain injury defense becomes quite useful when applicable. In such cases, one is arguing that either because of the injury the person failed to understand the impact or meaning of the behavior or that the person misinterpreted the situation because of the injury.

In the first circumstance, we had a patient who after a frontal injury would offer cattle or crops as collateral for loans and then when he needed more money later would sell the collateral without repaying the loans. In such a case, the patient was unable to understand the link between offering the merchandise as collateral and not being able to sell it later. This was despite the fact that prior to the injury the person had 20 years of perfect performance as a farmer and businessman. Even after the case was brought against him, he failed to understand the relationship between his behavior and the charges.

In the second circumstance, we defended a patient with a massive frontal infarct who had shot her husband. She argues it was done out of self defense because he was going to kill her, while the prosecution argued that this was untrue and that while he had made threats she was in no danger. Among other testimony, we were able to show that with her injury she would overgeneralize and take threats much more seriously than others would. We were also able to show that she was physically incapable of doing the crime in the method suggested by the prosecution. This impaired the case in that it argued against their claim of premeditation as well as the idea that she had ambushed her husband in some manner.

Whenever using a neuropsychological defense, the case must be tailored to the specific facts of the case. It is imperative to closely review all the details of the case to make sure that such a defense is likely to be accurate and to insure that the behavior of the patient falls within the limits of a person with a given injury. I have testified for the prosecution in several cases where the claims of a given brain injury are clearly contradicted by the history and facts of the case. In some cases making a decision may result almost in becoming a "detective" in recreating the crime in a meaningful manner consistent with the neuropsychological evaluation and the known facts.

There are drawbacks to this defense as well. Most importantly, one must recognize that a crime committed by a person with a brain injury may be committed again if the same circumstances arise as frontal patients fail to learn from experience. In the case of the farmer above, some banks continued to loan him money which he wasted despite my recommendation that a conservator be appointed for him because he was unable to enter such deals competently. This was later used to argue he was not really injured but doing things "on purpose". Thus, if the situation is likely to arise again, the competency of the individual and/or the safety of others may be endangered.

In such cases, whatever steps are available to prevent this must be recommended and pushed. For one of our patients who was truly dangerous, this meant "imprisonment" in a mental institution instead of a jail, likely for life. However this might bother someone, such outcomes may be inevitable consequences of the defense because of the need to protect society. In other cases, the loss of control over finances and such may be a severe psychological blow but it is unfortunately often a necessary one.

NEUROPSYCHOLOGY AND MEDICINE

Perhaps the most common attack on the credibility of an otherwise qualified neuropsychologist is that he or she is not a physician. This can be simply in the form of the question, "Now you are not really a physician, are you?" or "You are not a real doctor, correct?" This also takes the bizarre line of attack, "Now, you are really just a doctor of philosophy, aren't you?" One lawyer asked, "Can you tell me how many philosophy courses you've taken?" This line of attack is often used just to get you rattled and the questions should be answered simply and without combativeness. If you are asked an open ended question, one can explain one's training and background; otherwise, answering yes or no is the simplest approach.

A similar problem arises when one is told "Well, a neurologist could diagnose this better than a neuropsychologist, couldn't he?" The answer to this is a simple "No". From my perspective, I don't testify on anything I do not believe I can give true expert testimony. If someone else could present a point better, I tell the lawyer to get someone else. In those few cases where the testimony overlaps into medication or an area I am not an expert, one simply needs to say "That question would be better answered by a physician." There is no need to claim omnipotence but there is also no need to denigrate what a well trained neuropsychologist can contribute.

FINAL COMMENT

For those looking for a more general information text on forensic psychology including details of the courtroom, we suggest Theodores Blau's book: "The Psychologist as Expert Witness" published by Wiley (1984).

SEVERE HEAD TRAUMA IN A CASE

WITH PREMORBID DISABILITIES

Jeffrey Katz

Department of Psychiatry
University of Nebraska Medical Center
Omaha, Nebraska

One of the most difficult type of brain injury cases to work with is one in which there are substantial premorbid deficits. These deficits can be due to past neurological disease, past injury, or simply to a lack of environmental stimulation or training. Regardless of the etiology of such deficits, it is necessary to differentiate between neuropsychological deficits which are caused by a current injury which is being litigated and past deficits unrelated to the legal proceedings. The following patient illustrates such a problem in an accident case.

HISTORY

The patient is a thirty-two year old, right handed male with an employment history as a municipal laborer. Although he was awarded a high school diploma, he never learned how to read or write. Despite repeating the second grade, his academic performance had always been marginal. He is married and has two children. He had no prior psychiatric history and rarely drank alcoholic beverages. Approximately two years before the evaluation, the patient and two of his co-workers were involved in an accident while on the job. He was working near a brick wall that held a telephone cable. The wall was not sturdy enough to tolerate the stress imposed on it by the attached telephone cable and it collapsed.

The patient was hit on the head and body with flying debris from the wall, was knocked down to the ground and was rendered unconscious for several minutes. The patient was taken to a nearby hospital and released that same day. At that time, it was noted that the patient was confused and had suffered scalp and shoulder lacerations. Shortly after the initial emergency room visit, the patient developed episodic dizziness, headache, and numbness and tingling of both hands. Such symptoms prompted him to see a neurologist who diagnosed a left lumbar herniated disc, bilateral carpel syndrome and right occipital neuritis. Several weeks later, the patient started to complain of concentration difficulties, irritability and poor memory. A CAT scan of the head was subsequently performed which yielded negative findings.

Along with his co-workers, the patient retained an attorney to sue the telephone company, which had connected the cable to the wall, for personal damages. The plaintiff contended that the telephone company was cognizant of the fact that the wall was not structurally strong enough to support the cable and they were therefore legally negligent and liable for any physical or psychological damages incurred as a result of the accident. To determine the presence, extent and severity of brain and/or psychological injury, the plaintiff requested a neuropsychological evaluation. The task of the neuropsychologist was to assess for damages and, if observed, to determine the causal relationship between the accident and such damages.

The following methods and psychological tests were employed in the evaluation of Mr. M: Halstead-Reitan Neuropsychological Battery; Nebraska Neuropsychological Battery; Wisconsin Card Sort Test; Wechsler Memory Scale; Wechsler Adult Intelligence Scale-Revised; RANDT Memory Test; Wide Range Achievement Test; Minnesota Multiphasic Personality Inventory; Rorschach Inkblot Test; Pain Evaluation; Clinical Interview of the Patient; Clinical Interview of the Patient's Wife.

OBSERVATIONS AND INTERVIEW RESULTS

The patient is a large man who appeared older than his stated age of 32. At the time of the evaluation, he had been working as a supervisor of a municipal sewer maintenance crew for approximately one year. He was taking propranolol and aspirin to treat his headache. The patient complained of loss of pleasure and interest in his job. He reported that prior to the accident, he was able to successfully manage three jobs with relatively little difficulty and had derived enjoyment from all three. He was, however, struggling with his one new job and was not able to perform up to his own standard.

He claimed that his memory was poor and was impeding his job performance. He stated that he was afraid of losing his job. He also complained of being more irascible and easily angered since the accident and less able to get along with his co-workers. His irritability and short temper were apparent to the patient, his wife and children which stood in sharp contrast to his once mild disposition. The patient's wife indicated that their relationship had deteriorated since the accident and was characterized by frequent arguing and poor sexual relations. With some embarrassment, the patient conceded that he had recently struck his wife for the first time. He stated that he was less interested in his children. His diminished level of tolerance for his children resulted in frequent anger outbursts. The patient had indicated that prior to the accident, he took pride in the ability to assemble machine parts that had been disassembled several days beforehand. He complained that since the accident, he was less able to accomplish this task. A similar complaint was voiced by his wife. She reported that her husband was unable to help her father repair tractor engines and other farm equipment although he had done so in the past. The patient also mentioned that he had recently gotten lost while driving to work.

In addition to the symptoms enumerated above, the patient had complained of a dramatic increase in social isolation, a reduced tolerance for loud noises, poor concentration, emotional lability, diminished self control, insomnia and anxiety. Furthermore, he was unable to provide a detailed account of the events which had preceded the accident and was unable to describe the events which had followed the accident (after he regained consciousness), suggesting mild retrograde and anterograde amnestic disorders.

A mental status examination revealed that the patient was alert and oriented to person, place and time. His speech was slow but audible and intelligible. He rarely spoke spontaneously and offered relatively few elaborations with his responses to questions. There were no word finding difficulties noted. Thought processes were generally coherent with no evidence of a thought disorder. Associations were few, however, logical and relevant. Energy level was normal. Mood was depressed and affect was generally constricted, however, appropriate to context of thought. Thought content was free of suicide or paranoid ideation. Judgment and insight were grossly intact. The patient remained cooperative and motivated throughout the course of the evaluation. Vegetative signs included episodic insomnia and decreased libido. Appetite was reportedly adequate.

Table 1: WAIS-R and WRAT Results

Subtest	Raw Score	Scaled Score
WAIS-R:		
Information	11	6
Digit Span	12	8
Vocabulary	34	7
Arithmetic	6	6
Comprehension	15	7
Similarities	16	8
Picture Completion	17	11
Picture Arrangement	13	9
Block Design	24	8
Object Assembly	32	10
Digit Symbol	29	4

Verbal Intelligence Quotient: 81
Performance Intelligence Quotient: 89
Full Scale Intelligence Quotient: 83

WRAT:		
Reading	46	
Spelling	50	
Arithmetic	67	

TEST RESULTS

On the WAIS-R (see Table 1), the patient obtained a Verbal IQ of 81, a Performance IQ of 89 and a Full Scale IQ of 83, which placed his level of intellectual functioning in the low average range. His Verbal subtest profile contained relatively little scatter across measures. His Information and Vocabulary subtest scaled scores of 6 and 7, respectively, which are putative 'hold measures' and were judged to be consistent with low-average, premorbid level of intelligence, given his academic history. In contrast to the Verbal profile, his Performance subtest profile contained significant variability across subscales. There was a relative strength in Picture Completion (scaled score=11), suggesting intact nonverbal logical analysis and good attention to detail.

He achieved a scaled score of 4 on Digit Symbol which represented a statistically significant decrement in symbol manipulation ability which was consistent with his essential premorbid dyslexia and dysgraphia.

The results of the WRAT (Table 1) indicated that the patient's general academic skills were below the level of ability of ninety-nine percent of those in the standardization sample. His obtained standard scores on reading, spelling and arithmetic were 46, 50 and 67 respectively, which were all significantly below his Verbal IQ indicating a long standing learning disability.

Table 2: Nebraska Neuropsychological Examination Results*

Scale	Total	T	Scale	Total	T
1	6	88	22	0	96
2	1	86	23	47	99
3	2	90	24	2	81
4	0	92	25	25	119
5	8	83	26	0	92
6	1	91	27	31	111
7	9	96	28	113	115
8	0	82	29	1	90
9	0	95	30	6	88
10	4	104	31	7	90
11	4	96	32	12	97
12	1	86	33	7	82
13	3	100	34	5	96
14	1	91	35	21	100
15	6	90	36	3	96
16	9	102	37	3	95
17	97	100	38		96
18	1	96	39		90
19	0	95	40		92
20	7	97	41		104
21	4	96	42		90

*Critical level is 99.

His performance on the Nebraska Neuropsychological
Examination (Table 2) defined a number of prominent cognitive
deficits. His ability to sustain attention for moderately long
time intervals was suppressed and there was evidence of poor
concentration and depressed mental control, substantiating the
patient's presenting complaints. Bilateral and unilateral fine
and gross motor coordination of the hands were intact. He was
able to initiate, regulate and inhibit voluntary motor movements
successfully and there were no dyspraxias or tremors observed.
Complex oral-motor movements were executed normally. A mixed
tactile sensation picture was demonstrated. Although simple and
complex tactile sensation processes were intact for the right
side, simple tactile perception of the left side was impaired,
with complex tactile perception for the left side stimulation
falling within normal limits. Two-point discrimination was
suppressed bilaterally and simultaneous stimulation of the left
hand and cheek produced suppression of left hand sensation.
Basic visual analytic and more complex visual-spatial operations
were performed at the expected level. His performance on a test
measuring visual-motor efficiency, conceptual flexibility and
complex sequencing of symbols was deficient. His abilities to
discriminate and analyze phonemes, to comprehend simple and
complex sentences, to repeat words and sentences and to name
pictures of objects upon visual confrontation and from their
functional description were preserved. Oral expression of
automated, over-learned material was intact, however, he
experienced difficulty generating ideas orally both in a
structured condition and extemporaneously.

On the Halstead-Reitan Neuropsychological Battery (Table
3), the patient obtained a prorated Halstead Impairment Index of
0.8 which fell within the impaired statistical range. However,
his inability to read and to write were factors which
considerably contributed to this elevated value. Essentially,
his performance on the Halstead-Reitan Battery was consistent

Table 3: Halstead-Reitan Neuropsychological Battery Results

Impairment Index	.8
Tactual Performance Test	
Total Time	19'45"
Memory	8
Localization	4
Seashore Rhythm Test	8
Speech Sounds Perception Test	37
Finger Oscillation Test	53
Categories Test	52
Trail Making Test	
Trails A	41"
Trails B	104"
Aphasia Screening Test	11
Strength of Grip	
Right	140 Dyns
Left	140 Dyns
Wisconsin Card Sorting Test	
Errors	46
Categories	5

with his performance profile on the Nebraska Neuropsychological Examination suggesting intact bilateral motor strength and speed (Finger Oscillation and Hand Dynometer), inefficient and belabored complex sequencing ability, intact nominative language and suppressed ability to sustain attention in a low structure situation. His performance on the time component of the Tactual Performance Test, an index of nonverbal problem solving, tactile and kinesthetic integrity and motor dexterity, was impaired. While the incidental memory component for individual items was intact, his ability to conceptualize the spatial relationship between the items (Localization) was impaired.

The patient's performance on the Categories Test and the Wisconsin Card Sort Test (and Trails A and B) demonstrated compromised ability to formulate concepts and difficulty transferring from one conceptual set to another.

On the Wechsler Memory Scale (Table 4), the patient achieved a Memory Quotient of 86 which was commensurate with his IQ. Long term memory was normal, however, his knowledge of current information was below expectations. He experienced little difficulty counting down from twenty and counting up by threes. However, it was interesting to note that he did not know six letters of the alphabet. Logical Memory, Digit Span and Visual Reproduction were all within normal limits. However, on learning a series of word pairs, he fared well at learning easy word pairs (for example, up-down) but evidenced problems learning difficult word associations (for example, obey-inch). Such a differential suggests that the patient was unable to formulate semantic strategies to encode this information.

On the RANDT Memory Test (Table 4), the patient achieved an Acquisition and Recall Score of 64 (a measure of immediate memory with interference conditions), a Delayed Recall Score of 70 (an indicator of intermediate memory with varying time intervals) and a Memory Index of 62 (a composite score

Table 4: Memory Test Results

Wechsler Memory Scale

Information	3
Orientation	5
Mental Control	2
Memory Passages	8
Digits Total	10
Visual Reproduction	8
Associate Language	16
Memory Quotient	86

RANDT Memory Test

Acquisition and Recall	64
Delayed Recall	70
Memory Index	62

suggesting overall memory functioning that is analogous to an IQ), placing his memory functioning within the impaired range. An analysis of the subtests which contribute to these composite scores revealed that the patient's difficulty learning a series of word pairs significantly suppressed his Acquisition and Recall Score and that his poor recall of the details and theme of a short story, significantly reduced the derived Delayed Recall Score. All other subtests essentially fell within the normal range.

The results of personality testing (Table 5) provided evidence to determine that the patient was experiencing marked psychological distress characterized by depression, anxiety, agitation and social withdrawal. He was prone to ruminate and worry excessively and he maintained a poor self concept. Although adequate psychological resources to modulate his emotions were available to him most of the time, there was data to suggest that when involved in demanding and ambiguous situations, he was disposed to emotional lability and sudden emotional outburst.

The results of the pain evaluation implied that the patient's personality features were consistent with those who have difficulty tolerating stress and coping with pain and are predisposed to develop a chronic pain syndrome. Data indicated that the patient was experiencing significant headache in the base of the occipital area and severe back pain which was, purportedly, functionally disruptive and generally unmanageable.

DISCUSSION AND CONCLUSIONS

A comprehensive evaluation of this individual's neuropsychological status revealed dysfunction of a number of higher cortical processes. There was general impairment in generating complex language and in analyzing complex verbal material which adversely affected the patient's ability to encode and recall some verbal information, as illustrated in his poor performance in learning word pairs. Although these

Table 5: MMPI Results

Scale	T Score
L	53
F	63
K	46
Hs	88
D	110
Hy	80
Pd	55
Mf	74
Pa	56
Pt	87
Sc	75
Ma	46
Si	78

deficits were reliably observed in his performance, it was difficult to argue that they were causally related to the patient's head injury, given his questionable verbal analytic skills premorbidly as reflected in his long-standing dyslexia and dysgraphia.

Nevertheless, there was an interesting finding which when examined within the context of the patient's post-accident symptoms and stated premorbid skills, constituted a deficit which can be argued to the court to be related to the accident in question. Although slow, the patient proved to be able to analyze and integrate spatial information when a visual model was provided (i.e., Object Assembly).

He exhibited significant difficulty conceptualizing the spatial relationship between distinct items when a visual display was unavailable (localization), although he was able to conceptualize and recall the items individually (Memory component of Tactual Performance). This deficit was consistent with the patient's complaint of diminished ability to put together the separate components of disassembled machinery, which constituted a relative premorbid strength of this individual given his work history. The patient's impaired abilities to concentrate, to sustain attention and to shift conceptual set denoted a related constellation of deficits, implying dysfunction of the regulatory system of the brain which includes the frontal lobes. The fact that the patient did not demonstrate any significant motor deficits suggests that the anterior aspects of the frontal lobes were involved.

Furthermore, his report of extreme irritability and his tendency to emotional discharge are personality changes that developed after the accident and are also consistent with regulatory/frontal lobe dysfunction. With this clinical picture, it can be cogently argued to the court that the possibility exists that projection fibers between some subcortical structures (i.e., limbic) and the frontal lobes were disrupted. Indeed, such an occurrence is not unusual in closed head trauma which often produces shearing of subcortical white matter. An attenuation of perception of cutaneous stimulation presented to the left hand was evidenced suggesting equivocal conclusions in this case. Although this deficit may represent an insult to the right parietal area, one can argue that this finding can be attributed to this patient's diagnosed peripheral nerve disorder (Carpel Tunnel Syndrome), even though one would expect this disorder to produce bilateral sensory deficits of the hands.

To summarize, although there was evidence suggesting deficits in complex speech generation, complex verbal analysis and verbal memory, it was difficult to argue that they were accident related injuries given the patient's premorbid dysgraphia and dyslexia. Although the two sets of deficits may be represented by related functional systems, the possibility exists that the constellation of deficits not identified premorbidly (complex speech, verbal analysis and verbal memory) are accident related and share a common underlying dysfunctional factor (i.e., left prefrontal area). Nevertheless, such a possibility will remain remote in the eyes of a jury and will be difficult to defend.

COGNITIVE AND EMOTIONAL PROBLEMS

ARISING FROM A HEAD INJURY

Elizabeth Teegarden

Department of Psychiatry
University of Nebraska Medical Center
Omaha, Nebraska

As noted in the previous paper by Katz, three men were injured in the accident suffered by that patient. Each of these patients is interesting because each reacted quite uniquely to a very similar experience. A presentation of each of these cases is instructive in examining the forensic consequences of head injuries.

In this case, the patient is a 42 year old, right-handed man who completed nine years of formal schooling and a GED and who was employed as a foreman on a powerline crew. In June 1983, he and another foreman were walking past a city warehouse on their coffee break. Inside, there was a work crew operating a paint compressor from a cherry picker. The crew asked the patient and his friend to help them move the compressor. While they were moving it, the person operating the cherry picker hit an overhead telephone cable which was attached to the warehouse. This caused the upper portion of the brick building to fall, striking the patient and his friend.

The patient was hit on the right side of his neck, his head and back. He was unconscious for a few minutes and hospitalized for eight days with left hemiparesis and neck pain. After discharge, he continued to complain of memory loss for the accident, personality changes (paranoia and irritability), tremors of the upper extremities, headaches and slowed cognitive responses. He was readmitted to the hospital in August 1983, because of exacerbated neck pain. A CT evaluation, with and without contrast, showed a slight increase in attenuation in the right parietal lobe with no shift of midline structures or the lateral ventricles. X-rays showed a cervical subluxation and in September 1983, a posterior vertebral fusion of C5-C7 was performed.

During his second hospital admission, the patient was given a psychological assessment. On the WAIS, he obtained a Full Scale IQ of 79, a Verbal IQ of 82 and a Performance IQ of 78. Scores were uniformly low across subtests. Most of his responses on the Rorschach were perseverative "butterflies". On the MMPI he had elevations on scales 1, 2, 3, 7 and 8.

Prior to the accident, there were no job-related difficulties or medical/emotional problems. Family and social relationships were stable and he was actively involved in various hobbies and outdoor activities. Following the accident, he often got lost in his relatively small home town, was unable to read the many magazines to which he subscribed, nor could he perform mechanical repairs on cars because he couldn't remember how the parts fit back together. He was very reluctant to leave his house, avoided talking to lifelong friends and walking near buildings, and became upset when his wife left him alone.

Because of his impaired emotional and intellectual functioning, he was unable to return to his former job and was subsequently fired, receiving $180 per week from Workman's Compensation. In 1984, he and the other injured parties hired an attorney to sue the telephone company that had attached the cable to the wall. The suit claimed that the telephone company was negligent and thus liable for personal damages since they had attached the cable to a wall that was not structurally sound enough to support it.

A major emphasis in the case would be to show that the patient's cognitive and emotional functioning was severely impaired and that this impairment was caused by the accident. Along with other expert witnesses, the attorney hired two neuropsychologists to assess the presence/absence and severity of brain impairment. He thought that two would be preferable in order to better educate and persuade a jury, given the nature of the injuries. He also wanted to have an evaluation completed just prior to the actual trial date since the first assessment was completed 1 1/2 years before the trial. The first assessment was completed in October 1984 and this assessment was done in October 1985. It was felt that the same tests should be used in the second evaluation in order to assess similarities and/or changes in functioning. Other tests were also used to provide a more complete picture of his emotional and cognitive functioning.

ASSESSMENT RESULTS

Behavioral Observations

The patient appeared to be much older than his stated age and walked with a slight limp. Spontaneous speech was somewhat terse with dysnomia and thought blocking evident. His affect was blunted but he did joke from time to time. Tremors of the head and hands were observed, especially during the testing situation. He was oriented to person and place but not to time in that he did not know the date or his date of birth. He displayed a lack of concern and understanding about his family, current events and his future.

Neuropsychological Evaluation

The patient's performance on neuropsychological testing indicated deficits in most areas of brain-related functioning. On the Nebraska Neuropsychological Examination, 21 of the 37 scales were elevated above the critical level. On fine and gross motor coordination tasks, his movements were stiff, slow

and awkward with associated tremors and he was usually unable to
perform the required sequences. When drawing or writing, he
showed tremors and produced enlarged designs and letters which
were difficult to read.

When listening to beeps and patterns of rhythms on a tape,
he was unable to distinguish between differing patterns or
intensities and was unable to accurately count the number of
beeps heard even while using his fingers to count. He was
unable to tap various rhythmic patterns.

Overall tactile functioning was intact but he was slow to
respond when naming objects placed in his hands and perseverated
with the same incorrect response when asked to identify letters,
numbers and shapes drawn on his left hand. On visual processing
tasks, he was able to identify pictures of objects but often
could not think of the correct name within the allotted time.
He was unable to do most visual-spatial tasks, including
identifying directions on a map or drawing the time on a blank
clock.

Receptive speech was within normal limits. He experienced
difficulty with many expressive speech tasks in that he was slow
to respond, his rate of speech was slow and production was
limited. On arithmetic items, he was able to solve most simple
one-digit addition, subtraction and multiplication problems by
writing them out and then counting on his fingers.

Table 1: Nebraska Neuropsychological Evaluation (NENE)*

Scale	T-Score	Scale	T-Score
1	115	22	96
2	121	23	110
3	121	24	81
4	97	25	102
5	105	26	103
6	109	27	97
7	124	28	95
8	90	29	93
9	101	30	105
10	103	31	101
11	86	32	100
12	113	33	108
13	88	34	113
14	102	35	109
15	111	36	96
16	98	37	105
17	175	F1	99
18	98	F2	90
19	96	F3	123
20	99	F4	104
21	94	F5	99

*Patient's critical level was 100.

Mr. G.'s verbal memory was somewhat better than his visual memory but both were within the impaired range. On visual items, he did better with meaningful stimuli in contrast to designs. On verbal items, his immediate and delayed memory for discrete words was adequate but he had difficulty remembering numbers, sentences and the content of paragraphs.

On general intellectual items, he was unable to say how things are alike or different, what various common sayings meant or mentally solve arithmetic problems. It took him a long time to respond to questions and he tried to use visual gestures with his hands in order to elicit the word/idea he was trying to say.

On the Halstead-Reitan (HRNB), his average impairment rating was 2.72 (out of 4) which is in the moderately impaired range. On the Category Test, it was difficult for him to guess the correct principle. Once he understood it, he usually perseverated with the same idea throughout most of the next subtest. On the Wisconsin Card Sort Test, he also perseverated with the idea from the previous principle, completing three categories. He finally became so frustrated and angry that he threatened to quit.

On the Tactual Performance Test, his total time was within normal limits. He was able to reproduce from (incidental) memory, six of the ten geometric shapes but only two were drawn in the correct spatial arrangement. Manual Finger Tapping elicited a superior performance of his nondominant left hand over his right hand although both were in the impaired range. This was unexpected since the dominant hand is usually superior and he had had a left hemiparesis following the accident.

He had 12 errors on Speech Sounds while discriminating between nonsense words. When listening to various same and different rhythmical pattern on the Seashore Rhythm Test, 29 of his 30 responses were "same". This was similar to his performance on the Nebraska Neuropsychological Examination in which he was unable to differentiate between similar patterns.

Table 2: Halstead-Reitan Results From 1984 and 1985

Subtest	October, 1984	October, 1985
Average Impairment Rating	3.45	2.72
Category Test (total errors)	114	88
TPT Time (total)	22.5	15.3
TPT Memory	3	6
TPT Location	0	2
Rhythm (errors)	15	16
Speech Sounds	17	12
Tapping (DH)	42.4	38.4
Tapping (NDH)	30.6	38.2
Trails A	175"	124"
Trails B	180"+	573"
Aphasia	9	8
Perceptual	not done	9

On the Trails Test, he had to stop after each line and repeat aloud the previous letters/numbers before he knew what the next letter/number should be. His errors on the Aphasia Screening Test were made on spelling and mathematical computation items. His performance on the Sensory-Perceptual Examination was normal.

Performance on the Wechsler Memory Scale and the Randt Memory Test indicated deficits in immediate, delayed and remote memory. If was difficult for him to remember words, numbers, paired words, sentences and the content of paragraphs. His memory for designs and pictures was somewhat better but also in the impaired range. When asked to recall auditory and visual items 24 hours after their presentation, he was unable to remember most of the items. He was unsure of his age, did not know his telephone number and could not remember the alphabet.

On the WAIS-R, his Verbal, Performance and Full Scale IQ's were in the borderline range of intellectual functioning with little scatter among subtests. He was slow to respond to both verbal and performance items and he attempted to use hand gestures to define words and concepts. Some of his responses to questions were personalized. For example, when asked to define the word "terminate", he promptly said, " I was involuntarily terminated from my job-the letter said so-I was fired".

Brief achievement testing on the Wide Range Achievement

Table 3: WAIS-R AND WRAT-R RESULTS

	October, 1984	October, 1985
WAIS-R*		
Information	6	6
Digit Span	6	5
Vocabulary	6	7
Arithmetic	4	4
Comprehension	4	5
Similarities	3	4
Picture Completion	2	2
Picture Arrangement	4	4
Block Design	5	6
Object Assembly	6	6
Digit Symbol	2	2
Verbal IQ	72	74
Performance IQ	70	71
Full Scale IQ	70	72
WRAT-R **		
Reading Recognition	2	5
Spelling	0.4	0.8
Arithmetic	0.5	0.08

* All WAIS-R scores are scale scores except for IQ.
** All WRAT-R scores are percentiles.

Test indicated significant impairment in spelling (0.8th percentile), arithmetic (0.08th %ile) and word recognition (5th percentile). He was able to spell only five words, unable to spell his last name and able to solve only a few arithmetic problems. This indicated a decrement in performance since the patient had, ten years previously, passed a GED exam without taking classes, had before the accident been an avid reader and kept track of the family's finances.

Personality testing suggested that Mr. G. was confused, depressed, indecisive, anxious and had a low frustration tolerance. On the Rorschach, 13 of his 15 responses were identical. Other indices indicated that his attempts to integrate exceeded his cognitive abilities and he had low self-esteem. He showed an indifference to conventionality and people even though predominantly stimulated from the environment rather than from within and he exerted excessive control over his impulses and emotions.

Additional Evaluations

As part of the total examination, the patient was also seen by a neurologist, a physical therapist, a pain center, and had a Magnetic Resonance Imaging (MRI).

The neurologist found some mild to moderate features of an involuntary movement disorder which was not debilitating. This was manifested by head titubation and a variably present tremor in the hands which went away with purposeful movement. There was also evidence of a thought disorder with slow cognition, inability to lay down new memory and an inability to concentrate. Speech was at times slightly dysarthric but otherwise normal.

His thoughts were fixed around the course of the accident and his operation. The neurologist concluded that there were

Table 5: MMPI RESULTS

Scale	October, 1984 T-Scores	October, 1985 T-Scores
L	63	63
F	>100	80
K	53	55
Hs	73	88
D	69	82
Hy	65	82
Pd	64	71
Mf	65	45
Pa	85	59
Pt	77	77
Sc	105	88
Ma	78	60
Si	61	61

definite difficulties with fronto-parietal lobe functions in terms of global dysfunction of information processing in all modalities. There was a medial-temporal dysfunction which was severe with an inability to accurately lay down new memory and recall recent memories. Finally, he felt that there was a strong overlay of personality and/or thought disorder coloring the nature and degree of his disability.

The pain evaluation revealed that he was experiencing numerous tension headaches which started when he tried to do light work. He also developed muscular pain in the back of his neck and shoulders which also prevented him from working. When he slept at night, he woke up many times due to the pain over his entire body. It was recommended that he enroll in a pain management program so that he could be taught the skills necessary to help him better cope with his chronic pain problem.

The Magnetic Resonance Images (MRI) of the head found a small area of increased signal intensity in the left frontal lobe. There was also asymmetry of the temporal lobes with the volume of white matter in the right temporal lobe decreased in size when compared to the left temporal lobe. No other abnormalities were found.

This evaluation found significant neuromuscular deficits which were evident in his legs, arms and hands. There were decreases in range of motion in the cervical and lumbar regions, balance difficulties and observed tremors.

CONCLUSIONS AND DISCUSSION

The patient's performance on the various psychological tests indicated diffuse brain dysfunction in the frontal and parieto-occipito-temporal areas. Tests of fine and gross motor functioning, auditory discrimination, left-sided tactile perception, and visual-perceptual synthesis and organization indicated performance in the impaired range. His verbal fluency, problem-solving and reasoning abilities, and ability to encode and recall information were also substantially impaired. These findings were in agreement with the neurological and radiological assessments.

The patient also showed the emotional impairment often seen in this type of brain injury, i.e., inflexibility, emotional flatness and a lack of concern about some aspects of daily living. These findings were consistent with his markedly diminished level of functioning. Before the accident, he held a responsible job, engaged in many hobbies and traveled throughout the midwest. He was no longer able to function independently because of the deficits enumerated above, all of which developed post-injury.

There was some minor improvement in functioning in the elapsed year between assessments. The improved scores were elicited on the Category Test, on the HRNB impairment index and on the time taken to perform Trails A and the TPT. These general indicators of brain dysfunction generally improve spontaneously over time while remaining in the impaired range. During the time following the accident and up to the second evaluation, the patient had refused psychotherapy and cognitive rehabilitation.

It was felt that this was due, in large part, to his poor judgment and feelings of alternating depression and apathy concerning his many deficits. Thus, it was not surprising that in 2 1/2 years following the accident, there was little recovery of the various cognitive dysfunctions because of the emotional deficits which were incurred from the accident. The patient was depressed about his substantial impairments and chronic pain. Therapeutic intervention was recommended in order to help him cope with his feelings about his injury and subsequent deficits, even though he had refused this intervention in the past. In addition, a pain management program was recommended so that he could learn to handle his pain in a more effective way.

The refusal of the patient to seek treatment brings up an important issue in many forensic cases. Because of the nature of their injuries, many patients with poor judgment secondary to the injury will refuse treatment unless coerced. In general, both professionals and families are reluctant to do this, seeing the patient as free to choose whether to enter treatment. This leads to a variety of serious problems including cases which get considerably worse over time as emotional and cognitive problems interact with environmental problems (such as loss of the job, irritation and loss of a spouse, and reluctance of friends to come around) to create even more massive deficits.

In many of these cases, early intervention and treatment could stop some of the secondary problems which later appear. However, to get the patient into treatment takes firm handling and demands by both the professionals and family along with a tolerance of the abuse from the patient likely to result from such pressure. The treatment, if given properly, can be useful in mitigating the extent of damages. The authors have seen many cases where such treatment is denied by insurance carriers only to result in much worse damage and higher settlements than were necessary. In other cases, early treatment has stopped the development of problems similar to the ones described in this case.

PRE-EXISTING ALCOHOLISM FOLLOWED

BY HEAD AND BODY TRAUMA

George Archibald

Department of Psychiatry
University of Nebraska Medical Center
Omaha, Nebraska

This is the third of the cases injured in the same accident involing a cherry picker and a telephone line. This case was complicated by preexisting alcoholism as well as an inability of the patient to recognize the presence of his deficits.

The patient was a 49 year old, right-handed male with a high school education who was employed as an electrical lineman. His history included chronic alcohol dependence and a closed head trauma which occurred approximately 2 1/2 years before the neuropsychological evaluation. The patient reported that the while at work, the upper portion of an exterior wall was dislodged by a crew working from a "bucket" truck when the boom of the truck struck an overhead cable and dislodged the upper exterior wall of a building.

The dislodged bricks struck the patient and the medical records indicate that he sustained: 1) a right linear skull fracture (extending from the occiput to the temporal fossa traversing the skull at approximately the level of the sulvanian fissure). A CAT scan was read as indicating a right subdural hematoma with low grade shift of the midline structures from right to left and compression of the right lateral ventricle, 2) a cervical spine fracture of C6 and C7 (not detected until 4 months post injury when a CT scan was performed subsequent to complaints of numbness and tingling in the lower arms and hands), and 3) a phalengeal fracture of the great right toe.

The patient reports a brief period of unconsciousness after the injury. He was taken to a local hospital where vital signs were stabilized and then he was transferred to a larger medical center. Medical records indicate a dilated left pupil, bradycardia and subjective complaints of distress. A change in status necessitated a craniotomy and evacuation of the subdural hematoma, and medical records indicate considerable contusion and petechial hemorrhage of the anterior right temporal lobe. He also underwent a spinal fusion of C6 and C7 with subsequent bracing with a halo, and the phalengeal fracture was operatively reduced and pinned.

At the time of the testing, the patient reported a loss of acuity for smell, difficulties concentrating and remembering, a loss in efficiency and ability to perform mechanical tasks, fatigue, a "don't care" attitude, depression, pain in the lower back, neck and foot with physical exertion, and numbness and tension in the right frontotemporal scalp region. The patient denied or minimized adjustment difficulties and the extent of his impairments, however, his wife reports significant withdrawal from social activities, restlessness, sleep difficulties, a decrease in sexual activity, a lack of concern over finances and child discipline, marked inefficiency in performing household repairs, difficulties in verbal expression including tangential and sporadic recall of past events, stuttering when under stress and a decrease in functional vocabulary and word finding. The patient's wife also corroborated the patient's complaints of memory and concentration difficulties and apathy.

FORENSIC ISSUES

The patient was referred for a neuropsychological evaluation by his attorney to obtain information in preparation for a personal injury suit. The attorney had requested a re-evaluation of the patient as a prior neuropsychological assessment, one year previously, had indicated substantial deficits. In addition, it was considered important to have two expert witnesses, given the difficulties anticipated with establishing a causal connection between the injury and current functional impairments. Thus, the current assessment was directed at: 1) longitudinally assessing neuropsychological and concomitant emotional dysfunction following the injury, 2) establishing the extent of the patient's current occupational capabilities and life skills, and 3) determining the appropriate rehabilitation treatment regime.

There were several forensic issues involved in this case which are illustrative of a number of personal injury cases and thus, they will be discussed briefly. Of primary concern was the issue of whether the neuropsychological deficits and concomitant emotional difficulties could be causally linked to the head trauma. A collateral report from a psychiatrist treating the patient post injury expressed the opinion that the patient's presenting difficulties of low self-esteem and depression were not caused by the injury but reflected a "long time personality problem" that led to the history of alcohol dependence and current difficulties.

In general, there are often attempts by defense attorneys to discredit neuropsychological testimony by raising doubts about the validity of the instruments and questioning the causal connections between subjective complaints consistent with a "post-concussion syndrome" (e.g., headaches, nightmares, poor concentration, memory dysfunction, decreased efficiency, decreased sexual interest, sleep disorders, etc.). These attempts generally take the form of arguments which link current dysfunctions to a presumed premorbid personality disorder or malingering and question the validity of psychological and neuropsychological test findings.

In this case, collateral diagnostic procedures (MRI,

Regional Cerebral Blood Flow) were used to corroborate the neuropsychological test results. In addition, the internal consistency of the results and their correspondence to the research literature on the constellation of deficits, which correlate with the site of injury, were utilized to establish a causal connection. It should be noted that the neurological consult alone would have been insufficient in this case, as it concluded that the patient exhibited classic personality changes consistent with a post traumatic syndrome.

As indicated above, this diagnosis can be challenged by recourse to premorbid personality disorders and attacks on the validity of psychological and neuropsychological test results. The utility of utilizing additional, objective, diagnostic procedures such as the MRI is thus illustrated by this case.

This case also illustrates one among many role conflicts that a neuropsychologist can face when involved with forensic assessment. Specifically, the conflict can involve the role of the neuropsychologist as an expert witness in a legal case and the role incumbent on the neuropsychologist as a practicing mental health professional. For example, is it the role of the neuropsychologist to argue for a disposition that results in the greatest treatment benefit, or is it the responsibility of the neuropsychologist, in the role of "expert witness", to present the facts of the case in an adversarial setting, so that compensation will be commensurate with the assessed and experienced deficits?

It could be argued that testimony which emphasizes functional losses and argues for a large settlement would not be of optimal benefit as the patient would, in essence, be "encouraged" to remain unemployed and his self-image, already depressed, would be further eroded by testimony that concludes that he is brain-injured and not fully competent or functional.

Table 1: WAIS-R Results From Two Testings

Subtest	First Testing	Current
INFORMATION:	10	7
DIGIT SPAN:	7	10
VOCABULARY:	10	8
ARITHMETIC:	8	8
COMPREHENSION:	13	8
SIMILARITIES:	11	13
PICTURE COMPLETION:	11	9
PICTURE ARRANGEMENT:	10	10
BLOCK DESIGN:	12	9
OBJECT ASSEMBLY:	12	11
DIGIT SYMBOL:	6	6
VERBAL IQ:	100	96
PERFORMANCE IQ:	112	104
FULL-SCALE IQ:	106	98

On the other hand, presenting testimony where functional losses are balanced with capabilities and optimistic predictions of treatment outcome are put forth, may undermine the legal case and the award of compensation for treatment and losses may not be forthcoming.

CURRENT NEUROPSYCHOLOGICAL TEST FINDINGS

On the WAIS-R (Table 1) the patient achieved a Verbal IQ of 100, a Performance IQ of 112, and a Full Scale IQ of 106. The Full Scale IQ is in the average range of general intellectual functioning. The patient's performance, however, is not consistent across subtests. Digit Span elicited 6 digits forward and 3 backward indicating a relatively depressed performance on the more demanding backward series. On Digit Symbol the speed of performance was significantly less than expected. On the Arithmetic subtest performance was below average. This triad of subtest weaknesses indicates decreased mental efficiency and less than intact attention and concentration.

Verbal responses on Information, Vocabulary, and Similarities were brief and unelaborated with average response latencies. When performance was stressed, however, by requiring more lengthy verbal responses to analytic questions on Comprehension, numerous hesitations, repetitions and decreases in voice projection were observed.

On the Halstead-Reitan Neuropsychological Battery (Table 2), the Category Test was in the impaired range with performance characterized by difficulties abstracting the correct principle and numerous incidences of perseverative responding. On the

Table 2: Halstead-Reitan Neuropsychological Battery

Subtest	First Testing	Current Testing
CATEGORY TEST:	115 errors	79 errors
TACTUAL PERFORMANCE		
TOTAL TIME:	16.6 min.	6.6 min.
MEMORY:	9 correct	7 correct
LOCALIZATION:	6 correct	1 correct
SEASHORE RHYTHM:	27 raw score	25 raw score
SPEECH SOUNDS:	4 errors	5 errors
FINGER OSCILLATION		
RIGHT:	55	62
LEFT:	56	55
TRAIL MAKING		
PART A:	54"	26"
PART B:	85"	109"
APHASIA SCREENING: 4 errors		0 errors
WISCONSIN CARD SORT:		
CORRECT:	79	79
ERRORS:	49	49
NONPERSEVERATIVE ERRORS:	17	31
PERSEVERATIVE ERRORS:	32	18
CATEGORIES:	1	3

Memory Localization component of the Tactual Performance Test, the patient had significant difficulties and was unable to reproduce the correct spatial arrangement of 9 out of 10 geometric shapes. Performance in the impaired range was also evident on the Seashore Rhythm Test and Part B of Trail Making.

Finger Oscillation elicited the expected superiority of the dominant over the nondominant hand and performance was within expectations. On the Tactual Performance Test, however, the nondominant hand performance was well below expectations. Performance on Speech Sounds Perception, Part A of Trail Making, and Aphasia Screening was within the expected range. The sensory-perceptual exam revealed an absence of tactile, auditory or visual suppressions, intact tactile form recognition, stereognosis and finger recognition but some difficulties with finger tip number writing on the right (dominant) hand.

On the Nebraska Neuropsychological Examination, which provides a more discrete analysis of neuropsychological performance by utilizing items tapping basic functional abilities, the obtained profile is in the borderline range with several scales (right and left complex tactile, bilateral tactile, trails, and stroop) at or near the critical level. There is also evidence of impairment when performance is evaluated qualitatively with attention to behaviors indicative of compromised executive functions.

Table 3: Nebraska Neuropsychological Examination

Scale	Score*	Scale	Score*
1	88	22	96
2	93	23	89
3	90	24	80
4	95	25	92
5	90	26	94
6	93	27	94
7	96	28	91
8	88	29	88
9	96	30	94
10	95	31	92
11	99	32	95
12	100	33	102
13	100	34	91
14	94	35	89
15	90	36	94
16	93	37	95
17	99	F1	95
18	97	F2	83
19	95	F3	92
20	100	F4	94
21	94	F5	96

*Critical level is 100.

Specifically, the patient took an inordinate amount of time to formulate answers to some relatively simple questions and exhibited difficulties on those items that required cognitive flexibility and the utilization of self-monitoring to guide performance. Associated with the above were difficulties with inhibiting, switching, sustaining and initiating responses. The maintenance of memory traces when interference was present was also problematic.

Verbal abilities were intact on tasks which assessed confrontation naming (Boston Naming Test) and nonverbal identification of word meaning (Peabody Picture Vocabulary Test). However, when verbal task complexity was increased by including a memory or affective component, there were notable repetitions, hesitations and formulation difficulties. For example, with the immediate and delayed recall of short stories, verbal fluency and organization was impaired. Similarly, when discussing emotionally distressing events or when responding to ambiguous stimuli on the Rorschach, verbal difficulties were evident.

Performance on visuospatial tasks revealed a similar pattern, i.e., the patient's responses to discrete, simple, unstressed tasks were within normal limits but deficits are apparent with increased complexity and task demands. Thus, performance on the Benton Visual Retention Test and the Hooper Visual Organization Test was without significant difficulties. When a complex figure copying task was presented (Rey-Osterrieth Complex Figure), however, there was a considerable loss of internal details on the immediate and delayed recall conditions.

Performance on the Wechsler Memory Scale (WMS) (Table 4) and Randt Memory Test indicate intact rote memory for simple material when external structure and cues are provided. In fact, on the more structured WMS, the patient's overall score is in the average range. However, when memory tasks are complex, involve interference or require sustained mental effort performance is impaired. Thus, on the WMS, performance on the Mental Control subtest and part B of Memory for Passages is impaired. Similarly, on the Randt Memory Test, memory is intact on the immediate recall of digits and simple verbal passages.

Nonetheless, memory impairments are evident when there is delayed recall with intervening interference (acquisition and recall of paired words) or when the patient is not specifically

Table 4: Wechsler Memory Scale

	First Testing	Last Testing
INFORMATION:	5	6
ORIENTATION:	5	5
MENTAL CONTROL:	4	4
MEMORY PASSAGES:	6.5	7
DIGITS TOTAL:	11	11
VISUAL REPRODUCTION:	9	11
ASSOCIATE LEARNING:	13	12
MQ	97	100

Table 5: MMPI Results

Scale	First Testing	Second Testing
L	30	40
F	60	64
K	44	44
Hs	59	67
D	94	94
Hy	58	56
Pd	62	60
Mf	67	71
Pa	50	44
Pt	75	73
Sc	71	84
Ma	60	65
Si	70	77

cued to remember certain items (incidental learning and delayed recall of picture names). Thus, the overall score on the less structured Randt Memory Test is in the impaired range.

The patient's responses to the MMPI (Table 5) are consonant with individuals who are experiencing marked psychological deficits characterized by a loss of efficiency, stereotyped approaches to solving problems, difficulties with concentration and memory. These are associated with withdrawal, substantial depressive emotions and confusion.

On the Rorschach, the patient exhibited extreme difficulty in formulating responses as indicated by the inordinately long reaction times and limited number of responses. This is consistent with the MMPI profile indicating impairments in mental efficiency and depressive affect. Because of the limited number of responses statistical indices of personality functioning can not be applied. Nonetheless, the obtained protocol does rule out a formal thought disorder and indicates that the above MMPI profile, which is indicative of substantial impairment, is not the result of psychotic thought processes.

Longitudinal Assessment

A comparison of the testing performed at 15 and 28 months post injury reveals a marked consistency in the findings with some relative difference that can be accounted for by the margin of error contained in the standard error of measurement or by relative shifts in functional abilities.

Neurological Findings

The patient was assessed by a consulting neurologist who reported no positive neurological findings except for a decrease in olfactory acuity. The physical and general neurological exam, motor, tactile, parietal and frontal lobe functions, Cranial Nerves II - XII were assessed as within normal limits. The neurologist did note, however, that the patient's history and subjective complaints indicating personality changes were consistent with a post traumatic syndrome.

Diagnostic Medical Findings

The Regional Cerebral Blood Flow Study utilizing the Xenon 133 inhalation method was read as within normal limits for gray and white matter flow in the right and left cerebral hemispheres. In addition, a MRI of the head and cervical spine was obtained. The T1 weighted images of the brain scan revealed areas of decreased signal intensity in the posterior lateral and inferior aspect of the right temporal lobe and the inferior portion of the left temporal lobe. The T2 weighted images showed increased signal intensity bilaterally.

The findings were read as consistent with an infarct or gliosis from a previous trauma. The MRI of the cervical spine revealed a metal rod in the posterior elements of the cervical spine (from a previous spinal fusion of C6 and C7), a central herniated nucleus pulposus in the C3-4 interspace and an impression of the posterior aspect of the dural sac at C5.

A Physical Therapy Evaluation was conducted and indicated no gross neuromuscular deficits, however, significant losses in musculoskeletal functioning were detected including: limitations in trunk rotation, side bending, lumbar extension and lordosis, and a greater than normal amount of lumbar muscle tone. A Pain Assessment indicated chronic back, neck and head pain that was consistent with a chronic pain disorder.

CONCLUSIONS

The results of the neuropsychological evaluation indicate several constellations of impairments which are entirely consistent with the history and site of brain trauma. Medical records at the time of injury document a right subdural hematoma and skull fracture with observable damage to the right anterior temporal lobe and adjacent structures. With such an injury, it would be predicted that there would be injury to: 1) the right frontal-temporal brain areas, 2) the contralateral (left) hemisphere opposite the the site of impact due to contra coup effects, and 3) potential damage to subcortical white matter and the basil areas of the brain because of rotational shearing forces. The results of the MRI confirm physical damage to the anterior temporal and dorsolateral frontal areas of both cerebral hemispheres.

The constellation of deficits evident on the neuropsychological tests correspond to the expected areas of brain damage, given the site and nature of the insult. The patient exhibits deficits in functions associated with the dorsolateral and basal frontal lobes including: decreased mental efficiency, difficulties with sustained attention and concentration, deficits in cognitive flexibility (manifested by deficits maintaining and switching cognitive sets required to reason and solve problems, and subtle difficulties in initiating and inhibiting on-going behavior), memory impairments most evident when there is a lack of external structure or cues to guide encoding and recall, or when interference is present including that produced when task demands are multifaceted (e.g., reading a newspaper article and trying to understand the main points and remember them at the same time).

In addition, the patient presents with the "classic" constellation of emotional and adjustment impairments associated with the dorsolateral, frontal brain areas: apathy, a lack of drive, indifference or unconcern for functional impairments and life tasks, and depressed affect. The above is seen, as expected, in the presence of intact intellectual abilities as measured by formal intelligence tests and intact performance on verbal and visuospatial tasks which do not demand significant "executive" control provided by the frontal brain areas.

The reported loss of acuity in the sense of smell corresponds with shearing of the olfactory filaments located on the basal surface of the frontal lobes. In addition, deficits with complex verbal and visuospatial tasks can be accounted for by damage to the frontal and right and left temporal areas of the brain. The above resulting from the site of impact, counter coup and rotational shearing.

Although the above cognitive impairments are relatively subtle or absent when assessed by performance on simple, discrete tasks on neuropsychological measures, they become pronounced when sustained complex activity is required such as that involved in vocational pursuits and adaptive and functional social interactions. The patient's reports of difficulties in completing household repair tasks including: losing tools, difficulties re-assembling mechanical parts, decreased ability to concentrate and remember task sequences, and neck, back, foot and head pain that increases with physical exertion are explainable as a result of the injury and illustrate the occupational disabilities that would be evident if this patient returned to his preinjury vocation.

SUMMARY OF FORENSIC ISSUES

The results of the neuropsychological, psychological, and medical-diagnostic procedures are in substantial agreement and document functional losses as a result of the work related injury. A longitudinal assessment reveals a relatively stable pattern of deficits over time. The internal consistency of the neuropsychological and psychological test results, and the correspondence of the assessed deficits to the site and nature of the injury, with corroboration by the MRI of structural damage to the cerebral cortex, provide a firm basis for testimony by the neuropsychologist. If the MRI had been nonconfirmatory, the neuropsychologist would be more open to refutation by potential arguments that a "post traumatic disorder" is at best an educated guess and the pattern of deficits could have resulted from premorbid personality and cognitive deficits.

This case also illustrates that a potential role conflict that can result from the position of the neuropsychologist as a mental health professional and an "expert witness" can be resolved. In this case it was decided that the patient's inability to acknowledge his functional losses and thus a corresponding unwillingness to enter treatment was the primary dispositional issue. The neuropsychologist, as a mental health professional, would thus attempt to confront the patient with the seriousness of his current emotional and cognitive impairments as a prerequisite for treatment compliance. The role of the neuropsychologist as "expert witness" in an adversarial process does not conflict, as the testimony presented would serve the purpose of establishing the seriousness of the neuropsychological deficits that have resulted from the injury.

It was recommended that the patient undergo treatment in a multidisciplinary brain rehabilitation program that included interventions that would also address the chronic pain disorder and emotional dysfunctions.

HEAD TRAUMA IN A HIGH SCHOOL GIRL

WITH SUBTLE RESIDUAL SYMPTOMS

Iris Rucker

Department of Psychiatry
University of Nebraska Medical Center
Omaha, Nebraska

In many cases of brain dysfunction, physicians will dismiss patients as cured despite the continued existence of some subtle and sometimes not so subtle cognitive and motor deficits. Such patients generally later have substantial problems in attempting to return to normal life. However, because they have been dismissed as "cured" by a neurosurgeon or neurologist, such cases can present a difficult problem for the neuropsychologist must contradict the "medical authorities". The following case represents such a case, as well as illustrates the potential value of rehabilitation treatment when such cases are identified.

HISTORY

The patient, KK, was a twenty year old, right-handed, single, caucasian female who was a high school graduate and had completed one and one-half years of college at a small, four-year state university. Her high school grades were As and Bs; she graduated salutatorian of her class of twenty students. Throughout her public school years, she was evaluated, on several occasions, with the Henmon-Nelson Tests of Mental Ability, producing an IQ of 111 in 1975, an IQ of 112 in 1977 and an IQ of 109 in 1980.

In October of 1982, KK completed the American College Testing Program test for college admission and produced the following standard scores: 20 in English; 11 in Math; 14 in Social Sciences; 18 in Natural Sciences and a composite score of 16. These standard scores represent the following percentiles for college bound students: 64 for English; 26 for Math; 40 for Social Sciences; 37 for Natural Sciences and 39 for the composite percentile.

This young woman reports that prior to her injury, she was socially active and well-liked by her peers. She enjoyed groups and was able to make new friends easily. Additionally, KK states that she was a quick and entertaining conversationalist. She made decisions easily and was firm in her opinion once she had decided an issue for herself. KK described herself as able to problem-solve and able to easily arrive at solutions. She worked with her family on the farm, doing chores as facilely as any one. While she was capable of reacting to specific situations with great anger, that wasn't usually her first reaction. KK described herself as "happy and fairly easy-going".

During the evening of July 23, 1983, she attended a party at "the sand pit", a gathering place of young people of the area which is on the outskirts of the town in which KK lived. She states that she knew she was going to have a beer or two so she did not drive but had her brother drop her at the party and would walk home since it wasn't very far, it was warm weather and the exercise would be good for her. At approximately midnight, it started to rain so KK decided to leave the party and go home. She was walking by the side of the road when she was struck by a pickup truck driven by a neighbor boy with two of his friends as passengers.

Reportedly, they did not realize they had hit any one and drove on into town. Within thirty to forty-five minutes, they returned to the spot of the accident, located KK, picked her up and put her in the back of the truck and drove, speedily, into town again. As they were rounding a corner, KK fell from the truck; the young man who was riding with her in the back also fell out, as did a beer keg that they were carrying. The beer keg, in it's fall, fell onto KK. The boys picked her up again and drove to the sheriff's office. He called the rescue squad (it was 12:50 AM when the EMS unit received the call) and KK was transported by ambulance to the emergency room of the hospital in a nearby town (it was 1:46 AM when the unit arrived at the hospital).

MEDICAL TREATMENT

On examination at the hospital, her pulse was 88, blood pressure was 160/90 and respirations were regular at approximately 20. No blood was noted behind the TM's. There was a large (approximately 3 inch) laceration above the left eye; it appeared to go all the way to the bone but without major muscle involvement. Her pupils were equal and round and reacted somewhat sluggishly to light. There was a very large laceration at the junction of the buccal mucosa and gingiva anteriorly and extending around to the left. A "fair" amount of blood was noted in the pharynx which required periodic suctioning.

The cervical spine was x-rayed and verified as intact. Abrasions were noted over the left side of the face; abrasions were also noted on the upper extremities. Both lungs had rhonchi, assumed to have been caused by the aspiration of blood. Her heart had a regular tachycardia while her abdomen and pelvis seemed normal. Decorticate posturing was noted on the left side and there was a large, deep abrasion on the right great toe which appeared to extend down to the tendon, leaving the distal phalanx visualized. KK would withdraw from painful stimuli on the right side but her left side gave variable responses to painful stimuli - occasionally she would withdraw but usually she would produce movement on the contralateral side with grimacing. She displayed sustained clonus at the left ankle while the left biceps, tendon and reflex appeared normal.

An endotracheal tube was placed through the nasal route because of the persistent need to suction her mouth and the apparent blood aspirations. Blood gases were then obtained and were reported as: Ph=7.41, CO2=29 and PO2=124. A right pneumothorax was observed when her chest was x-rayed to determine the position of the endotracheal tube. She was given a 10mg Decadron IV push to prevent/reduce cerebral edema. A second chest tube was placed, at the request of the helicopter medical crew, so that changing altitudes would not expand the pneumothorax. She was transferred by helicopter to the nearest large city hospital so that treatment could be more comprehensive. The transfer was begun at 8:30 AM.

When KK arrived at the second hospital at approximately 11:00 AM, she was responsive to requests for hand squeeze, pupils were reactive to light with the left pupil slightly larger than the right and her skin was pale and warm and diaphoretic. She was agitated, had a blood pressure of 130/95, pulse of 110 and respirations were controlled on the ventilator.

CT scan of the head revealed mild brain edema with no midline shifts; fractures in the left maxillary sinus were noted. During the exploratory abdominal surgery, a small hemoperitoneum and a 10 cc hematoma at the splenic hilum was observed. There was no active bleeding, at that time, therefore, the hematoma was not removed. Simultaneously, a LAD intracranial pressure monitor was placed in the right frontal area. Initially, her intracranial pressure was in the upper 20s mm mercury (up to 15 mm mercury is considered normal for a healthy adult) and Mannitol was administered. Slowly, over the next two days her neurological status improved, she was extubated and on her third hospital day, the LAD monitor was removed. Even so, her neurological progress was reported to be "fairly slow".

A consultation by the Oral Surgery Department was initiated for evaluation of the facial bone fractures. It was determined that she had a left mallear complex fracture with a blow out fracture of the left orbit. On 8/4/83 an open reduction with internal fixation of the fractures was completed. When postoperative facial edema resolved, it was noted that the peripheral left seventh cranial nerve was malfunctional. An Ear, Nose, Throat (ENT) consult recommended that this malfunctioning just be observed and they hypothesized that proper nerve performance would return spontaneously. Further evaluation by the ENT group, located a nasal frontal ethmoid fracture; it was recommended that KK be followed up by an ENT group in her hometown since she was at risk for further frontal sinus or nasal frontal duct problems. At the time of this consult, it was noted that she had an ulceration of her right vocal cord secondary to prolonged endotracheal intubation. A Vanceril inhaler was prescribed for this problem.

KK received physical therapy (PT) during her hospitalization on a daily basis unless she was restricted to her bed by additional surgeries and/or other treatment which contraindicated PT. Both parents were instructed in the exercises that she was to continue at home. Additionally, she was to be followed by a physical therapist in her home town.

At the time of discharge, her neurosurgeon reported that she had made "considerable" progress from a neurological point of view, i.e., she was alert, oriented and conversive. She continued to exhibit occasional periods of agitation and there was "some residual left sided hemiparesis but fine motor function seemed to be intact". Diagnoses were multiple traumatic injuries as follow:

1. Closed head injury with residual left hemiparesis
2. Left peripheral seventh cranial nerve paresis
3. Right pneumothorax, resolved
4. Left orbital blow out fracture
5. Splenic hematoma

KK was seen in September of 1983 for follow-up by her neurosurgeon. She reported to him that she did not remember being in the hospital at all and her first memory after being discharged was of a time when some calves she had been raising were shown (there was no record of how long a time period this encompassed). She explained to the physician that she was having trouble remembering recent things, not things in the past. Even so, she believed that this problem was getting better. KK had no memory of the accident or of the day of the accident. In fact, she states that her memory closest to the date of the accident was of the fourth of July weekend. Her parents confirmed that she was having memory difficulties but they explained that regarding the time between her memory of the fourth of July and the accident, there was nothing much exciting going on for her to remember.

KK reported having mild headaches, at this time, but stated that these were not a new phenomenon, she had had mild headaches prior to the accident. She was continuing to attend physical therapy twice a week at a local hospital and was doing the recommended exercises at home. She believed that her strength was gradually returning. KK planned to begin college in the winter term and wanted to take a course in the meantime, in high school English, just to see how she would do.

At the time of follow-up, the neurosurgeon reported that KK's voice was still somewhat hoarse but she displayed no gross evidence of speech difficulties. The facial incisions were clean and well-healed. Her face appeared to be symmetrical, but on command and with emotion, there was slight left side weakness. There was no nystagmus. Pupillary response to light was within the normal range. There was some decreased sensitivity to pin prick on the left side of the chin that did not involve the upper lip and did not involve her tongue. Her jaw tended to deviate to the right when she opened her mouth.

She walked with a normal based gait but without associated movement of the left arm; there was a slight circumduction of the left leg. Deep tendon reflexes in the upper extremities were quite active with the left more active than the right. She had a slight Hoffman response on the left. Rapid alternating movements of the left upper extremity were definitely awkward compared to the right. There was a slight pronation and drift when she held her arms extended in front of her with her eyes shut. There was no grossly demonstrable muscle weakness; the difficulty with shoulder movement seemed obviously connected to the acromioclavicular separation of the left shoulder.

Knee jerks were both hyperactive, with the left more active than the right. Both ankle jerks were also hyperactive but there was no obvious difference between the sides. There was a poor response on plantar stimulation and there was definitely no Babinski elicited.

KK was admitted to the hospital (the same large city comprehensive care facility she was flown to post-accident) in November of 1983 to have the separation of her left acromioclavicular joint repaired. The orthopedic surgeon, in his presurgery workup, stated that KK had an obviously deformed left shoulder, that is, it was not square and it dropped off in a rounded fashion. The acromial head of the clavicle protruded up from this area. It was palpable approximately 2 cm above the acromian process of the scapula.

She had decreased ability to elevate her left shoulder girdle and also to abduct the left shoulder (limit was approximately 30 degrees). Even so, she had normal extension and flexion around the shoulder joint; the internal and external rotations were 70 degrees and 50 degrees, respectively. These were considered, for the most part, normal. No muscular atrophy was observed, however, the left quadriceps strength was decreased somewhat when compared to the right quadriceps but not markedly so. KK walked with a slight limp, favoring her left leg; an antalgic gait was not noted. The neurological exam was significant for decreased sensation to soft touch over the area of the submental 5th nerve branch on the left side. Aside from this finding, cranial nerves and the remainder of the neurological exam were considered normal.

A resection of the distal left clavicle with acromioclavicular ligament repair was completed without incident and KK's postoperative course was unremarkable. Two days post surgery, she was ready to begin range of motion exercises with her shoulder and it was arranged that she be followed up for this treatment in her hometown.

REFERRAL AND LEGAL CONSIDERATIONS

The attorney representing this young girl requested a reevaluation of her by her neurosurgeon in May of 1985. As a part of this reevaluation, a neuropsychological as well as psychological evaluation was completed as a consultation to the neurosurgeon. These evaluations were performed in preparation for a claim for personal injuries resulting from the accident of July 1983.

The primary legal considerations in a psychological/ neuropsychological evaluation for an attorney in a personal injury claim are: Is there brain damage/injury? Can brain injury be clearly demonstrated? And/or how clearly can brain injury, as a result of the accident, be demonstrated? How will the injury affect the lifestyle of the injured person and how will that new lifestyle be different from and/or vary from a normal lifestyle? What basic day-to-day things are different for this person as result of the injury and which of these day-to-day things, when emphasized, are most likely to impress a jury with the extent of and/or the seriousness of the consequences of the injury?

If the injured person's injuries are only psychological, e.g., in whiplash cases, the jury is usually not as impressed/sympathetic. This is because "psychological only" injuries are subjective injuries and are more likely to be the result of malingering or an unconscious desire for injury so that the person can receive some compensation for his/her pain and suffering. The goal of the neuropsychological assessment was to determine whether KK had experienced brain functioning deficits as a result of the previously described trauma; whether emotional/psychological changes and/or problems were linked to the injuries she sustained; in what way were her deficits likely to affect her functioning - occupationally, socially and academically; what rehabilitative treatments would be most beneficial; and approximately what would be the expectant length of time committed to such a program and/or programs.

PRESENTING COMPLAINTS

KK stated that prior to the accident, she was making (high school) grades of A's and B's with little study; after the accident, she said that her grades (college) were C's or lower. Her college major was elementary education. She described her personality as more mature and then further explained that she behaved less spontaneously than she did prior to the accident and no longer liked to do things that have not been planned. She also stated that her sense of humor was no longer as good as it had been. Friends and acquaintances have told her that she was "different" - before she was fun to be with and afterwards, it seemed to them that all KK did was fight with them.

Regarding her ability to contribute her fair share of the farm chores, she noted that she was not as physically strong as before and was unable to hold "things" steady. Prior to the accident, she worked as a secretary in the town courthouse and after the accident, she noted that she typed much slower because her left hand didn't move very fast. She described herself as thinking and reacting much more slowly than she did before. Her emotional reaction to these changes was sadness; she said she felt especially sad when her brother, to whom she had always felt very close, would get angry with her because of the decrements in her chore skills.

KK reported that, on a scale of 1 to 10, her energy level before the accident was an 8 or 9 but subsequent to the accident was closer to a 5 or 6. This young woman also described herself as having a much reduced self-confidence. She said, in fact, she had no confidence at all in herself, in even the smallest things, e.g., in letter writing. She would make mistakes, whereas before, she possessed a skill of which she was quite proud. Further, her handwriting was poor now and she would find herself saying things that she did not mean.

The patient described various sources of physical pain:

1. Left shoulder - not a daily pain but 1-2X/week; it's an aching pain on the top of the shoulder; at times the pain will travel down the arm and/or go up the neck to the ear; sometimes

the pain is accompanied by a heavy feeling; the pain gets worse
if KK walks on rough terrain so she tries to walk smoothly and
if the arm is held against the body, as if in a sling or in some
other steady position, it hurts less; the intensity of the pain
is worse if the weather is cold; pain seems to be precipitated
by carrying something heavy and also can be begun if she braces
herself on arm with pressure (as a person would if they were
reading a book while lying on their stomach.

2. Leg/hip - when hip hurts, the leg hurts; pain from the
hip goes down the leg; it's an aching pain, not sharp; a dull
pain, similar to what one would feel if very tired; when it
hurts it feels as if the leg won't move as fast; in fact, when
walking, the leg feels as if it drags a bit if walking slowly
and drags more if walking fast or running; pain can be
precipitated by riding 2 hours or more in a car, sitting in one
position too long and by cold weather; sometimes a popping is
experienced, it does not necessarily hurt but it is a little
disconcerting to hear and "feel your hip pop"; this happens
either when sitting or walking.

3. Headaches - less frequent now than in the beginning;
initially, when would wake and get up a headache would be
located behind left eye; KK has wondered whether headaches in
that location could be due to the "plate" that's in that area;
she has learned that if she has a headache and she lies back
down for approximately 15 minutes with eyes closed, the pain
will go away.

4. Jaw - presently not excessively painful; it will pop
sometimes and sometimes it will catch (which is "scary") and she
is afraid her mouth won't close; occasionally the pop is
accompanied by pain immediately beside her ear on the right
side; not a lasting pain, it's sharp and then goes away.

5. Vocal cords - pain only occurs when KK must sing,
especially, if the notes to be sung are high notes; voice will
feel quite tight; has been told not to yell; she doesn't get a
sore throat, it just tightens and now this occurs less than
before. KK described how her hands feel more cold now than
before the accident. Her right hand feels colder to her than
her left. The phenomena of cold hands was quite worrisome to KK
because when her hands were cold, they felt clammy as well. She
had tried wearing mittens but that did not help; her hands still
felt cold and they still would sweat. She had tried rubbing her
hands and that did not help either. Her perceived temperature
of her feet did not change.

Hand-eye coordination tasks were problematic for this
woman. She said that her typing was much improved compared to
last April but it was quite inferior to her original skill
level. She had taken typing in high school and had received an
award for typing 60-70 words/minute. Additionally, she played
ping-pong with a much reduced skill and grace level than she did
before her injury. She stated that she is better now than when
she was first out of the hospital; she doesn't feel as awkward
but she was still unable to play well enough to win a game.

Dancing was another coordination task that produced a
diminished skill level in this patient. She stated that she was
no longer able to dance; it seemed that her feet don't move on

the beat. She said it is as if the message of the beat is delayed. She felt awkward. In her head, she had the "right" beat but couldn't get it translated quickly enough to dance. She described how she was able to clap her hands to a beat if it wasn't too fast; KK gave as an example a religious song that requires a rapid clapping pattern and stated that she had difficulty clapping rapidly and keeping the increasingly complex pattern of claps in her head.

This young woman described several incidents that occurred in her classes that have had a great effect on her and on her emotional state, as well as on her already decreased self-esteem. On these occasions, she and her classmates were learning and practicing specific exercises that an elementary school teacher would have to demonstrate to her pupils; KK was humiliated by the fact that all of her classmates could easily complete these exercises and she alone was unable to do them. On other occasions she has had to stop the exercises that the others were doing because she was experiencing such great pain. Additional problems at school include difficulties she has experienced in her English class. In her high school, she was in the top five in all of the English classes and now she reported difficulties developing themes for her papers, difficulties finding the right word to use and difficulties clarifying her opinions and ideas so that they are understandable to others.

Additional problem areas included: increased sensitivity regarding what she thought people were saying about her as a result of their observation of her diminished skills; decreased ability to make decisions, even simple ones, e.g., where to go for supper; having word finding difficulties when speaking as well as writing; severe problems understanding what people were saying to her but feeling so badly regarding this difficulty that she told no one; the more complex the verbal communication the greater her difficulty; decreased ability to control and modulate emotional reactions; much lower frustration tolerance; decreased ability to make friends; increased tendency to worry over things that never mattered before; more easily influenced by others now, especially when she is having trouble making a decision; experiencing severe problems processing information quickly, i.e., when she and her boyfriend saw a comedy at the movies, she was unable to "catch" the total plot much less the jokes; no longer feels comfortable in a group of people; feels she can no longer relate to people.

TEST RESULTS

On the Wechsler Adult Intelligence Scale-Revised (WAIS-R), Ms. K produced a verbal IQ of 89, a performance IQ of 83 and a full scale IQ of 85. Her performance on the individual subtests is reported in Table 1. Her performance on the Digit Symbol subtest, predominantly a test of motor ability and requiring visual acuity as well as visual-motor coordination and a compulsive need to conform, was significantly better than other performance tasks. KK's mother, on the WAIS-R, produced a verbal IQ of 95, a performance IQ of 100 and a full scale IQ of 97. Her father, however, produced a verbal IQ of 100, a performance IQ of 113 and a full scale IQ of 106.

Table I: WAIS-R Findings

Subtest	Scaled Score
Information	7
Digit Span	8
Vocabulary	10
Arithmetic	6
Comprehension	9
Similarities	9
Picture Completion	6
Picture Arrangement	8
Block Design	8
Object Assembly	6
Digit Symbol	12

This young woman's memory functioning, as measured by the Randt Memory test, is shown in Table 2.

On the Wisconsin Card Sorting Test, KK produced 69 correct responses, 10 errors, 6 perseverative responses and 6 of 6 categories. The Category Test (Booklet Form) was completed with a total of 44 errors. Both performances are within low normal limits.

The results of formal personality profiles confirm the clinical picture of this woman, that is, she is feeling quite alienated and misunderstood, is withdrawn from others and is

Table 2: Randt Memory Test Results

Subtest	Scaled Score
Acquisition and Recall:	
Five Items	7
Paired Words	11
Story Verbatim	8
Digit Span	6
Incidental Learning	10
Delayed Recall:	
Five Items	9
Paired Words	12
Short Story	10
Picture Recognition	16
General Information	1

Acquisition and Recall (Standard Score): 86
Delayed Recall (Standard Score): 96
Memory Index (Standard Score): 90

quite occupied with private fantasy and daydreams. She may be seen by others as ruminative, obsessive and lacking poise, especially in group situations. She appears to be having feelings of inadequacy and, at this time, she emanates a passive-dependent adjustment to life, displaying the concomitant anger that often/usually accompanies dependency.

The T scores on the various tests of personality can be found in Table 3. As can be seen, the MMPI produced elevations on paranoia, pschasthenia and schizophrenia. The profile is best clasified as an 87, a very unsual pattern to find in a normal young woman. On the Millon, the highest elevation is on the dependent scale, a result inconsistent with her previous history. The Interpersonal Behavior Survey showed highest scores on the dependence and shyness scales, a result consistent with the findings on the Millon. This is also consistent with the mild elevation of the Si scale on the MMPI which along with Depression scale was just under the 70 cutoff.

Neuropsychological testing reflects very mild deficits as exhibited in the T scores on the Nebraska Neuropsychological Evaluation Battery reported in Table 4 below. The critical level on this protocol is 97, meaning that scores at or above 97 are abnormal. Six scores were elevated according to this rule, a finding consistent with a diagnosis of continuing brain impairment.

CONCLUSIONS

KK presented as a person experiencing mild brain deficits.

Table 3: Results of Personality Tests

MMPI	Score	MCMI	Score	IBS	Score
L	46	Schizoid	35	Denial	37
F	73	Avoidant	59	Infrequency	47
K	51	Dependent	112	Imprs. Mgmt	37
Hs	64	Histrionic	38	Gen Aggres	47
D	69	Narcissistic	<30	Hostile	51
Hy	59	Antisocial	<30	Expr Anger	50
Pd	60	Compulsive	72	Disregrd Rts	52
Mf	51	Passive Aggrs	<30	Verb Aggres	49
Pa	70	Schizotypal	52	Phys Aggres	42
Pt	73	Borderline	38	Pass Aggres	42
Sc	77	Paranoid	<30	Gen Assert	33
Ma	45	Anxiety	52	Self-Conf	33
Si	67	Somatoform	61	Init Assert	34
		Hypomania	40	Defen Assert	27
		Dysthymia	43	Frankness	51
		Alcohol Abuse	40	Praise Give	56
		Drug Abuse	<30	Request Help	36
		Psychotic Thkg	58	Refus Demand	37
		Psych Depress	49	Confl Avoid	54
		Psych Delusion	40	Dependency	65
				Shyness	62

Table 4: Nebraska Neuropsychological Evaluation

Scale	Score	Scale	Score
1	82	22	96
2	83	23	99*
3	96	24	80
4	92	25	83
5	97*	26	92
6	97*	27	93
7	95	28	91
8	90	29	93
9	95	30	91
10	95	31	94
11	83	32	99*
12	83	33	84
13	88	34	100*
14	91	35	100*
15	90	36	94
16	93	37	95
17	96	38(F1)	95
18	96	39(F2)	84
19	95	40(F3)	91
20	96	41(F4)	94
21	92	42(F5)	90

She had difficulties with selected motor tasks, including drawing, rapid fine motor movements requiring the rapid processing of both linguistic and numerical symbols, oral motor movements and left hand and finger motor tasks. This young woman performed at a lower than expected level on certain language tasks: speeded verbal repetition and complex auditory comprehension. Additionally, she displayed deficits on tasks of verbal memory, intellectual analysis and integration tasks and exercises requiring general intelligence and orientation.

While the neuropsychological testing reflected only mild deficits, it was clear that KK had experienced structural brain damage. Her intellectual functioning level, at the time of testing, was at the lower end of the low average range. This functioning level was quite reduced from her preaccident capabilities. Premorbidly, this young woman's academic and scholastic skill levels were those of a person functioning at the upper end of the average range or the lower end of the high average range. Her ability to perform tasks of memory, especially tasks of acquisition and immediate recall, was less than would be expected of a person of her former mental ability. KK's memory index score of 90 was a negative 2/3's of a standard deviation below the mean expected of her same age group. This score placed her at the 25th percentile regarding memory functioning.

Even though KK's neuropsychological deficits appeared mild, the very fact that she experienced the decrements had precipitated psychological problems which, in turn, had exacerbated her deficits, both the physical and the mental ones. At the time of this evaluation, this young woman kept herself more isolated than she had prior to her accident and she had become hypervigilent regarding people recognizing her diminished capabilities and her reduced facility to understand and integrate what was happening around her. These behaviors were noticed by others, misunderstood and/or misinterpreted and precipitated less social acceptance of her and this, as previously stated, exacerbated her difficulties.

While KK's family was quite supportive of her, they often unwittingly contributed to her not recognizing the extent of her difficulties and, thus, not seeking assistance to better deal with them. For example, instead of indicating to her and to her physician that she was having memory problems, they commented that there really were not many things happening for her to remember, thus dismissing the significance of the lengthy time span of her first memory post injury.

It seemed unlikely that her parents ever verbalized the attitude that "the least said, the soonest mended", but somewhere, somehow KK came to this stance and, initially, during this evaluation, she refused to verbalize that there were problems much less what the specific problems might be. It was only over a period of time, after rapport was established, that this young woman was willing to expose herself by revealing the problems that she considered great weaknesses, to a stranger who might not understand or empathize, but who in fact, might pity her, thus increasing her sense of "shame" over her diminished functioning and decrease her already negligible self-esteem.

Subsequent to her injury, KK engaged in self-defeating behaviors. That is, in her college classes, when she was unable to perform well the tasks that the others in the class could, she would simply not attend the class for several days. While she may have behaved in this manner prior to the accident, the damage she experienced as a result of that accident reduced her ability to efficiently engage in tasks requiring cognitive flexibility, planning, adapting to cognitive stress, problem-solving and creativity, thus making it more likely for her to behave, impulsively, in ways which would be maladaptive for her in the long run.

It was recommended that KK become reinvolved in a course of physical therapy until she was able to learn how to more completely manage her physical changes and the pain that accompanied those changes. Additionally, it was suggested that this young woman would benefit from a structured, cognitive rehabilitation program assisting her with techniques to improve her verbal memory, to increase her ability to comprehend complex auditory material, and to more effectively deal with the emotions and the problems precipitated by those emotions subsequent to her injury.

Follow Up Care.

KK did admit herself, at the urgings of her parents, to a center for treatment of chronic pain; this facility also treated selected aspects of her brain dysfunction. She participated in a full course of treatment which was four weeks, ten hours/day, five days/week.

The initial physical therapy evaluation revealed abnormal

pelvic positioning, a weaker than normal left shoulder, pain in the right temporomandibular joint, less than normal range of motion on opening of the temporomandibular joint, muscle tone of the lumbar and hip region higher than normal, a gait pattern with different stride lenghts and rhythms, and unequal arm swings. On admission, she was able to ride an exercise bicycle for ten minutes, twice daily, climb ten flights of stairs three times daily and walk briskly for fifteen minutes three times each day. She was placed on a weight lifting program involving progressive resistance for the gross shoulder motions of internal rotation, external rotation and flexion. Elbow flexion and extension and knee flexion and extension was also a part of the resistance exercise program.

At the time of discharge, KK was able to ride an exercise bike for twenty minutes twice daily, climb twenty flights of stairs three times daily and walk briskly for twenty-one minutes three times each day. Her posture and gait pattern were considered significantly improved and her flexibility was judged to be moderately improved.

On admission to this facility, on the Psychological Stress Profile, KK's hand temperature and frontalis muscle EMG readings were monitored across three conditions. Her hand temperatures ranged from 78.3 to 82.1 degrees F., representing a less than adequate vascular relaxation response. During the initial rest phase, her EMG readings were 10.3 to 12.1 microvolt (mv); during the stress condition (serial 7's, subtracting 7 from 900 on a continuous basis), the range was from 10.8 to 14.5mv; and the range was 10.9 to 15.9mv during the subsequent rest and recovery phase. These EMG readings were indicative of a moderate level of muscular tension in the frontalis muscles. On the facility's equipment, the ideal readings were 2.0mv or below.

As a part of treatment, she was taught the proper method of deep breathing, the use of visual imagery, progressive muscle relaxation, EMG and hand temperature biofeedback to facilitate her relaxation efforts. At the time of discharge, she could consistently, raise her hand temperature to 93 to 94 degrees F. Additionally, her EMG readings were reduced to between 5.4 to 4.5mv, reflecting a much lessened tension level.

On admission to the chronic pain treatment unit, KK completed another MMPI. On this MMPI she was described as appearing as if she were a "psychopathic" personality who in some way had been "caught" by the "law" or the treatment facility. In fact, later in treatment, she stated that she had not wanted to attend this treatment program and had only agreed to come to please her parents. Clearly, initially, she was feeling sad and angry. It was likely that her sadness would abate when she was able to escape her stress, i.e., treatment. She was likely to display good insight and genuinely, "talk a good story" regarding how she would do all that was asked of her so that she would "get better", but the long-range prognosis for behavior change was poor.

During her treatment, KK overtly presented herself as a pleasant person who really had no problems except the physical ones that were observable. She was polite but guarded in most of her interpersonal interactions with both staff and fellow patients. As rapport developed, this young woman verbalized areas of concern, including: separation and individuation problems resulting from her accident and from family dynamics; her diminished ability to communicate resulting from her accident and the concommitant feelings of isolation and estrangement; her lack of appropriate assertiveness and her diminished feelings of comfort in social situations. Supportive and role-play techniques were used to encourage her to produce her own solutions to problems using problem-solving strategies and review of probable consequences for the generated solutions.

KK's family was supportive of her throughout this treatment and participated with her on two occasions. This seemed to have both some positive and some negative effects.

At the time of discharge, this woman appeared to have made improvements. She stated that her atitude toward her family and toward most aspects of her life had improved. She believed she was more able to effectively communicate with others, including her mother with whom she formerly believed there had been a significant communication problem. She stated that she was becoming more aware of others and was focusing on what they said to her so that she was more able to respond to them in a "normal" manner. Additionally, KK said she felt she was behaving in a more assertive fashion, giving her opinions and making decisions that previously had been quite difficult for her. Her discharge MMPI indicated that KK was still quite angry, rebellious and experiencing familial conflict, as well as having feelings of being alienated and misunderstood by those around her. She continued to view the world as a rejecting and hostile place, showing others her anger for them and thus, precipitating their being angry, in return, with her and in this manner, setting up the condition for a self-fulfilling prophecy which reinforced her alienation from others.

It was recommended that her progress be considered more "apparent" than "real" since she continued to have a diminished self-esteem and her verbalized view of the world seemed different from her internalized view of it. It was predicted that as long as "things" in KK's life went along smoothly, she would not display difficulties. However, it was hypothesized that she was still unable to modulate her behavior in a predictable and adaptive fashion; she continued to have subtle communication problems, poor social intelligence and difficulties experiencing empathy for others and while she stated that family conflicts were reduced, they were still unresolved. It was recommended that treatment continue, at least intermittently, for a time.

In October and in November of 1985, KK requested return appointments to work on areas that had become quite problematic as a result of her heavy academic load, the stress concommittant with that load and her own diminished abilities to cope with cognitive stress in an adaptive fashion. In October, she described her problems as: getting confused; forgetting things, even when she wrote them down; experiencing sleep disturbance after being late for several appointments (she would get up several times during the night to check the clock to see whether the time was correct and then she would worry that what she had seen was in some way in error); problems understanding, "screening" and/or integrating verbal material; difficulties "getting close to people"; and wanting more self-esteem.

KK reported that after this first appointment, she did well for approximately two days but then things began to deteriorate once again. When she arrived for the October appointment, she indicated that she had waited far too long before she called and requested help. She realized that not only was she forgetting things, etc., she was reacting emotionally, fearing that she was "losing her mind" and/or "getting worse", thus making her situation even worse than it was in an ever increasing downward spiral.

The problems KK described in November were much the same as those in October, including: she had forgotten (memory) to attend a compulsory lab; she had studied for a test and couldn't understand (comprehension and integration) the material; became aware of self being rude (decreased ability to modulate behavior and emotional reactions) to a friend when he called and she was tired; and had experienced "dizzy" spells. Once again, time was spent developing problem-solving strategies and alternative solutions to difficulties posed. Techniques for memory improvement were detailed and tasks for increasing understanding and integrating of complex verbal material were designed. KK was encouraged to seek medical attention for the "dizzy" spells if they did not spontaneously remit within one week. This young woman was urged to continue to use and practice the tasks and skills she was taught. She was also encouraged to become more aware of clues/signs indicating things might not be going as well as she would have them go and to call for a "tune-up" appointment rather than wait and need a "major over-haul".

It was recommended that KK become involved with a local psychologist/neuropsychologist for a combination of: therapy to aid her with the emotional adjustments she would continue to make as time post injury progressed and to guide, monitor and update the rehabilitation tasks necessary for her continued improvement in the previously delineated deficit areas. The therapist chosen should have experience with brain injured people. Experience and specialized training would be necessary to maintain the most advantageous mix of knowledge, empathy and understanding to encourage and sustain the patient's motivation for and progress on tasks that are, at best, difficult for them.

EFFECTS OF HEAD TRAUMA IN A FOUR-AND-ONE-HALF-YEAR-

OLD CHILD: DEVELOPMENTAL ISSUES

Jane Crowley

Department of Psychiatry
University of Nebraska Medical Center
Omaha, Nebraska

Evaluation of children represents one of the most difficult challenges to the neuropsychologist. Not only is it necessary to evaluate where the child is at the present time, but it is necessary to predict how the child's injuries will interact with normal developmental processes to predict how the child will be as an adult. The present case illustrates some of these issues.

Miss D. is a right-handed Caucasian female child presented at age 6 years, 7 months for evaluation upon referral of her attorney. At the age of 4 1/2 she was struck by a car while crossing the street and litigation has been initiated around the damage suffered by the child as a result of the accident.

This case will be presented in a number of sections. First, some general considerations in the forensic evaluation of a young child will be detailed. From there, the case presentation begins with medical background, report of previous evaluations, school information and current complaints. Next the results of the evaluation are presented to illustrate the nature of this child's injury. The results are presented primarily for the reader's benefit and are therefore not in a form typical of a forensic report, as indications are given for the choice of the instruments utilized among other issues. However, the conclusions and recommendations section and the one detailing prognosis are written as would be appropriate in a report to legal personnel. Finally, a summary is given to highlight some of the issues unique to this case, as well as typical to evaluation of head-injured children in general.

GENERAL CONSIDERATIONS

The evaluation of this case involved the consideration of a number of factors that serve to highlight the interplay of forensic and clinical issues in a case of closed head trauma in a young child.

As always in the assessment of a legal case, the role of the neuropsychologist involves not only the assessment of neuropsychological sequelae from the accident and remediative planning but also assisting the attorney in the determination of damages. Both these tasks involve ascertaining premorbid functioning which presents unique issues in a preschool child.

In the determination of premorbid status in an adult, work and educational history are used (and any previous testing if it exists). In a school-age child, educational history is the major source of information on premorbid functioning. Not only do such sources provide actual data, in the form of grades, work ratings, etc., but also provide a source of third party input (i.e. outside of the family) that is arguably more objective than family input, both from the standpoint of the assessment itself as well as in a court presentation.

In a child injured prior to beginning school, there is a reduced likelihood that they have had experience in structured group situations outside of the home and therefore estimates of premorbid functioning must be approached in a different manner. Even if a child has attended a structured preschool of some sort, though this can provide qualitative data about premorbid intellectual and behavioral functioning, it is seldom available in the quantified and peer-referenced manner represented in grades and group achievement scores. A preschool teacher's comments about drawing ability or math readiness skills may be useful clinically, but such information is not as acceptable in litigation as psychometric test results demonstrating the degree of damage sustained.

Therefore, an alternative method for estimating premorbid functioning in such children must be utilized. With known correlations of nearly .50 between natural parents' IQ and their children's and .50 between siblings' IQ, the use of intellectual and/or achievement testing of blood relatives becomes useful in providing an objective basis on which to base estimates of potential prior to the trauma. Further, such information becomes essential in determining the degree of "lost" occupational and educational attainment as a result of the injury.

As in all cases of forensic evaluation of children, regardless of age, traditional personality assessment of the parents and siblings should be done to determine the degree of their need for ongoing, adjunctive professional support, which needs to be included in the damages sought. Most often this includes instruction in parenting techniques as a child's behavior is markedly changed after a severe head trauma and parents struggle to adjust to a "new" child who is often behaviorally quite disruptive. Additionally, depending on the factors delineated below, professional assistance with the emotional adjustment of the family itself to the stress of the trauma is often necessary.

Assessment of the child's emotional/personality development is also important. In a child of any age, the possibility of a handicap raises the central issues of the handicap's effect on the developing self-concept of the child. In closed head injured children, epilepsy is a frequently occurring neurological sequelae and the range of possible neuropsychological deficits is broad. With the latter category, the child's ability to interpret his/her world has been impaired, so the effect on their perceptions as the basis for their self-esteem becomes complex. As such, if therapeutic assistance is required, it often requires a specialist who can incorporate an understanding of the child's capabilities into whatever therapy modality used.

For example, a child whose auditory processing capabilities are limited should be approached through either visually oriented techniques (videotape) perhaps with behavioral rehearsal, or play techniques, depending on the issues to be worked on. This interplay of the cause of the difficulty hampering the child's ability to understand the treatment is a major challenge presented by such children.

Critical factors that need to be included in such an assessment are: degree of social support from friends and family (especially as respite care sources), guilt around the occurrence of the child's injury, present understanding of the child's physical and cognitive deficits from the accident (e.g., epilepsy), current behavioral presentation, parental discipline techniques, educational/remediative efforts since the accident (particularly parental perception of school placement if the child has since become of school age), and sibling response to the injured child.

Such information is as essential in the consideration of formalized out-of-home programming (day school vs. residential placement vs. public school placement) as is the actual evaluation of the child's neuropsychological deficits. The relevance of both current placement as well as predicted future needs is, of course, prominent in the determination of damages to be sought.

This consideration of family status is of primary importance as these factors interact with the objective evaluation of a child's deficits, as families differ widely in their ability to tolerate the inevitable behavioral/medical sequelae of a serious head injury. History of parental attempts to deal with systems outside the family (e.g., medical, educational) in attempts to secure ongoing treatment for the child are often sources of significant stress and will require professional intervention. For example, school systems can be reluctant to acknowledge the special educational needs of these children as they fail to fit into established categories.

Conversely, though a school's attempts may be well-intentioned, they may be inappropriate, as an individual school system is unlikely to have had significant experience in dealing with traumatically brain-injured children. In either case, it sometimes becomes necessary to secure adjunctive remediative services from private speech, physical and/or occupational therapists. Parents may have to engage in a protracted process with a school system to secure proper resources for their child, in and of itself a stressful experience. This becomes another consideration in the determination of damages to be sought.

CASE PRESENTATION

Medical Background

Upon admission to the hospital at the time of the accident, Miss D. was comatose but would react to painful stimuli. She remained in a coma for 10 days, with the diagnosis of closed head trauma with cerebral/brainstem contusion. Additionally, she suffered a fractured right elbow, fractured right hip, fractured pelvis, right pulmonary contusion and an apparent renal contusion.

Hospital course included a series of CT scans which demonstrated initially a mild right periventricular temporal horn hemorrhage and zones of intracranial hemorrhage in the right frontal region, as well as bilaterally around the lateral ventricles. An interim CT scan demonstrated a bilateral subdural hygroma in the frontal horns with a mild left to right shift. Upon discharge, there was believed to be a complete resolution of the subdural collections of fluid noted previously. Initial EEG demonstrated abnormal slowing of left occipital rhythm, which severe severe, substantially resolved on discharge EEG, with no epileptiform activity being seen on either EEG. Though neurological findings were noted as markedly improved, upon discharge it was noted that she was still having significant difficulty with speech.

An EEG done 5 months after the trauma showed epileptiform activity in the right posterior region for which Miss D. was begun on Tegretol, to which Depakene was subsequently added; diagnosis of complex partial seizure was made. A subsequent EEG at 9 months post trauma was interpreted as demonstrating some risk for seizures with a right posterior spike wave discharge. CT scan done 7 months post trauma demonstrated a mild degree of atrophy in the left frontal area. A subsequent CT scan done at 9 months post accident was read as normal, showing no evidence of localized atrophy.

Neurological exams subsequent to hospital discharge showed mild dyspraxic speech, dystaxic gait, right facial weakness, mild left hemiparesis, left Horner's syndrome post motor vehicle accident and tongue deviation to the left (ascribed to an upper motor neuron lesion). Attention deficit disorder was also noted upon clinical exam and a "loss of higher cortical functions". This continued to be the presenting clinical picture at the time of evaluation here.

Previous Evaluations

Prior to the testing detailed here, Miss D. had been evaluated at two other facilities, at 9 and 18 months post accident. At the time of the first evaluation, her WPPSI Verbal IQ = 97, Performance IQ = 99, Full Scale IQ = 97. Her second intellectual evaluation yielded WISC-R score of Verbal IQ = 85, Performance IQ = 84, Full Scale IQ = 83. Speech evaluations at both times indicated expressive one-word capability at or above age level, with marked deficits in receptive speech (with score 18 months below her age peers) and in more complex expressive productions. Gross, fine motor and visual-motor evaluations indicated an age equivalent two years below her age peers.

School Placement

At the time of this evaluation, Miss D. had been placed in a regular kindergarten class. During the previous school year, she had been placed in a self-contained behaviorally impaired unit with weekly occupational therapy contact and brief (4-5 min.) weekly contacts with a physical therapist.

Miss D. is the youngest of three children (one full sibling, one half-sibling) living with her natural parents.

Presenting Complaints

Upon presentation for her evaluation (two years post trauma), problems noted were poor attention span, temper tantrums, impulsivity, emotional lability, slurred speech, right facial weakness, gait problems, memory problems and cognitive deterioration from her status prior to the accident. She continues with a diagnosis of partial complex seizure disorder, for which she currently is on Tegretol and Depakene.

EVALUATION

Behavioral Observations

Miss D. presented in the testing situation as an extremely active child demonstrating both motoric overactivity during the two days of testing and observation, as well as a short attention span. She required frequent and firm redirection to attend to the test materials and often engaged in manipulative behavior in an effort to avoid task performance.

Motivation to perform was extremely variable even with the use of concrete reinforcements. Miss D. was accessible to social reinforcement but to maintain maximal effort, concrete reinforcements had to be used. Her ability to work for a delayed reward was not consistent, though when the contingency was restated, she could renew her efforts.

An instance of possible seizure activity occurred with a notable period of post-ictal confusion. An intentional tremor in her left hand was observed intermittently.

Speech was notable for slurring but grammar and syntax were generally within age appropriate levels. Miss D.'s speech becomes less intelligible in social situations, as opposed to the actual testing situation. She is less deliberate in these settings, and this results in a reduction of intelligibility from 85% during the evaluation to 60% in casual speech. A significant amount of irrelevant speech to task demand was noted, with duration increasing on those tasks where Miss D. was unsure of the answer. Verbal cueing was often used. Capacity to self-correct was extremely limited.

Miss D.'s discomfort and anxiety about her behavior was apparent as she frequently responded to redirection with apologies and requests to ensure that the examiner " still liked her". In general, it was clear that even with the high amount of structure imposed in the testing situation, Miss D.'s adaptive behavioral competency is quite impaired. Concrete rewards were needed to maintain motivation, though even with this technique, consistent capacity to perform was limited.

Test Results

Miss D.'s scores on the LNNB are given below. It should be noted that she was administered a form of the test standardized for preschool children, which though analogous to the current Children's Revision, is an expanded version being used currently by our clinic.

Miss D.'s performance on the LNNB (Table 1) is clearly indicative of brain damage, with a total of nine elevations above the critical level. The Right Hemisphere scale is elevated both above the critical level as well as significantly above the Left Hemisphere scale, indicative of lateralization of brain damage more to the right, at least in terms of motor and sensory loss. Elevation of the Pathognomonic Scale is further indication of brain damage but due to the height of this elevation, demonstrates that relatively little compensatory mechanisms have evolved in the two years since the accident. The elevations of Visual, Receptive and Expressive Speech, Writing, Reading, Arithmetic and Intelligence will be examined in more detail below, primarily examining her performance item by item.

Fine motor movements were somewhat awkward and slow, though Miss D. was generally able to perform the sequences required. Oral motor capabilties were quite limited with difficulties noted most on the right side of the face. In drawing and other visual-motor tasks, Miss D. was only intermittently capable of good control with her dominant (right) hand so that some productions were quite poor. Problems with inhibition of fine motor movement were most apparent, as well as demonstration of motor overflow.

Basic sensory capabilities were intact, with Miss D.'s problems again apparent at that point where integration of sensory modalities was required (visual-verbal, auditory-

Table 1: Luria-Nebraska Neuropsychological Battery (Under 8)*

Scale	Raw Score	T Score
Motor	32	78
Rhythm	9	76
Tactile	7	65
Visual	10	95
Receptive Speech	11	89
Expressive Speech	17	92
Writing	29	221
Reading	12	97
Arithmetic	18	110
Memory	10	76
Intelligence	20	100
Pathognomonic	25	106
Left Hemisphere	5	75
Right Hemisphere	8	97

* Critical Level = 82 (T-Score)

verbal). Complex visual stimuli present problems for Miss D. but it is difficult to ascertain if this is a problem with visual analysis per se or reflects her high level of distractibility, as she can become distracted by elements of the stimulus itself.

Receptive speech capabilities were intact for simple commands but notably disturbed when two commands were given or any degree of complexity in the language was introduced. A lack of mastery of basic linguistic concepts (for example, same and different) was apparent. She has problems tracking longer stimuli and perseverative responding was seen. Often Miss D. would only respond to a single word from a command.

Expressive speech was quite slurred but generally intelligible. This articulatory difficulty is due to oral motor problems noted above. However, Miss D.'s ability to formulate speech was quite impaired, with circumlocutions noted as well as inability to keep responses targeted to stimuli. Generally, she was more capable in overlearned material. Again, attentional components were seen when she would respond only to a portion of the stimulus.

Miss D.'s performance on the more academically oriented portions of the LNNB indicates, in general, her difficulty with cognitive processes requiring any integration capabilities. Basic grasp of letters was superior to numbers, with Miss D. often producing forms that were grossly distorted as numbers. Most of her knowledge of letters seemed to be on a rote basis with no understanding of phonics, or even a rudimentary grasp of the concept of letters as symbols when the demand includes that she generate her own response completely (as opposed to being cued by response alternatives). Her difficulties with fine motor control as well as visual-spatial skills was apparent in all her productions in this portion of the test.

Memory capabilities were often marked by confabulations

Table 2: Intellectual Test Results

	Scale Score		Scale Score
WISC-R:			
Information	8	Picture Completion	13
Similarities	3	Picture Arrangement	8
Arithmetic	7	Block Design	6
Vocabulary	7	Object Assembly	6
Comprehension	6	Coding	7
Digit Span	6	Mazes	8
Verbal IQ = 77			
Performance IQ = 75			
Full Scale IQ = 73			
McCarthy Scale of Children's Abilities (Raw Scores):			
Leg Coordination		7	
Arm Coordination		2	

particularly as stimuli became more complex or longer. Demands for preschool children on the test are quite limited and though Miss D. performed within the average range, it should be noted that this was accomplished by extensive structuring and frequent redirection.

Intellectual scale performance (Table 2) is commensurate with Miss D.'s scores on the WISC-R Verbal Scale. Her grasp of linguistic concepts that underlie the capacity for abstract and symbolic reasoning was quite limited in items about group membership beyond those relationships that are apparent on a physical level and to which she has been exposed repeatedly through direct experience. Any items that required verbal reasoning, even on the most rudimentary, level presented difficulty for her.

Miss D.'s scores on the WISC-R indicate a global decrement in more complex tasks and demonstrate general intellectual functioning in the deficient range in both verbal and nonverbal tasks. Verbal abilities are consistent, save for Similarities. Miss D.'s difficulty with basic receptive speech capacity is seen, as she was unable to grasp the task demand of this subtest and instead responded with irrelevant speech to these items. Nonverbal abilities were also consistent save Picture Completion, which demonstrate, consistent with the LNNB, the intactness of basic visual analysis.

Qualitative analysis of Miss D.'s responses to the WISC-R showed again perseveration, circumlocution, verbal cueing, as well as some left/right confusion (notable on Picture Arrangement). Her approach to most of the nonverbal tasks was quite poor, comprised essentially of an unsophisticated attempt at trial-and-error. On Block Design she would habitually begin an item by forming the block in some approximation of the design within the overall configuration.

It is important to note that the scores obtained on the WISC-R were done with the imposition of high degrees of structure, requiring constant redirection to task and frequent breaks.

McCarthy subtests were administered to evaluate gross motor capabilites. These skills are severely deficient, with Miss D.'s scores on both subtests indicative of severe impairment. Academic readiness was evaluated using the PIAT, with the scores as given below.

Table 3: Achievement Test Scores (PIAT)

Subtest	Age Equiv.	Grade Equiv.
Mathematics	5-5	.4
Reading Recognition	6-2	1.1
Reading Comprehension	No Score	No Score
Spelling	6-0	1.0
General Information	6-2	1.0
Total Test	<5.6	.4

Miss D.'s scores on the PIAT (Table 3) for the reading-related skills are within a borderline acceptable range. Math skills are significantly delayed. These scores are notable, as Miss D. is presently in the middle third of her second year in kindergarten, with her previous year having been in a specialized placement with a high degree of structure. The PIAT was chosen for inclusion in the battery of tests given as there is no demand for written work, in order to remove the decrement possible due to her poor fine motor control.

However, particularly for Miss D., the additional structure and cueing provided by the multiple choice format of the test is no doubt responsible for her improved performance on this instrument, relative to her LNNB and WISC-R scores. Again, her problems with visual-spatial relations were apparent in her choices of responses to particularly the mathematics items.

Parental responses to the Personality Inventory for Children were indicative of the perception of many areas of impairment. These include problems with academics, social skills, self-control, attention span, emotional lability, acquisition of developmental milestones and bizarre behaviors. The Personality Inventory for Children is useful in gathering daily functioning information in cases where the respondent may have a "response set", as it contains validity scales analogous to those on the MMPI to indicate inconsistent or exaggerated complaints.

Upon interview with her parents, they provided examples of the above behaviors and the general impression gained was one of significant confusion and frustration in dealing with their daughter and the changes in her behavior since the trauma.

The next two sections are presented in a form more typical of that which would be included in a report to legal personnel.

CONCLUSIONS AND RECOMMENDATIONS

Miss D. presents with a picture quite typical of a child who has sustained significant brain damage. Though basic sensory modalities are intact, fine motor capability has been significantly impaired, with problems in control and speed in both hands. Beyond the simple uni-modality of these skills, Miss D. is not demonstrating the beginning capacity for the integration of modalities that is the cornerstone of academic skills. Visual-motor skills essential for any written productions are impaired as are most other cross-modality capacities.

The most serious of her deficits, as well as the one with the broadest impact for her functioning, is her poor attention span and high distractibility. Considerable evidence is apparent that Miss D.'s ability further to inhibit activity to accomplish a targeted goal has been severely compromised. Her ability to self-monitor her behavior or to benefit from feedback from others and correct herself has also been severely compromised. It is this disinhibition of those mechanisms that a normal brain inhibits routinely that most seriously affects the broad range of Miss D.'s functioning, both academically and socially.

The result of these impairments is seen when evaluating her progress since the accident as demonstrated by her testing scores from the two previous evaluations performed since the accident. Her Full Scale IQ has decreased steadily from 97 in October 1983 (9 mos. post trauma) to 83 in August 1984 (18 months post trauma) to 73 in the current evaluation. Examination of performance on each subtest within the intelligence tests given does not indicate a loss of growth in absolute terms, which might be incorrectly inferred on the basis of the decrease in IQ scores. What this does indicate is much slower progress in Miss D.'s development than occurs with a normal child as they get older. This will result in an ever-widening gap between Miss D. and her peers as measured by IQ testing. This will mean that there will be a steady decrease in Miss D.'s IQ over time.

However, this further reduction does not indicate a decrease in absolute level of functioning. There has been no decrease in Miss D.'s functioning since the accident and there is none expected. Instead, this indicates the effect of the loss of more "executive" capacities of the brain that are needed as the demands for competent living increase as Miss D. gets older. These demands include the integration of single modalities (e.g., visual, auditory, tactile, motor) with other modalities that are required for acquisition of academic skills like reading and math. Due to her brain damage, these skills are not being acquired because of the barriers to effective learning represented by her neuropsychological deficits.

Essentially, though there has been no decrease in functional capabilites since the accident, there has been little progress despite a year and a half of academic exposure, with one year having been in a special educational context. For the testing here to be completed, it should be noted that a considerable amount of structure was necessary. The testing was done in a quiet room on a one-to-one basis and significant difficulties with attention and motivation were still encountered. This will be greatly multiplied in a classroom setting where the amount of distractors is much greater. Rewards had to be used often to maintain compliance and this is reported as the main problem in the classroom. Additionally, Miss D.'s current classroom is a kindergarten placement, where the demands for individual work are much less than on even the elementary school level.

Intellectual testing of Miss D.'s blood relatives (mother, father, brother) provides a reference point from which to estimate Miss D.'s premorbid IQ (i.e. before the accident). This testing yielded Full Scale IQ's of 102, 115 and 118 respectively. Essentially, this reflects in functional terms the difference between average to bright average intellectual functioning (by her immediate family members) and mentally deficient functioning by Miss D. Her premorbid functioning is thereby estimated to have been at a level commensurate with a Full Scale IQ of 100-120. This stands in marked contrast to her present measured level of 73.

Achievement testing further documents the delays apparent in the IQ testing. Though reading skills are at an academic readiness level generally, her math readiness skills are significantly deficient. In this area, Miss D. is not only behind other children her age but is behind even other kindergarten children.

Recommendations include:

1) Continued medical follow-up in reference to suspected seizure seen during evaluation.

2) Specialized academic programming with extensive behavioral modification approach. A highly structured educational approach will be required on a full-time basis. Unlike a classroom oriented for behavioral control strictly, Miss D.'s needs are distinctly different, with the primary need being for training in the self-monitoring and self-control that she no longer can exert due to her neuropsychological deficits. As such, either a day school with parent retraining to ensure continuation of programming at home or on a residential basis will be required. Due to the global effect of the disinhibition Miss D. exhibits, social skills training will be necessary as well. This must become the prime focus of treatment at the earliest possible time.

3) Increase in speech therapy to daily contacts of one hour duration to address the multidimensional nature of Miss D.'s speech and language deficits. These include problems with the actual control of her tongue and the musculature of the right side of her face, in addition to serious language deficits.

4) Both occupational and physical therapy to remediate as much as possible the fine and gross motor deficits that continue to persist. Fine motor and visual-motor competency will have a particularly profound effect on academic skills as it is essential for the mastery of all writing tasks.

5) Appropriate group activities should be secured for Miss D. Obviously, these will need to take place in a structured setting where adult supervision is guaranteed. This will be important for the development of Miss D.'s social skills. Again, the group appropriate for Miss D. would be other brain-impaired children and not behaviorally impaired children in such an experience. The mastery experience this could afford Miss D. would also be essential, as a critical dimension for her will be building a good self-image in the face of a marked impairment which will always be a difference between herself and her peers.

    Further, an experience in group oriented, nonacademic tasks would be useful year round, as well as an extracurricular activity. If not in a full-time residential program, this should be secured for Miss D. after her regular schooling time. Such a supervised experience will provide Miss D. with an opportunity to socialize with peers that does not occur naturally now, due to her problems in relating to other children.

6) The continuation of therapy contacts with additional individual focus on Miss D. Gradually over time, Miss D. will need help understanding what is wrong with her and why she is different from other children. Her understanding and then acceptance of the life-long challenges this creates for her will require considerable exposures over time. Psychotherapy with

brain-damaged children takes special expertise and requires a specialist in the field.

It is typically difficult for any public school system to meet the needs of a child whose brain impairment covers the scope of difficulty that Miss D.'s does. As outlined above, she requires extensive multidisciplinary assistance to maximize her capabilites and allow her to even progress at a level to maintain her present general level of functioning (borderline deficient). As such, these services will need to be secured on a private basis and Miss D.'s progress will require ongoing monitoring to direct the efforts appropriately.

Extensive coordination between home and school is vital to ensure that behavioral programming at the school is continued at home as well.

PROGNOSIS

From experience with other children with similar problems and the results of current testing, prognosis for Miss D. is judged to be maximal functioning at a borderline deficient level. This is to say that, with the proper treatment as outlined above, Miss D. will make progress. However, with these remediative efforts, this progress will have its limits due to the brain damage apparent from this evaluation.

In real-life terms the maximal level of functioning as given above will mean that Miss D. will, as an adult, be able to function only on a semi-independent level. This would mean either independent living with regular supervision or residence in a group home setting.

In terms of possible employment, again with the optimal treatment, Miss D.'s options will be severely limited. She could likely be able to work at a job where the structure was high and no demands for decision-making by her were made.

The treatment outlined above will need to occur on a structured basis for at least the period of time commensurate with the regular educational period (12 years), although some aspects may change over time as Miss D. reaches maximal levels (for example, in speech therapy). This child will likely require assistance for the rest of her life.

Cost for the program outlined above at current dollar values is estimated as:

1) If a residential program is chosen, from $2500-$4500 a month depending on the institution chosen.

2) If a day program is chosen monthly, cost from $250-600.

3) If a day program is chosen, her parents will need professional help on an ongoing basis to be able to cope with Miss D., at an average cost of $7000 a year.

4) After reaching majority age, cost of supervised boarding homes range from $1000-$2000 a month. If Miss D. lives independently, cost of supervision would be about $300-500 at

present dollar value.

5) A further element to consider is the issue of lost wages to Miss D. With the estimate of premorbid IQ as given above as 100-120, she could likely have earned a salary commensurate with her father's earnings, or at least the average for a U.S. citizen.

With her injury, she will at best be able to hold a job at minimum wage or in a sheltered workshop. This results in a loss of at least $10,000-$20,000 in wages in current dollar value per year.

We would expect as she was in good health prior to the accident, that her working life would have been 40-45 years. There is nothing to suggest that she will not live a full life span of an average American female, at present about 72 years.

SUMMARY

It is important to note that in the concomitant evaluations of the other family members, Miss D.'s mother and brother were both diagnosed as suffering from post-traumatic stress disorder-chronic. With her mother, the impact of guilt around the circumstances of the injury and subsequent dealing with the school system around her daughter's educational needs were particularly cogent factors. In preschool children, who are not assumed to "know better", the possibility for guilt on the parents' part becomes exacerbated considerably.

This family was receiving assistance prior to the evaluation, with a focus on the mother. However, in our experience this is unusual. More typically, the parents' guilt prevents them from seeking assistance for themselves, as they feel this would be selfish and that, in some way, enduring their discomfort is their "just desserts" for not being more careful with their child.

However, quite typically in such cases, the injured child here was not included in the treatment as she was too disruptive. As indicated earlier, such children are unique challenges and, as such, are often avoided in the treatment process by therapists unacquainted with brain-damaged children.

For Miss D.'s brother, the fact that he witnessed his sister being struck by the car resulted in nightmares and increased anxiety in the ensuing two years. This highlights the necessity for a family focus to such an assessment and is indicative of the wide range effects of this kind of tragedy in a family. Competent clinical practice alone would dictate the need for such an evaluation. However, forensic assessment adds the additional demand in the determination of damages so that all sequelae to the trauma are highlighted. The family can then receive sufficient financial compensation to address the multifaceted impact of their child's injury.

Finally, the ongoing need for the involvement of neuropsychological consultation should be apparent from this case. As the field of neuropsychology is a relatively new specialization, interpretation of results from such an evaluation can only be done be personnel competent to understand the longitudinal effects of such an injury. Expectations must be modified throughout the child's development and specialized programming must be developed, among other issues. It is unlikely, particularly if services must be secured piecemeal for a child, that the role of coordinator could be assigned to another professional whose overall perspective could match that of a neuropsychologist.

DEPOSITION IN A CASE INVOLVING

BRAIN INJURY AND NEUROPSYCHOLOGY

Charles J. Golden

Department of Psychiatry
University of Nebraska Medical Center
Omaha, Nebraska

The following represents a complete deposition which
represents some of the kinds of questions one is likely to be
asked. I first considered editing the deposition to make myself
look better but we decided to present this without any changes
except of names and places to avoid recognition of the case. It
should be noted as discussed earlier, that a deposition such as
this which was for discovery allows more leeway than does court
testimony for both the professional as well as the lawyers. The
original typing and spelling errors have been preserved for the
sake of interest.

DIRECT EXAMINATION

Mr. Clark (Q). State your name, please.

A. Dr. Charles Golden, G O L D E N.

Q. How much do you charge for your deposition time?

A. $150.00 an hour when I'm in Omaha.

Q. How much are you going to charge for trial, days in
Arizona?

A. I charge per day $1,200 plus expenses based on an
eight hour day.

Q. How much have you charged Mr. Frost so far in this
case?

A. Two thousand dollars, plus, I guess, he owes me for
half an hour of talk which could be another $75.

Q. So that half an hour of time was time you spent just
prior to this deposition?

A. Yes, sir.

Q. If you would, please, tell me what you and Mr. Frost
talked about prior to the deposition? Well, besides tennis.

A. We didn't talk about tennis at all.

Q. Amazing.

A. We talked about -- I just told him that there was nothing I needed to ask him. That everything was okay, and he didn't need to be nervous, that the test results in the case were very straight forward. We discussed a little bit of just the liability end of the case, just out of my own interests, and we discussed the fact that he has a friend that owns the Denver Broncos, and I was trying to think if there was anything that they could do for me, which I hadn't thought of, still haven't, and we discussed the fall, the turning of the leaves.

Q. Did you discuss your opinions at all?

A. Not really. I just told him -- I just told him, basically, that I thought she was very damaged and that she was going to need a lot of help which I've already told him earlier.

Q. I'm sorry.

A. Which I had already told him earlier.

Q. When was that?

A. On the phone.

Q. When did you first form your opinions in this case?

A. After seeing the patient.

Q. When was that?

A. About -- you've actually got all of this stuff that's dated there. It was about two or three weeks ago. If you want an exact date, I'd have to look. It was September 14th, 15th that we were out there -- I believe, were the days. Let me check my calendar, too, just to be precise. Yes, September 15 -- 16th, I'm sorry. We had all the testing done by the morning of the -- yes, by the 16th and formed our opinions shortly thereafter.

Q. All right. So not until September 17th were you able to form your opinions in this case?

A. A definite opinion. I had read the records and stuff before.

Q. There is an IEP which I understand -- if I understand right, stands for Individualized Education Program?

A. That's what I think it does stand for.

Q. Do you know where that is from? It's dated September 27, 1984.

A. I assume it would be from the school that she was in, which is the one in Margayia.

106

Q.   Which is what school?

A.   The one in Margayia that she's bused to from her house. I don't remember the exact name of the town -- in the Eden, Margayia area.

Q.   Do you have other records from her Eden, Margayia.

A.   All records that we have are right -- are there.

Q.   Doctor, have you had your deposition taken before?

A.   Uh-huh.

Q.   I just remind you that you have to answer audibly, and that you have to wait until I finish my question before you answer, otherwise the court reporter will not be able to take it down appropriately.

A.   I'm sorry if I bothered you.

Q.   You didn't bother me. It just wouldn't look right on the record. Will you tell me everything you have from Margayia, please?

A.   All of the testing was done in Margayia.

Q.   All of your testing was performed in Margayia?

A.   All of our testing was done in Margayia.

Q.   What I'm trying to segregate, though, is the records which you have from the Margayia school which LL KK attends versus records you have from your testing.

A.   I think since you just went through it, found the record, I'm not quite sure -- these are -- this is some testing they did that Mr. Frost sent me, and this is some testing that was done at the Easter Seal School. The rest of the records that I have copies of is all there. I've seen more records. I've met with Mr. Frost and his staff in Honolulu and looked at some other things, but I don't have copies of anything else.

Q.   Do you recall what else you looked at?

A.   No. I couldn't tell you in detail.

Q.   Anything that you looked at that you think -- that you don't have here that you think is important to your opinions today?

A.   That it was just -- no, not really. Most of what I got from them was a history, which I got, again, from the parents.

Q.   As far as I can tell, we have from Margayia OLSIST-F test plus the IEP dated September 27, 1984, and a test for auditory comprehension of language, 9-17-84. Do you have anything else from Margayia that you've reviewed in this case?

A.   Not that I have in my records. As I just told you, I looked at Richard's file, but I couldn't tell you all the things that was in it.

Q. You can't tell me of anything in that file that was important to your opinion?

A. Our opinions are based largely on our own history and the testing.

Q. Are you familiar with the facilities available to LL KK at the present time?

A. I'm, basically, familiar with special education facilities in the United States including Margayia.

Q. What is your understanding of what facilities are presently available to LL?

A. She's in a special education class in the school district which is attempting to provide training for her, and as you could see from the IEP and the variety of areas for her speech, her academic kinds of things, her physical needs, basically, Margayia has the same services available that are required by 94-42 that are available across the country.

Q. Do they have anything else to your knowledge?

A. There are private kinds of places that you can go to and stuff, but the school systems have, basically, the same available that other school systems do.

Q. How do you know that?

A. Because I've work with a number of the school systems in the state. I've had lots of cases there. I'm from Margayia, too, which helps somewhat. Lived there for 22 years, and I visit there quite frequently.

Q. Have you ever worked in Margayia?

A. Oh, yes.

Q. When?

A. I haven't -- as a psychologist, I've worked there as a consultant in a number of cases over the past ten years since I've gotten my degree. I worked for the United States Post Office. I did tutoring of children and things like that. Just little jobs as I went through school to support myself.

Q. So you never worked as a psychologist there?

A. I have worked as a psychologist since my degree. Not full time, but I do go in as a consultant to hospitals, talks, seminars, training sessions, things like that.

Q. Why don't you tell me about all of your experience in Margayia starting with the most recent?

Mr. Frost: As best you can.

Witness: I can't tell you every case I've been in in

Margayia. I do not have that information in front of me. I've seen probably about 30 to 40 cases in Margayia.

I've given talks in all of the major cities in Margayia on neuropsychology in adults and children and the treatment rehabilitation and assessment to people with brain injuries. I've done that about 15 times probably in Margayia, although that's an approximation.

Like I said, I don't keep records like that. I've been a consultant to University of Southern Margayia, to U Margayia. I'm going to be giving a -- a workshop at the University of Margayia on brain dysfunction, and I've spoke to the Margayia State Psychological Association and other groups in the state who have been meeting in Margayia.

Mr. Clark: All right. Now, the 30 to 40 cases that you've consulted on in Margayia, have any of those resulted in your making recommendations for placement somewhere in Margayia?

A. Certainly.

Q. What kind of recommendations have you made?

A. Well, it depends on the case. It could be recommendations to a State hospital, to a private psychological facility. We've referred people out to our own treatment facilities out here. We suggested people go to places like the Brown schools where they're appropriate for the case. We've suggested that people stay with their local school district in cases of children, and in adults we've referred them to some of the hospital rehabilitation facilities that exist in the state where they're appropriate.

Q. Have you consulted on cases in Margayia where children such as LL were involved?

A. Sure.

Q. How many times?

A. I would guess that of the cases we've had in Margayia probably about half of them were children.

Q. 15 to 20?

A. Yes, somewhere in there.

Q. All of them similar to LL in terms of needs?

A. Well, I see each case as individual. LL is on the fairly severe end of intellectual impairment in that she is much worse off than most of the kids I see. Physically, she's a little bit better than some of the kids I've seen. She isn't paralyzed. She's able to walk, things like that.

Q. All right. I don't understand what facilities are available to a child like LL in Margayia. You mentioned, generally, those that are required by the government. Can you tell me what is required by the government, then?

A. The government -- the law just requires that the school provide appropriate help for a child to maximize the amount of learning and education that they can get and has been ruled by the courts, as I'm sure that you're aware, that that includes a wide range of services ranging from academic tutoring to physical therapy, and such like that, when physical problems interfere with school performance.

Where the parents live now, they're in a school district that does have a very high level of function and is able to provide all the basic services she needs at the moment at this age, at the age of 10 1/2.

Q. Okay. What basic services do you believe she presently needs?

A. She needs an extensive education program very much like the one they're providing. They're doing an excellent job with her at the moment. Right now, I think the school district is doing as good a job as anyone could do.

Q. Have you ever rendered a report to Mr. Frost?

A. No.

Q. Have you been asked not to?

A. No.

Q. When were you first contacted by Mr. Frost or someone from his office?

A. About six months ago -- six, eight months ago. Sometime early in the year.

A. No. I visited with them, one of my visits to Honolulu.

Q. How did that come about?

A. I was in Honolulu, and I think Dr. Marvett (phonetic), Dr. Robert Marvett, said that there was some cases that he thought I could be useful in helping with and if I would be willing to meet with them, and I said, "yes", and so he arranged for us to meet for dinner.

Q. Who's Dr. Marvett?

A. He's a psychiatrist at Honolulu.

Q. A friend of yours?

A. I hope so.

Q. All right. You had dinner with who, Mr. Frost?

A. Mr. Frost and some of his people, and I don't remember all the names.

Q. And when was that?

A.   About six months ago, like I said.

Q.   Was this case specifically brought up?

A.   Yes.

Q.   Did you agree at that dinner with Mr. Frost and his associates to work on this case?

A.   I said I was more than glad to evaluate her, that it wouldn't be a problem.

Q.   When was your next contact concerning this case?

A.   We've had phone calls back and forth since then.

Q.   Do you keep a record of that?

A.   No.

Q.   How do you keep track of your time?

A.   I just usually charged him for the evaluation.   I told them I'd charge them a flat rate which I did.

Q.   Flat rate of $2,000.?

A.   Right.   Including all of our expenses.

Q.   What was your expenses?

A.   Flying out to Eden, airplane fees, hotel, that kind of thing.

Q.   How much?

A.   I couldn't even tell you for sure.   Not all the bills are in.   Probably about half of the $2,000, more than likely, but   that's just a guess.

Q.   So $3,000 total so far?

A.   Oh, no, no.   There are no additional -- the $2000 includes the expenses.   When I set a flat rate, I set a flat rate.

Mr. Frost: That's what you said.

Witness: That is what I said.   No.   It was just $2000. That we do the case for $2,000 period, whatever it cost us for the evaluation part.

Mr. Clark.   And we've already talked about what you charged if you go to trial?

A.   Yes.

Q.   Have you worked with Mr. Frost on any other cases?

A.   We had one other case together.

Q. Have you been deposed in that case?

A. No. I was not deposed in that case.

Q. Is your deposition scheduled?

A. No. The case has settled. The lawyers on the other side did phone me, but I never had a formal deposition.

Q. Any other case with any other members with Mr. Frost's firm?

A. I don't believe so. I don't know. Who are all the people -- I have -- actually, we do have one outgoing case. I take that back -- yes. We do have one other adult case. I just remembered.

Q. Would you tell me what you know about that case?

A. It is just a case that they asked me to evaluate. The man had some kind of an injury in a sea accident, and we brought him here to Omaha for an evaluation and for treatment, and he's brain damaged.

Mr. Frost: I didn't even know they were here.

Witness: They came here. They didn't tell you?

Mr. Clark: Have you been deposed in that case?

A. No. And there's nothing scheduled at the moment.

Q. How many times have you had your deposition taken in the past?

A. 50 times, 45 times, something like that, maybe in the last ten years.

Q. Always as an expert in this type of case?

A. As an expert and sometimes -- usually either brain injury or pain cases or cases involving significant psychological disturbance. I've done criminal cases as well as civil cases.

Q. How many civil cases have you been deposed in?

A. Thirty maybe. These are guesses. I do not certify the accuracy of these numbers. I've never counted.

Q. Have those cases been for the Plaintiff or Defendant?

A. Both.

Q. How many times?

A. It's about half and half.

Q. Do you have any copies of depositions you've given in the past on behalf of the Defense in brain damage cases?

A.   Not -- no, I don't think so. We don't keep many --
once a case is settled, we usually get rid of the files.

Q.   Do you have any depositions from your past cases that
you've given?

A.   They might, but I would not know for sure. My
secretary would have to look through the files.

Q.   Is that here?

A.   The files that we can get our hands on are here.

Q.   Could you ask her to do that, please? Let's take a
break. You can ask her to do that. Maybe she'll find them
before we're finished.

A.   I'm not sure she would be able to identify a brain
injury case from any other kind of case.

Q.   That's all right. If she can bring in the depositions,
we can identify the brain injury through you.

A.   Right. Do you want copies of this?

Q.   Maybe, maybe not.

A.   Right. I would just have to state on the record, we
would have to charge you for copies for any of these things.

(A short recess was taken.)

Mr. Frost: I think he was saying he doesn't get copies of
all the depositions. Let me know just so the record is clear,
to try to accommodate your schedule, we moved the depo up and
already limited my time in discussing the case to something
less than half an hour.

Mr. Clark: Now, you say you performed testing on LL in
September of 1985; right?

A.   Yes.

Q.   And that was in Margayia?

A.   Yes.

Q.   Did you also perform testing on her siblings?

A.   Yes.

Q.   Same days?

A.   Yes.

Q.   What tests did you give her brother and sister?

A.   Basically, the Wechsler's Intelligence Test for
Children, revised, plus a -- well, that's all they got. The
mother filled out a personality test, and we also did an

achievement test, the Woodcock-Johnson Test.

Q. You did the WISC-R for the brother and sister?

A. And the Woodcock-Johnson, and the mother filled -- the parents filled out a personality inventory on the children. The WISC-R is the main test.

Q. Did you meet with the mother and the father?

A. Oh, yes.

Q. Tell me how long you met with -- strike that. Did you meet with the mother and father individually and together or --

A. Yes.

Q. How long did you meet with the mother?

A. Several hours. I didn't time it.

Q. How long with the father?

A. Same thing.

Q. And how long together?

A. Again, I met with the mother, then I met with them together, and then I met with the father for awhile, and then I met with the mother, again, and I can't tell you the exact times. I spent about five hours in all of that.

Q. Did you take notes at all of those meetings?

A. No. It inhibits people when you take notes.

Q. What did you talk about at those meetings?

A. LL.

Q. Tell me what you can recall.

A. We talked about LL's history, and they told me about the manner of her birth, the fact that she was born prematurely during an elective caesarean. The mother told me that she had -- the baby was in the hospital for about a month. That after she came out of the hospital, a couple weeks later, she suddenly developed a severe disorder which was identified as meningitis. That afterwards, that her developing properly, that she had trouble with motor, with her visual functions, with language, with cognition, and that she had not met any of her normal milestones developmentally, and they gave me just a little history. That they had moved to Hawaii, and that they decided to move to Margayia because they offered better educational services there. I also watched them at the same time interacting with LL and with the other children.

Q. Did they know you were watching?

A. Yes, yes. There were no two-way mirrors in the hours.

Q. Oh, this was at their house?

A. yes.

Q. Did you review any medical records?

A. I did in Mr. Frost's office.

Q. But again, you can't recall what you reviewed, and it's not important to your opinion?

A. It's not important to my opinions. I'm not testifying on the adequacies on the medical care.

Q. If the medical problems had any affect on her, you can't testify to that?

A. I can, depending on how you phrase that question.

Q. Well, why don't you tell me what you can testify to?

Mr. Frost: Let me object. That's so vague and open. I don't think that can get a meaningful answer. I have no idea, personally, what you're after on that question.

Mr. Clark: Go ahead, Doctor. He makes objections that don't really sound like objections to anybody else but him, but that's okay.

Mr. Frost: I object. Vague and ambiguous. If you can answer it, fine, but my objection will be, no matter what the answer is, I don't think it can be responsiveness.

Witness: I can admit to being confused at this time.

Mr. Frost: If you are confused, ask him to restate it.

Witness: I can't testify in the medical care at all in whether it was adequate or the right medical care or anything else. I can testify on the relationship of psychological test results to the reported types of disorders and problems that she had.

Mr. Clark: Could you elaborate on that, please?

A. The parents identify that she had been born prematurely, was in intensive NICU for a month and perinatal intensive care unit for a month, and, secondly, she had meningitis, which from their description followed a fairly typical course for that type of meningitis, and one can relate what her symptoms are now to those events back then and to the rest of the history that they gave. They did not report -- yes, to the rest of the history that they gave.

Q. What can you relate to prematurity?

A. Basically, in a child who's born premature with Highland Membrane Disease, if we see deficits in the children, they tend to be what we call diffuse deficits. They were not focal in nature as a rule. They tend to show some background lowering of the behavior competence of the brain and a higher

115

susceptibility to the development of learning problems later on and to the failure to meet development milestones and the like.

Q. Do you agree that not all premature infants who have respiratory distress syndrome have any type of brain damage?

A. There is a minority of people that we cannot yet certainly identify it, however, we do know that the incidents of learning problems and of lower IQ in psychological problems, especially as they get older, is higher in those children than in children with a normal birth history, but as you said, not every child has been identified to have problems. No question about that.

Q. Is it your opinion that this child has some brain damage because she was premature?

A. It is my opinion that the child has brain damage due to both the fact that she is premature and the subsequent meningitis.

Q. Well, assume, Doctor, that she did not develop meningitis, is it your opinion that she would have been brain damaged?

A. From our test results, it is probable that she would have had some brain damage even without the meningitis.

Q. To what extent?

A. To a lesser extent than she has brain damage now, but probably she would have probably had an IQ of -- again, because we never got to observe her obviously. She was only six weeks old at the time that the meningitis -- one has to work on probability here, but chances are her IQ probably would have been in the 85, 90 range, and in school, she probably would have been identified as learning disabled.

Q. On what do you base that opinion?

A. Just on the results of the testing, the fact that I do know what children with meningitis look like afterwards as a group. I've seen a number of children who have had meningitis like LL did. We now the kind of test results they give. In LL's case, the test results are much more severe than is normally seen. It is out of the range that we would suspect to see. To say that it were properly medically treated, and from what I could tell, the meningitis itself was properly treated medically. That's not an expert opinion, but that's just what I've seen.

Q. Do you know what inappropriate ADH is?

A. What?

Q. Inappropriate ADH.

A. Again, I can talk about the appropriateness of the treatment of the meningitis.

Q. Do you know in your review of the medical records that

that was in the medical records?

Mr. Frost: It's a misstatement. There's no showing of any inappropriate treatment of the meningitis.

Witness: I did not see anything that mentioned inappropriate treatment of the meningitis.

Mr. Clark: Do you agree that if the meningitis was treated and there was inappropriate ADH or cerebral edema because of inappropriate treatment, that that could cause the extensive brain damage that you see rather than anything like prematurity?

Mr. Frost: Wait before you answer. Let me object that that misstates the facts in this case that there was any inappropriate ADH at all. Go ahead.

Witness: Cerebral edema typically does not produce the kind of test results that we're seeing here unless the child's brain is low through the tentorium or something like that, which, again, there was no mention of anything like that in the medical records that I know of.

Mr. Clark: What is your understanding of LL's condition when she was discharged from Bronson Hospital (phonetic) on March 2, 1975?

A. That was from the NICU unit you're talking about?

Q. Do you know?

A. I'm asking for a clarification. If I knew for sure --

Q. What was her condition in your opinion on March 2nd, 1975, Doctor?

A. Again, I can't tell you by the contact date, and if you won't clarify the question, I can't answer it.

Q. Would you disagree with all of the physicians who were treating her at that time if they said she was a normal healthy infant?

A. If you won't clarify the answer to my question, I can't answer any questions. If you're going to play games like this, we're not going to get anywhere.

Q. I'm not playing games.

A. I don't have the names of the hospitals memorized. Was it NICU? You refused to answer that. If you won't answer that, I can't answer your question.

Q. Doctor, please feel free to look at your records.

Q. I do not have the medical records in front of me. I told you that already. I don't know why you're doing this.

Q. All I'm trying to do is find out what you do know and what you don't know as you sit here today. You're the one that's rendering expert opinions and willing to testify on the cause of prematurity and the cause of brain damage.

A. But I'm not willing to render expert opinions on the exact dates that everything happened, and I don't have them in front of me, so if you would be kind enough to tell me that that was when she was leaving the NICU --

Q. Assuming that when this patient was discharged from the hospital after having been in the NICU, that all the treating physicians have testified that this was a normal healthy infant, would you disagree with those physicians?

A. I wasn't there at the time. I wouldn't agree or disagree. I can state, however, that a lot of psychological and cognitive problems don't show up until years later. There's no way a doctor after a child is a month born can make statements like that. There's all sorts of things that you cannot know at that point in time, and I'm sure if the doctors made that statement, they made it within the limits that they know, but that doesn't mean anything in terms of what was really going on.

Q. Those doctors at least had the benefits of having examined the patients.

A. There is -- they can't make a better prediction having identified her than I could. Learning disabilities and other problems show up years later, and the predictability of what you're like at one month of age as to what you're going to be at twelve is zero. There's no prediction between the two, and nobody is competent to make predictions like that.

Mr. Clark: Move to strike as nonresponsive.

Mr. Frost: That is exactly what he asked.

Mr. Clark: Do you agree that those doctors had the benefit of an examination and you did not?

A. Yes, that I agree to.

Q. It would be a lot shorter if you just answer "yes" or "no" when you can. They had --

Mr. Frost: Let me object to the argument nature. I think he's being very responsiveness. I think maybe you're getting an answer, and he's elaborating. Maybe you're getting more information than you want, so if --

Mr. Clark: Anyway, they had the benefit of the examination and you did not. They felt she was a normal healthy infant, and you feel that she had some brain damage at that time, is that true, when she left?

Mr. Frost: Asked and answered several times.

Witness: Yes.

Mr. Clark: And again, all I want to know, everything that you base that opinion on, anything in the physical findings as she left the NICU, anything in the observations of any of the physicians that in your opinion causes you to think that there

118

was brain damage at that time.

Mr. Frost: Asked and answered. He talked about correlation.

Witness: No.

Mr. Clark: So you don't base your opinion at all on the medical records; is that true?

A. No. That's not true, either.

Q. What is it about the medical records, Doctor, that you see that causes you to think that this infant, this particular infant, had some brain damage when she left the NICU?

Mr. Frost: Let me object. He's already answered that in detail about the prematurity. Do you want him to do it, again?

Mr. Clark: Go ahead.

Witness: Premature children who are born with poor Apgar scores, cognitive dysfunction of a diffused nature, that does not show up until the child is considerably older. The -- there is nothing in the medical records that contradicts that.

The rest of the opinion is based upon, again, the rest of her medical history, the meningitis, her subsequent history, and the current test results based on the fact that we work with -- and there's both a literature on it, that we work with these children with meningitis are going to look like later, depending on what they look like before. We can look at these test results and a lot of it clearly is due to the meningitis, but, also, again, her injuries are much more diffuse and much more serious than we see with cases of this type of meningitis, therefore, there has to be another factor. The only other identifiable factor in her history is the premature birth.

Mr. Clark: What do you feel is a poor Apgar score?

Mr. Frost: If you feel you're an expert.

Witness: If the child is not at nine or ten after five minutes, I would consider it poor.

Mr. Clark: So you disagree with all of her treating physicians if they said she had good Apgar scores at eight at five minutes?

A. That might be good for a premature child. But, again, in the literature relating to this psychological functioning, what we find, if the child does not get up to nine or ten after five minutes, the child is, again, at higher risk. The difference between making a prediction to the child's physical outcome, whether she's going to have problem in the hospital versus whether she's going to have cognitive problems in life. I'm interested in something different than what the doctors are interested in.

Q. So you think anything under nine at five minutes is a poor Apgar score?

Mr. Frost: Let me object. He just answered that exact question.

Mr. Clark: Can you answer it "yes" or "no"? If you feel --

A. In terms of their psychological outcome, we consider it a poor score, yes.

Q. And would you say that any infant that has an Apgar score between nine and ten is probably going to have some focal impairment as you called it or some brain damage?

Mr. Frost: That isn't what he said.

Witness: That's a complete misstatement of what I said.

Mr. Clark: So you don't feel that?

Witness: No. You just misstated my whole position.

Mr. Clark: All you got to do is answer my question "yes" or "no". I don't understand it over here, where you're coming from, and you have much more knowledge in this area than I do, and all I'm trying to do is understand it. Is it your opinion, just "yes" or "no", that if an infant has an Apgar score of under nine or ten, that she's probably going to have some brain damage?

Mr. Frost: That's not what he said.

Mr. Clark: I didn't say -- I just asked him if that was his opinion.

Witness: No.

Mr. Clark: Is it your opinion that any premature child who has an Apgar score of under nine or ten is going to have some lowered IQ in brain damage?

Mr. Frost: Asked and answered.

Witness: No.

Mr. Clark: What is it, then, about this child besides the IQ -- excuse me, strike that. What is it about this child, then, besides the fact that she had an Apgar of eight at five minutes that makes you feel that this child would have had some brain damage besides the fact that she was premature and she had an Apgar of eight.

Mr. Frost: We went through that for the last 15 minutes. I guess, do it again.

Witness: If you rule out all of the causes for seeing her at risk, then, there is no reason to see her at risk, which you've just done.

Mr. Clark: So those are the only two?

A. Those are the two I stated, yes.

Q. But we do know and you agree that not all premature children who have Apgars of eight have some lowering of IQ or brain damage?

Mr. Frost: Asked and answered.

Witness: Yes.

Mr. Clark: Doctor, you've agreed to testify as an expert in this case at the time of trial?

A. Yes.

Q. Tell me what opinions you have in this case. Just run through them all, please.

A. Actually, just one basic opinion, that LL has severe brain damage that's resulted in a drop of IQ at least 50 to 60 points, and that she will be forever unable to take care of herself or live an independent situation or hold any kind of competitive job. Also, that related to that is just that the quality of her life has already been severely impaired and will be continued to be very poor in the future.

Q. Now, that doesn't include the things that we've just been talking about. Did you leave that out because we just talked about it or that's really not a part of your opinion?

A. We already talked about it.

Q. I really want everything, whether we've talked about it or not, just go through the list.

A. Well --

Mr. Frost: Let me object to rehashing things we've just spent most of the deposition time on already, but go ahead, again, Doctor.

Witness: That LL has severe brain damage that is due to a combination of her meningitis and the prematurity of her birth.

Mr. Clark: Is that everything, now?

A. That's everything.

Q. Can you separate, Doctor, what is due to meningitis and what is due to prematurity?

Mr. Frost: He's done that.

Witness: To the degree that I've already done it?

Mr. Clark: I must have missed it.

Mr. Frost: Let me object. I don't mind going --

Mr. Clark: If you'd up, we'd get this thing done. Make

your objection and that's it.

Mr. Frost: We'd get it done if you'd ask one question. Are you trying to catch him or what?

Mr. Clark: I'm just trying to understand.

Mr. Frost: If the questions aren't exactly the same, and you're trying for impeachment at trial, and you keep asking the question over and over hoping you'll get a different answer. You're at least as bright as I am, and you heard what he said.

Witness: Children with meningitis typically show areas in cognitive functioning of specific focal types of damage that generally --

Mr. Clark: Let me just rephrase the question. Apparently you don't understand where I'm going. Maybe that's why Mr. Frost keeps objecting. You say that she has a drop of IQ of 50 to 60 points?

A. Yes.

Q. I'm trying to figure out in terms of quantifying how much is due to the meningitis, how much is due to the prematurity.

Mr. Frost: Asked and answered, again.

Witness: Typically a child with meningitis that we see, this type of meningitis, will have sometimes no drop in IQ at all, but a maximum drop usually in the 20 point range. For the child to lose as much as 50 to 60 points due to the meningitis suggests that the child had some pre-existing brain damage, because in this case of the prematurity and that at least the child's brain was much more susceptible to the affects of the meningitis at the time.

Generally, the less developed the child's brain is at the time the meningitis occurs, the worse off the child is going to be. By being born prematurely, her brain did at least -- did not have adequate time to fully develop, which means the diseases that she catches at a different age are going to be much more severe to her than diseases to another child who was born at the right time is going to have. When you're talking about brain age, you're talking about age since cessation, her age since birth because she was born early was actually that of a newborn and that made her much more -- at least that made her much more susceptible to injury. It is probably also true, though, that because of the prematurity, because of the Apgar scores, we know that statistically those children are at a higher risk that will show up later in life given the test results that we have now.

Mr. Clark: How many cases of early onset group B streptococcal meningitis have you seen?

A. Probably five to ten.

Q. And how many late onset group B streptococcal meningitis patients have you seen?

A. We see probably about three to eight meningitis cases a year, so we would be doing this -- we're probably talking about 20 to 50 cases, 30 to 50 cases probably.

Q. Of late onset?

A. Well, late onset or later than LL's age, let's put it that way.

Q. Maybe that's where we're falling off?

A. What do you mean by --

Q. Do you understand early onset to mean the first seven days of life?

A. I understand it -- I can understand it to mean whatever you like. Different doctors use the term in different ways.

Q. What is your definition of early onset?

A. I was using just the first two months of life.

Q. So you do not separate it first seven days versus seven days to three months?

A. I could if you wanted me to, but, no, I won't do that.

Q. Then, that's not a part of what you normally do in your definition?

A. No. As I said, I just --

Q. So you group early onset and late onset together, if the definition is first seven days early onset and seven days to three months as late onset?

A. If we're doing it that way, you're trying to classify LL as late onset?

Q. Do you believe that she is?

A. No. I'm just trying to get it straight. If it is late onset, most of the seven days to three month range, so almost all of them would fall in that range. I see very few kids with meningitis right at birth in the first seven days.

Q. Were you classifying LL as early onset?

A. Just for -- for my psychological purposes, the first two or three months are the key, but I will admit, again, our cases tend to be in the four to eight weeks, four to twelve week range. We see very few early onset cases.

Q. Do you agree that there are some differences in the virulency of the group B streptococcal meningitis in the patients that you see?

Mr. Frost: I don't understand that question.

Witness: I think he means the severity. Some are more virulent than others. Some are more severe than others, yes.

Mr. Clark: And, therefore, some cause a greater loss in IQ than others?

A. Probably, yes. There's a statistical mean and standard deviation associated with it.

Q. Have you ever had a child who you later found out had group B streptococcal type 3, and then did some testing at age 9 or 10 and found that he or she had a 50 to 60 drop in IQ?

A. For kids with onsets and the ranges that we typically see, I've never had a kid with an IQ this low. The lowest that I can recall is about 75 to 80. I have seen some kids who were born with severe meningitis who were worse, but as I said, we see very few of those, and they typically -- the ones that I've seen have been so wiped out, I wouldn't have evaluated them, anyway.

Q. Tell me what tests you performed with Lisa and what her scores were. I know you said the WISC-R. Tell me what her score was on the WISC-R, and I have some stuff.

A. You messed up my files, yes. Lisa's IQ overall was 112 on the Woodcock-Johnson, and the achievement test, her achievement was all in the fifth to sixth grade range.

Q. How old was Lisa when she was tested?

A. Lisa was twelve years and one month old, just starting the sixth grade, so her IQ was above average and her achievement scores are slightly above average on the whole.

Q. What were the subscores on the WISC-R?

A. All of them?

Q. Uh-huh. Well, I'm going to get a copy of it. i was looking for the scaled score. She had a verbal 63, performance 55, and full scale 118, and the scaled score and the IQ was 115, verbal, performance 106, and full scale 112?

A. Uh-huh.

Mr. Frost: the doctor doesn't have it. I'll vouch that he's reading this correctly.

Witness: That's fine.

Mr. Clark: And Jason?

A. Jason's verbal IQ was 103, performance 135, full scale 121, and Jason's achievement test scores were all in the second to third grade level, and his exact age was seven years and six months, and just starting the second grade, so Jason's achievement scores and IQ were all well above average.

Q. Tell me what tests you performed with LL and what her scores were.

A. Okay. LL had a verbal IQ of 57, performance IQ of 52, and a full scale IQ of 50. On several of the subtests, she simply got the minimum score possible. On the Stanford-Binet, she ended up with a 61 and a mental age of 6years 4 months. On the Peabody Picture Vocabulary Test, the revised version, she had an IQ of 49 and an age equivalent of four years, five months. On the Beery Development Visual-Motor Integration Test, she ended up with age equivalent of 5-7, and on the Vineland Adaptive Behavior Scale, she ended up with a chronological age of 4 years, 0 months, and at the time, she was 10 years and 7 months old, and on the Luria-Nebraska, she scored severely into the severe brain damaged range.

Q. Which is what? I don't understand.

A. Luria-Nebraska Neuropsychological Test. We gave her two forms of the test. One is the children's form, and the other is the extended form. On a normal person, if the scale on the test would have been 10 percent of the scale into the brain damaged range, LL had more like 75 percent of the scale in the brain damaged range.

Q. You say you gave two different forms of that test?

A. Yes.

Q. And they were both the same?

A. Yes. The forms are related to each other, so being the same is not a big surprise. There's nothing meaningful. We just happened to have given both forms. That, basically, is it. She just shows problem in all the higher cognitive areas. She can hear. She can see, although she has peripheral visual problems, as I'm sure you know, and she can do very basic things, but anything requiring judgment, abstraction, higher cognitive skills, reading, writing, arithmetic, evaluations, what's happening to her social judgment, is well beyond her.

Q. Well, let's start with the physical problems that you know, all right? You said peripheral vision; correct?

A. Yes.

Q. Anything else? In other words, motor function problems?

A. Well, she had difficulty with motor function. her right hand is somewhat more impaired than her left hand. Her bilateral coordination was poor. She had difficulty with movements of her mouth. She had difficulty with drawings. Drawings were very poor and slow, and then writing is a motor skill. She did very, very poor on that.

Q. Any other physical tests that you performed?

A. Well, we also performed tests of tactile sensitivity, and she can feel, touch. Then we did what we call a double tache sensation. You touch two places simultaneously. She's not able to do that properly. She has a lot of difficulty with that. Much more difficulty than other children her age.

Auditorally, she can hear and recognize basic sounds, and she can hear basic -- well, speech sounds and nonspeech sounds, but she can't deal with any kind of complex hearing task, but as far as we could tell, she can hear.

Q. What about her vision? Other than peripheral vision, did you note or did you see in any of the records what her vision was?

A. You mean the acuity of her vision?

Q. Yes.

A. No. I don't remember that. She could see adequately to see her images, and she had to look closer at the pages and at things, and she has some difficulty when she walks seeing sometimes things in her way and things like that, and I'm sure her vision and clearly her eyes did not move with each other in a coordinated fashion, and she had trouble with following any kind of moving object, so she did not see well, and she really had to concentrate on a piece of paper and look at it closely to see it.

Q. Do you know what her corrected vision is?

A. No. It didn't look great, but that's just a general observation.

Q. Now, as I understand it, there are certain categories of mental retardation that you, Doctor, sometimes refer to; is that right?

A. Right.

Q. Trainable, educable, profound. Could you just tell the ladies and gentlemen of the jury that might be hearing this later what that is, those categories?

A. Well, the categories that we typically use now is mild, moderate, severe. Now, the mild goes down to IQ from 55 to 70. Moderate is from 40 to 55. She falls into the moderate IQ range, which the other word for that is trainable, which means that she can be trained to do basic things, to take care of herself, comb her hair, things like that. She still can't tie her shoes, but, eventually, she should be able to do that, however, her judgment will never be very good. She'll never be able to take care of herself. She can't be expected, for example, to raise a family or be able to do anything like that nor can she be expected to be in any kind of competitive work situation, although she may be able to work in a sheltered workshop type of setting.

Q. Have you not had patients or seen patients in the trainable mentally handicapped range who have, in fact, gotten out and entered the competitive work force?

A. Under 55, that's very rare and almost only when someone just puts together a job for them, like cleaning up a room or something like that. It is almost because they knew someone or something like that. We do not attempt -- well, mild mental retardation people can get out into the competitive work about half or a third. When you get under an IQ of 55, the likelihood of that happening is very, very low. It's not possible, but I would not hold that out as a strong possibility to anybody.

Q. You said, at the present time, it's your opinion that LL is receiving adequate instruction and care in the school?

A. Yes.

Q. Before I get to that, did you test the parents at all in any way?

A. Yes.

Q. What test did you give the parents?

A. We gave them MMPI and the Wechsler's Adult Intelligence Scale.

Q. What were the scores?

A. Luana had an IQ verbal of 124, performance of 139, full scale IQ is 134, which would actually place her in the genius range, and Rod, her father, had a 115 variable, performance 111, full scale 115, which puts him in the superior range. Their MMPI's were both normal.

Q. At the present time, based upon your test, do you have any recommendations concerning any treatment for the parents?

A. No. The parents are very religious people who have taken on what's happened to them very well, and I think as long as they keep their faith in the future and their willingness to work without becoming depressed, I would not interfere at all with what they're doing.

Q. Now, you've stated that what LL is receiving at the present time is adequate. When do you think in your opinion that the school district will be unable to meet LL's needs, if ever?

A. Well, basically, the school district's only required by law to treat her through the upper age of 21 at all, and they do not treat children past 21, so that would be my definition. Our own feelings and our own way of handling these cases is that a child really ought to be out of the home by the time they're 18. There's a need for the child, especially the mentally retarded child, to develop some dependence.

She can go into a boarding house where she will be cared for. She needs to do that if she's going to reach her full potential to the degree that she'll be able to take care of herself. We usually recommend to the parents, regardless of what the school is doing, that the child be placed in an outside home by the age of 18, and if the school can continue to help them, that's fine. In LL's case, she's going to need basically self- help skills and training for working in a sheltered workshop situation, and I think that would be best gained outside the school in the workshop and in the group boarding home situation.

Q. I know some states provide sheltered workshops and, in fact, provide minimal payment for those in the sheltered workshop. Do you know whether Margayia, in fact, provides such a program?

A. As a rule, in Margayia, if there is a responsible party to pay for it, they expect you to do that. The other problem is that if you want the better facilities, you have to go to the private groups. The State run facilities are not very good, to put it nicely and --

Q. How much does the State require in terms of payment from someone in Rod K's income bracket?

A. That, I could not tell you for sure. I haven't looked at tables like that in a long time. The costs of the programs themselves, in a private setting, we're talking about a yearly cost starting at $30,000 in a state like Margayia and working your way up, of some them running as much as $60,000 a year.

Q. All right. Let's stay with the State for one minute. You have no idea what it would cost for LL to be in a sheltered workshop environment which is run by the State?

A. No. I never really considered that as an option because that's not what would make her develop the best she can. As I said, I've lived in Margayia, and I've gone to these places, and they're not very good.

Q. What's the difference between the State run and the private?

A. The State runs it as cheaply as humanly possible. They hire the people cheapest available who don't have any qualifications. They hire people for psychological people and evaluations who do not have adequate training and degrees in my opinion. They even hire physicians who could not practice legally, who could not get a license except in working for a State facility.

Q. What's the name of the State facility nearest Eden?

A. Well, if we're talking about a boarding home, they don't have names. Most of them are located in the larger cities.

Q. Where is the nearest workshop to the present home?

A. More than likely, Acronopolis.

Q. You don't know, though?

A. I couldn't tell you for sure. They tend to be concentrated in the larger cities.

Q. You have not gone to the nearest sheltered workshop, state run, and evaluated that workshop?

A. Not that specific one, no, but then there's no guarantee they will be living there in ten years either.

Q. So in terms of the quality of the people in the facilities at that location, you would not be able to testify, specifically, as to what's available?

Mr. Frost: Let me object. He's testified as to his knowledge of all the facilities he's examined in Margayia.

Witness: Well, it would be meaningless, first of all, because the turnover in those places in terms of staff is so high. What their quality of any one given program is is meaningless, but what is more important, and because you're talking about putting a person into the system for 50 years, is the overall quality and extended quality over time, and the State system just does not meet those requirements.

Mr. Clark: Is the short answer to my question you don't know what is available and what type of people are at that facility?

A. Today, no. I do not know who's there today.

Q. No, you don't know what the turnover is at that particular facility?

A. No. I don't know the turnover at that particular facility.

Q. What particular private school did you have in mind when you started talking about $30,000 a year?

A. I didn't have a particular one in mind.

Q. Which ones have you actually gone to, and give me the names of the ones you can tell me about that actually charge $30,000 per year.

Mr. Frost: Are we talking about schools or living facilities?

Mr. Clark: I think we're talking about sheltered workshops.

Witness: You're talking about whatever. It's your question.

Mr. Clark: I'm sorry.

A. It's your question. You're talking about whichever you wish to be talking about.

Q. Maybe we better get that clear. It was my understanding that when I asked you about State shops, something about $30,000 costs, do you recall that?

A. Yes.

Q. What was that for?

A. That was just the cost of placing another child that we were working with. That has been the lowest cost that we have placed a child in similar types of problems. I didn't have a specific name of a facility in mind.

Q. $30,000 for what, placed them where?

A.   In a boarding home type facility with adequate
supervision and training and vocational opportunity to the
person's best ability.

Q.   What all is provided at this boarding home?

A.   Well, the kinds of homes I'm talking about would
provide room and board, 24 hour a day supervision, would limit
the number of children living in any given setting to four to
six to eight maximum. We prefer four to six. They would
provide transportation of the individual where they need to go.
They would provide cultural outings, going to movies, shopping
centers, whatever it is people are doing for entertainment at
the time, and they would provide -- arrange for a job somewhere,
noncompetitive jobs that the individual could do to earn some
money on their own or a sheltered workshop type setting where
the person could work.

They would also provide training for the person, teaching
them how to make food, teaching them how to clean clothes,
teaching them how to do the dishes, teaching them how to take a
bus. It's kind of an extended ongoing school, and then, of
course, would protect them. people like LL have a great deal of
trouble, for example, when they reach adolescence with sexual
kinds of manners. They can easily have poor judgment. They can
get pregnant. All sorts of things can go wrong, and you need
adults who can help protect them from those kinds of problems,
usually multiple adults. Usually in these places, the staff-
patient ratio, there are more staff members than there are
patients.

Q.   How much would they earn at this noncompetitive
employment?

A.   Oh, sometimes they don't earn anything at all.
Sometimes it's fifty cents or a dollar an hour. It depends
where you are and stuff like that. It depends on your level of
skills as well.

Q.   You don't recall the name of the facility that you're
talking about that cost of $30,000 per year?

A.   No.

Q.   Can you give me the name of any facility in Margayia
near the KK's home, private or otherwise?

A.   No. I don't memorize facility names.

Q.   Do you remember the city in which this facility was
that you placed this whoever you were talking about?

A.   I couldn't -- I don't, again --

Q.   You don't remember names of cities, either?

A.   No. Not -- these things, I do too many cases, and I

have too many to be able to do that.

Q. How long ago was that?

A. We have placed cases in Margayia several times over the past ten years.

Q. I'm talking about the one that was $30,000.

A. I couldn't even tell you for sure which of the cases I told you was the $30,000. I just remember that was the one being the cheapest. We've also placed people in the Brown and Deveroe (phonetic) school which has ended up costing $60,000 to $80,000. I remember those because they were so impressively high.

Q. Where are those?

A. Brown school is in Texas, and Deveroe is out in Pennsylvania. Brown, as a matter of fact, has branches in Hawaii, and I think one in Margayia as well. We send people to those when the smaller facilities are not able to handle the person for one reason or another. We try to go with the cheaper places first.

Most of the time what we do in a case like this, if you want to, the procedures of going through this is when you decide the kind of facility, then we work with local social work agencies, private social work agencies, and things like that in the area the person lives in to identify possibilities within the area, and then the choices are made. I do not actually make the choice myself usually.

Q. Assume for a moment, Doctor, that Mr. and Mrs. KKdecide that they would like to keep LL in the home for as long as possible, and in that case, do you agree that the school would provide supervision for her until age 21?

A. Yes, they would, during the day.

Q. I'm sorry.

A. During the day, the school would provide classes for her.

Q. After age 21 and, again, assuming that Rod and Luana would like to keep their child with them so they can keep in touch and make sure that she's getting the care that they want, what kind of care would you envisage for her from the home and how much would it cost?

A. It's a difficult question because I've never let anybody do that. It's not in the child's best interest, and I'm very opposed to that. To answer your question, it would depend upon how much Rod and Lucy were willing to --

Mr. Frost: Luana?

Witness: Luana. I'm getting LL, Luana and all that mixed up, but it would depend how much they were willing to sacrifice their life. She will need constant supervision, and she's going to be attracted to boys, and they're going to be attracted to her, and the question is what is their breaking point. And I don't know that at this point in time.

Mr. Clark: Well, we know that at least Luana has exceptional ability in terms of IQ.

A. Yes. That doesn't tell us anything, but --

Q. And we know that she's a teacher; true?

A. Yes.

Q. And so we know with this exceptional ability and the training that she has, that she could probably provide some teaching and training for LL, could she not?

A. Again, we really go back to the same issue. The trouble is to train someone like LL to all the areas you want to do it, sometimes will make LL suffer a great deal and Luana is still her mother. We just do not recommend things like that while it's theoretically possible, if anyone was my patient, and I've indicated to the KK's that we would like to continue working with them, we would just simply not allow that to happen. It's too much pressure, too much attention. She would never reach her full potential under those kinds of circumstances. The KK's are very nice people, but they're still her parents.

Q. Yet, I have heard of cases, and maybe you can tell me whether you have, of the parents actually getting more out of a child than any institution could.

A. I'm not talking about putting her in an institution. You put her in a State institution in Margayia, and she would turn into a vegetable. That's, also, why I don't want to put her in a State workshop, for the same reasons. They are lousy places, but there are good places, but the good places can get more out of the child than the parents can. They're objective about it. They're willing to give the children more freedom, and they're emotionally going to get as messed up by problems happening to child.

Q. What is a good place in Margayia, something I can go to and I can say, now, this is what is going to be provided her, so I can go there and I can re-evaluate and so the ladies and gentlemen who are going to be hearing this testimony later --

A. We're talking about --

Mr. Frost: Let him finish.

Mr. Clark: -- can say this is the facility and this is what they need. They're going --

Witness: If we were going to place her tomorrow, but you're talking about placing her ten years from now, and there's no way I can go in there. It would be very expensive to identify the ideal facility. We'd have to have people look around and investigate it. It might be the ideal facility ten years from now. It would be purely speculation.

A.   Which facility is purely speculation. It may not be in existence. You're just too far into the future to make meaningful statements.

Q.   Would it be reasonable to talk about the State facilities in terms of where they're going to be in ten years, and they may be so far advanced that they may be better than the private schools?

A.   The trend in the State of Margayia -- Margayia used to have a very good mental health system. The last 15 years, they've been dismantling it. There's no evidence that's going to change. The system has been going downhill in Margayia. The likelihood that there's going to be a change in tax policies in the United States are such that suddenly we're going to be doubling taxes. To invest money in these things, again, is such a low probability that I just cannot entertain that as a strong possibility.

Q.   It would be purely speculation to try and compare State facilities and private facilities since we don't even know if the private facility is going to be there?

Mr. Frost: He's talking about generally, and I think that's been asked and answered in some detail.

Witness: I think for the general comparison, there's no problem. If you talk specifically this group, this State facility, that would be pure speculation, but in general, the private facilities, the good private facilities are much, much better than the good State facilities and , again, if I had a child, I would not even consider placement in a State facility if it was my child. That's what I have to go by.

Q.   All right. I need to understand what you believe LL is going to get in a private institution that she would not get first at home.

Mr. Frost: Asked and answered in some detail.

Witness: Again, we go back to that. A good facility will allow her to mature. It will not infantilize her as much as the --

Mr. Clark: I'm not talking about benefits to her. I'm talking, specifically, day to day. What are they going to do that a State facility is not going to do?

A.   They're going to give her better care. They're going to give her better trained people to work with her. They're going to protect her better. The State facilities have much higher rate of rape. All those kinds of things they try to shove under the carpet. They're going to give her better people work with. Better environment in terms of the physical environment itself, the kind of room that she's living in, better opportunity for outside events and things like that. The State facilities have largely been warehouses, and while they give you the minimum food to eat and a place to eat, they're not very pleasant places to eat.

Q. That's pretty general, again.

Mr. Frost: Let me object to your characterization, but go ahead and answer the question. I think he was very specific.

Mr. Clark: As I understand the process, I get to ask the question, and you object, not in the middle of my question but after the question. I'd appreciate it if you would follow that format.

Mr. Frost: Go ahead, but your comment that you started off with, I thought he was very specific. You're commenting that he was general.

Mr. Clark: Okay, Doctor, what is it that is going to be provided in terms of better care in a private facility versus at home?

A. Better trained attendants, better medical attention by more qualified people.

Q. That's what I'm trying to get. What better care on a day-to-day basis?

Mr. Frost: Are you asking State facility or home?

Mr. Clark: We're at home.

Mr. Frost: You were at State at the last question.

Mr. Clark: Okay. I stayed at the state, I thought.

Witness: You have me totally confused. What are you asking?

Mr. Clark: What in terms of better care is going to be provided in the private facility than the State facility?

Mr. Frost: Asked and answered.

Witness: Better care is having attendants who are more qualified. They know how to handle the child's problem. They can react objectively to what she is doing. They can allow her more freedom, more flexibility, more attempts to grow to an individual to the extent that she can, protection from other individuals who will be in the same home and have poor judgment, as well as protection from people in the outside who like to prey on people who are retarded and have emotional problems.

That they will provide better facilities, that means nicer food, nicer place to live, a cleaner place to live, and all the other, air conditioning, other kinds of things that we look upon that make a better house and a better facility, better medical care, quicker medical care when you need it.

By more qualified people, psychological care at the same level and counseling by people who have degrees and who, again, in my opinion are better qualified to do the kinds of work that they're doing, and, again, more opportunities, more flexibility, to do a wider range of things, and also responsiveness. The private facilities are much more responsive to the complaints of parents and the complaints of the people who live there in it in terms of improving, where the State facilities are not bound by rules. They're bound by regulation. They're limited by money, and they do not respond as well to changes that are necessary not the individual client.

Mr. Clark: Is this a State run school?

A. What?

Q. This school -- medical school.

A. The University is paid for half by outside fees and half by -- our treatment clinic is entirely paid for by private fees, 100 percent. The State would not fund it at an adequate level of a service that I would be willing to run.

Q. If I understand it, it is your opinion that to take care of LL KK adequately, starting at 18, she will need $30,000 a year?

A. No. I said that would be the minimum.

Q. I want to now how much you think it's going to cost.

A. I said it's going to be somewhere in the range of $30,000 to $60,000 a year. It will depend exactly on the current dollar. It will depend on the economic situations and what's available when she becomes 18, and I cannot get anymore precise than that at 8 years in advance.

Q. Now, do you think that this $30,000 to $60,000 will take care of everything that she needs from age 18 on?

A. Per year in current dollars, it is my anticipation that that should be adequate.

Q. Is LL presently attending school?

A. Yes.

Q. What school, Eden?

A. It's in the Eden school district. I forget the exact name of the school.

Q. How much time is she spending there?

A. Ponderosa is the name of the school.

Q. How much time is she spending in the regular classroom, and how much is she spending in the special ed. program?

A. I think she's 100 percent special ed.

Q. Do you know what her grades are?

A. I don't think they give meaningful grades. I think they say you're doing okay. You're doing nice. She can't read or write, and she's supposed -- they just make up a grade, make her happy. She's not performing anywhere beyond the first grade or kindergarten level. Not even that, really.

Q. Have you got any of her school records other than this on IEP?

A. No.

Q. Have you visited her school?

A. No.

Q. Have you seen any of the grades which you don't think are very meaningful?

A. They don't give grades in special education.

Q. How do you know?

A. Because I've worked with thousands and thousands. That's exaggerating. I've worked with hundreds of school districts with special education grades. If they give the grades, all they mean is that the child is living up to their potential. I happen to know LL's special potential grade in special ed. I've done more than enough cases that that's true in Margayia, but in a lot of states -- LL can't even write her name at this point in time.

Q. They do, in fact, give grades?

A. I don't even know for sure that's the grades. They don't, in most schools. They give satisfactory and things like that. They do not give them A, B, C's, D's, and that school is an exception, but even if it is, it still doesn't mean anything. To get an A meaning that you almost learn this year - that at the age of 11 to write your name is not a meaningful concept. If she was in a regular classroom, she would be getting all failures period. She can't -- like I said, she can't even write her own name properly. She can't read at all. She cannot do work with numbers. There is no school skill that she can do properly. She can't draw. She can't copy adequately.

Q. All right. Now, if I understand it right, Doctor, it's your opinion that LL would have had a 30 point drop in IQ even though she had not developed meningitis.

Mr. Frost: Asked and answered. Go ahead, Doctor.

Witness: You asked about an estimate, and we said around a 20 to 30 point drop.

Mr. Clark: Even without the meningitis?

A. Even without the meningitis she would have had learning problems in school.

Q. Do you think she would have been outside of the sheltered workshop?

A. Oh, of course.

Q. She would have been able to get employment outside of

the home?

A. Oh, yes. She would have been able to be able to. She wouldn't have been able to take care of herself. She wouldn't have been able to have a job above minimum wage level. She wouldn't have been a college professor or anything like that, but she would have been able to take care of herself.

Q. Basically, an average student?

A. No. I said a learning disability, again, at this minimal level of functioning. Typically, those kids can function. They don't do well in school. They, again, are able to get minimal type jobs and take care of themselves.

Q. When you say 20 to 30 percent drop, where are you starting from?

A. From about 110 to 115, so she would have been somewhere around 85.

Q. Is that above the level of the mental retarded range?

A. Yes. That starts at 70. No. Premature birth does not cause one to become mentally retarded. It can lower your IQ. It can result in learning disabilities and can result, again, in you being much more susceptible to other brain injuries later in life.

Q. What's the average IQ?

A. 100.

Q. Isn't there a range that is normally used?

a. That depends on who you talk to, but normally people say 90 to 110 is average. Some people will just say 85 to 100 is low average, and 100 to 115 is superior or high average. Different groups have classified things differently.

Q. How do you classify it? That's really what I'm asking.

A. I think from 90 to 110 is average -- is my own personal bias.

Q. I assume when you say 90 to 110 is average, I'm just -- I would probably fall in the average -- hopefully, presumably, in the average range, 90 to 110 as 90 percent of the population would?

A. Not unless you went to the -- the average lawyer has 118, 120 comparable to LL's parents.

Q. Let's just talk about the population.

A. From 90 to 110 is about 50 to 55 percent of the population.

Q. Doctor, have I covered all the opinions that you have in this case?

A.   As far as I can tell.

Mr. Clark: I don't have any other questions.

Mr. Frost: No questions.

(The deposition concluded at 11:45 p.m.)

EXAMPLE OF TEST RESEARCH INFORMATION

NECESSARY FOR FORENSIC TESTIMONY

Charles J. Golden

Department of Psychiatry
University of Nebraska Medical Center
Omaha, Nebraska

One of the greatest weaknesses of psychologists testifying is their own lack of knowledge about the tests they are using. For many of the tests still used today, there is not even a single accepted manual, let alone a relatively up to date summary of the literature on a test. The following is the summary of the LNNB which we use for such work (updating it as necessary). This represents the basic type of information which should be available on any test used in court.

If this information is absent or the "expert" is not aware of this information, a lawyer can effectively use interogation in these areas to discredit a witness. This is especially true if the lawyer can manage to appear more knowledgeable about the testing than the expert does. In other instances the expert must rely on his claim of expertise in the absence of better answers, an appropach which can make one look pompous at best and ignorant at worst. On the other hand, intelligent answers to psychometric questions will quickly lead lawyers to back off from such an approach. This can have the beneficial effect of them not asking some questions which may be harder to answer. What follows was the basis for part of the LNNB manual.

THE LNNB

The <u>Luria-Nebraska</u> <u>Neuropsychological</u> <u>Battery</u> (LNNB) is a multidimensional battery designed to assess a broad range of neuropsychological functions. Although it can be used as a neurological screening instrument, its primary purpose is to diagnose general and specific cognitive deficits, including lateralization and localization of focal brain impairments, and to aid in the planning and evaluation of rehabilitation programs. Based on the theories and diagnostic procedures of the Russian neuropsychologist A.R. Luria, the LNNB offers the benefits of standardized administration and scoring and makes Luria's highly respected clinical procedures more widely available to practitioners in clinical neuropsychology. The standardized version attempts to retain the qualitative aspects of Luria's clinical technique by varying specific aspects of tasks thought to be related to particular underlying neurological functions, by allowing considerable flexibility in the administration of items and by using both quantitative and qualitative scoring procedures.

GENERAL DESCRIPTION

The LNNB is a 269-item (Form I) or a 279-item (Form II), individually administered battery designed to measure various types of cognitive deficits in adults and adolescents, as an aid to neuropsychodiagnosis. The battery actually consists of over 700 discrete tasks, many of which are considered simultaneously in the scoring of an individual item. For each item, the client is assigned a score of 0 (normal), 1 (weak evidence of brain disorder), or 2 (strong evidence of brain disorder). These individual scores are then summed in various combinations and finally converted to overall T-scores for each scale.

The LNNB yields both quantitative and qualitative scores, both of which are important in assessing neuropsychological functioning. The quantitative scales are grouped into four major areas. The <u>clinical</u> scales comprise the original scales of the battery and assess a variety of sensorimotor, perceptual and cognitive abilities. The <u>summary</u> scales provide summary information regarding the discrimination between brain-injured and normal individuals, the severity of observed impairment, and lateralization. The <u>localization</u> scales are an empirically derived set of scales designed to aid in generating hypotheses about the nature of any focal deficits. The <u>factor</u> scales, developed using factor analysis, are useful in assessing specific neuropsychological functions, although considerable care must be used in their interpretation. A method for scoring each response qualitatively is also available. Overall, clinical interpretation of the LNNB is based on both the quantitative and qualitative scores, the pattern of the individual item responses, configural analysis, comparison of the obtained scores with the scale patterns for individuals with known localized brain dysfunction, and integration of the test data with information from other sources, including clinical observations and the results of other neurological tests.

There are two forms of the LNNB. Form I, consisting of 269 items, has been in general clinical use since 1980. Form II, which is largely a parallel form, consists of 279 items and was introduced in 1984. The two forms are not entirely independent. Of the 279 items on Form II, 84 (approximately 30%) are identical to items on Form I. The scales are similar for both forms except that one additional scale, C12 (Intermediate Memory) is added to Form II. This scale is intended to measure longer delays of recall than covered in the original memory scale, C10. A new, provisional scale, Delayed Memory, is also available for Form I, although this scale differs in some important respects from scale C12 for Form II. Another difference between Forms I and II is the set of stimulus cards used. Form II uses a separate set of stimulus cards which are more convenient to use since they are numbered to correspond to the item numbers, are bound into a booklet and use larger pictures. The other major difference between the two forms is

that <u>Form</u> <u>I</u> <u>can</u> <u>be</u> <u>either</u> <u>hand</u> <u>or</u> <u>computer</u> scored, whereas, <u>Form</u>
<u>II</u> <u>is</u> <u>computer</u> <u>scored</u> <u>only</u>.

The LNNB is a powerful tool to use in assessing cognitive
strengths and weaknesses. Unlike the other major
neuropsychological test batteries, the LNNB is easily
transportable and relatively inexpensive since it does not use
any elaborate hardware or medical procedures. It is easy to
administer and score, and can be used by trained technicians or
paraprofessionals under the supervision of a qualified
professional.

Although administration times vary for individual clients,
the total time required to administer the complete battery
averages about 2 1/2 hours for a typical brain-damaged client,
though the battery may be given in two or more sessions on
successive days. The range of time for test administration is
normally between 1 1/2 and 4 to 6 hours. This compares
favorably to other comprehensive batteries which can take up to
2 days to administer. Thus, the LNNB should prove useful in a
variety of settings where a detailed yet cost-efficient method
of assessing current neuropsychological functioning is required.

PURPOSES AND USES

The LNNB has been used for a variety of assessment
purposes. Specific uses include: (a) identifying brain damage
in individuals who have symptoms of uncertain etiology (e.g.,
differential diagnosis with functional psychiatric disorders);
(b) assessing the extent and nature of deficits in clients with
known lesions for forensic purposes and to plan appropriate
interventions; (c) evaluating the effects of specific
interventions or rehabilitation strategies on neuropsychological
functioning; (d) examining the effects of various types of brain
damage across different populations; and (e) testing theoretical
propositions about brain-behavior relationships to confirm,
expand or modify current models of brain function.

The LNNB has proven useful in a variety of settings dealing
with clinical neuropsychology. Typical settings which make use
of this kind of battery include inpatient and outpatient
psychiatric facilities, rehabilitation centers, hospitals,
health maintenance organizations and private practices in
neurology and neuropsychology. Potential users include advanced
professionals with specialized training in neuropsychology and
psychometricians under the supervision of a qualified
professional.

PRINCIPLES OF USE

<u>Respondent</u> <u>Population</u>

Designed for persons at least 15 years of age, the adult
version of the LNNB has also been used successfully with younger
adolescents, ages 13 and 14. A parallel children's version of
the battery for use with 8- to 12-year-olds is currently being
developed.

The use of flexible administration and scoring procedures
enables skilled users to obtain meaningful results even with

individuals who are considered "untestable" with other instruments. This feature is not automatic, however. The special needs of certain clients with sensory deficits, receptive or expressive speech disorders, reading disabilities, or impoverished educational backgrounds require particular sensitivity and skill on the part of the examiner to assess neuropsychological functioning independent of these factors. Although the LNNB contains some items which may be more culturally specific (e.g., reading "streptomycin-Massachusetts Episcopal"), many of the items do not require a verbal response and, thus, are less affected by cultural differences.

RELIABILITY

The reliability of the LNNB has been examined from a number of perspectives including interrater agreement, split-half reliability, internal consistency and test-retest reliability.

Interrater Reliability

An initial study (Golden, Hammeke, & Purisch, 1978) examined the interrater reliability of the LNNB. The battery was administered to five separate clients who were simultaneously scored by five independent pairs of examiners. The resulting 1,345 comparisons were then examined for level of agreement. Over 95% of the comparisons were identical, indicating a high level of interrater agreement.

In a follow-up study, Bach, Harowski, Kirby, Peterson, and Schulein (1981) examined interrater agreement among five raters under two conditions: (a) a normal range of responses, and (b) responses which were deliberately vague and difficult to score. To control for the level of agreement due to chance, coefficient kappa (Cohen, 1960) was used. This provides a lower-bound estimate interrater reliability. The kappa coefficients averaged over .80 which is well within acceptable limits for comparable tests. Predictably, lower levels of reliability were obtained for the condition in which the answers were intentionally vague.

Split-Half Reliability

Golden, Fross, and Graber (1981) examined the split-half reliability of the LNNB using odd-even comparisons. The sample consisted of 74 normal subjects, 83 psychiatric patients and 181 neurological patients (N=338). The resulting reliabilities ranged from .89 on scale C10 to .95 on scale C8. The same study also examined the item-scale correlations across the test. Examination of the correlations showed that an item was most highly correlated with the scale it was assigned to in 250 of the 269 items on the battery. The study also established that most items correlated significantly with more than one scale, emphasizing the fact that the items are indeed rather heterogeneous and assess overlapping areas.

Golden and Berg (1980a, 1980b, 1980c, 1980d, 1981a, 1981b, 1981c, 1982a, 1982b, 1983a, 1983b, 1983c) investigated relationships between each item and every other item on the LNNB using the results of the Golden, Fross, and Graber study. Significant correlations (p<.001) were found between nearly all items studied and items from other scales. As noted by the authors, the intercorrelations shed light on the abilities which are required to perform a given task. More importantly, the results are consistent with a functional systems theory of brain organization and predictions made from Luria's theory on these relationships.

Internal Consistency

Several recent studies have assessed internal consistency rather than split-half reliability. Internal consistency differs from split-half reliability in that it represents the average split-half reliability and, thus, tends to be more stable than any single reliability estimates based on split-half comparisons. Mikula (1981) obtained internal consistency estimates (alpha) ranging from .82 (on C2) to .94 (on Cl) for the original 14 clinical/summary scales on a sample of 146 brain-damaged patients and 74 medical controls. Moses, Johnson, and Lewis (1983c) calculated internal consistency for each of the major clinical scales. Based on a mixed sample of 285 patients (88 alcoholic, 101 schizophrenic or schizoaffective, and 89 brain damaged), they found average alpha coefficients in the mid-.80s (range of .78 to .88).

In a reanalysis of the previous study, Moses, Johnson, and Lewis (1983a, 1983b) reported internal consistency reliability for three different groups: mixed brain-damaged, alcoholic and psychotic (schizophrenic or schizoaffective) subjects. Alpha coefficients for the 14 original scales ranged from .80 to .92 for the brain-damaged group, from .48 to .82 for the alcoholic group and from .57 to .85 for the psychotic group. For the localization scales, the alpha reliabilities ranged from .77 to 0.89 for the brain-damaged group, from .49 to .81 for the alcoholic group and from .53 to .80 for the psychotic group. For the factor scales, the alpha coefficients ranged from .10 to 0.90 for the brain-damaged group, from -.50 to .88 for the alcoholic group, and from .005 to .88 for the psychotic group. Two of the factor scales (R5--Word Comprehension and R6--Logical Grammatical Relationships) were subsequently dropped due to low reliability.

Adequacy of the obtained alphas for the summary and localization scales was determined by whether they were at or above the level found in the previous study (Moses, Johnson, & Lewis, 1983c) (i.e., r = .80). The factor scale alphas were examined to determine if they were within the range which would suggest possible value for further research or clinical use (defined as .59 to .69 and >.70, respectively). Moses, Johnson, and Lewis concluded that the alphas were sufficiently high to justify the clinical use of the original 14 clinical/summary and eight localization scales with brain-damaged subjects.

More recently, Sawicki, Maruish, and Golden (1983) examined the internal consistency of the original 14 scales in a mixed sample of normal and brain-injured patients (n=559), as well as separate brain-impaired (n=451), schizophrenic (n=414), mixed psychiatric patient (n=128) and normative (n=108) samples. The correlations are generally quite high, with the lowest reliabilities occurring in the normal sample, probably due to the range restriction within this subgroup.

Test-Retest Reliability

An initial study of test-retest reliability was conducted by Golden, Berg, and Graber (1982). For this study, the investigators chose 27 patients exhibiting chronic, relatively stable head injuries whose initial test performances fell into the middle range of the normative distribution for the LNNB. The patients included neurological and psychiatric cases with testing done after resolution of any acute psychiatric symptoms. Intervals between test and retest averaged 167 days (SD=134 days) with a range from 10 to 469 days.

The lowest test-retest reliabilities, expressed as Pearson correlation coefficients, were found on C3(.78) and S3(.77). Other reliabilities ranged from .84 for C10 to a high of .96 for C9. Parceling out the variance contributed by the test-retest interval yielded little change in the resulting correlations, suggesting that the variable range of this interval was of little importance in chronic, static cases.

A further study of test-retest reliability was reported by Plaisted and Golden (1982). Test-retest reliability was calculated for the 14 original scales, the localization scales and the factor scales. The data were based on a sample of 30 patients with an average test-retest interval of 8.1 months (SD=6 months). All patients had emotional difficulties but did not show evidence of neurological problems. Test-retest reliabilities for the 14 original scales ranged from .83 to 96, with a mean of .89. The factor scale test-retest reliability coefficients ranged more widely (from .01 to .96) with an overall mean of .81 across the 30 scales. All the factor scales except two showed acceptable levels of correlation significant at the .001 level. These exceptions were R5 (Word Comprehension) and R6 (Logical Grammatical Relationships). When these two scales were deleted from the factor scales, the mean test-retest reliability increased slightly to 82.

STANDARD ERROR OF MEASUREMENT

The standard errors of measurement (SEMs) for the clinical summary, localization, and factor scales are summarized in the test manual. For example, the SEM for S3 is 3.00 T-score units, computed from the overall reliability estimate of .91 and a standard deviation of 10 (N=559). Thus, across a very large number of observations on the same individual, two-thirds of the scores for S3 should fall within 3 T-score units above or below the theoretical true score. The use of the standard error of measurement might be demonstrated in an evaluation of the size of pretreatment versus posttreatment changes in scaled scores for a patient following the start of a rehabilitation program. Suppose a patient had a T-score of 74 on S2 prior to treatment and 62 after 6 weeks. Because this difference of 12 T-score units is larger than the SEM for this particular scale, it is reasonably certain that a change in the patient's true score is taking place, rather than a random fluctuation in scores attributable to error variance. (Of course the key issue of whether or not this change is causally related to the rehabilitation program cannot be addressed due to the absence of an appropriate control condition).

DETERMINING STRENGTHS AND WEAKNESSES

Several authors have noted the potential usefulness of an "ipsative" approach for determining relative strengths and weaknesses within individual cases (Cattell, 1950; Sattler, 1982). The analytic strategy involves establishing a profile of statistically reliable deviations in an individual's score on a particular scale, based on that individual's mean score across all the scales for a particular group. Since this procedure involves multiple comparisons, all of which are interdependent, it is important to protect against overinterpretation of positive and negative deviations. One common procedure involves the use of Bonferroni's t statistic (Davis, 1959). In practice, this approach with the LNNB involves a three-step procedure: (a) calculate the mean T-score for a particular group of scales (e.g., clinical and summary, localization, or factor scales); (b) compute positive and negative deviations of the observed individual scale scores from this overall mean, and (c) look up the significance of these positive and negative deviations in separate ipsative tables for each group of scales. The formula for Bonferroni's t insures that the critical value for each scale varies as a function of the reliability for that scale, the sample size on which the original reliability estimate was based, and the total number of scales being compared simultaneously.

For the LNNB, three different sets of ipsative tables are available. Noting the potential usefulness of an ipsative approach to the LNNB, Reynolds (1982) used the split-half reliabilities reported by Golden, Fross, and Graber (1981) to calculate critical values for the 11 basic clinical scales at three different confidence levels. Moses (1983b) subsequently used the internal consistency estimates to compute ipsative tables for the 14 original clinical/summary scales and the eight localization scales. Since the split-half reliability estimates used by Reynolds in his computations are consistently higher than internal consistency estimates, Moses' tables of critical values are generally more conservative than those reported by Reynolds. Finally, an updated set of ipsative values based on internal consistency estimates for the mixed sample of brain-damaged and normal subjects (N=559) reported by Sawicki (1983) are reported in the test manual.

VALIDITY

Estimates of criterion-related, concurrent and construct validity of the LNNB have been obtained from a number of empirical studies. These studies have used a variety of approaches such as classification of brain-damaged versus other criterion groups, comparison of profile patterns for individuals with localized brain impairments and across different diagnostic groups, and comparison of the LNNB to other tests designed to measure similar constructs.

Classification of Brain-Damaged versus Other Criterion Groups

An initial study (Golden, Hammeke, & Purisch, 1978) examined the diagnostic efficiency of the test items in discriminating between brain-damaged and normal subjects. The diagnoses of the brain-injured patients in this study, as well as other studies discussed in this section, were made by the attending physician, usually a neurologist or neurosurgeon. The diagnoses were supported by such medical and laboratory data as CT scans, EEGs, angiograms, pneumoencephalograms, skull X-rays, neurological history, and/or surgery, according to the patient's condition. CT scans were the most frequently used technique, with CT scan data available for approximately 60% of the patients. Histories of the patients were also reviewed to ensure that there was no evidence of current or previous psychiatric disorder and to ensure that the history was compatible with the patient's neurological diagnosis.

The impaired group in the original study was comprised of 50 patients, 27 males and 23 females, and represented a range of neurological disorders. The group contained 15 patients with left hemisphere injury, 15 patients with right hemisphere injury and 20 patients with diffuse brain injury. The average age of the neurological patients was 44.3 years, with a standard deviation of 18.8 years. Their overall level of education averaged 10.3 years, with a standard deviation of 2.8.

The control subjects consisted of 50 patients, 26 females and 24 males, who were in the hospital for a variety of medical problems, including back injuries, infectious diseases and chronic pain. While most of these patients were referred from neurological and orthopedic wards, none had medical histories, symptoms or laboratory data suggestive of cerebral dysfunction in the opinion of the attending physician. The average age of the control patients was 42.0 years, with a standard deviation of 14.8 years. They averaged 12.2 years of education, with a standard deviation of 2.9 years.

There were no significant differences between control and neurological patients for age and sex, although the two groups did differ significantly in regard to education, $t(98)=3.51, p<.01$. Because of this difference, an analysis of covariance was used to examine the residual differences between the groups controlling for the effects of educational level. Of the 269 items in Form I, 252 discriminated significantly between the neurologically impaired and nonimpaired criterion groups at the .05 level or better.

Hammeke, Golden, and Purisch (1978) reported the first study evaluating the ability of the original 14 scales to differentiate brain-damaged from normal controls. This report stemmed from the first author's dissertation, which used the same neurological and control groups as described by Golden, Hammeke, and Purisch (1978). The study found significant differences ($p<.001$) in the performances of the neurological and control groups on all 14 original scales. To further evaluate the discriminative power of the scales, cutoff scores that maximized the percentage of total classification were chosen for each scale. Classification accuracies ("hit rates") for the individual scales ranged from 74% for C6 to 96% for C10 in the control group, and from 58% for C2 to 86% for C6 in the brain-injured group. Combined hit rates for both groups ranged from a low of 74% accuracy on C2 to a high of 86% on S1. A discriminant analysis using the 14 original scales was able to correctly classify all 50 of the control patients and 43 of the 50 brain-injured patients, for an overall hit rate of 93%.

To control for the differences in educational level, a different sample of neurological patients, matched for diagnosis and severity with the original sample, was created. The majority of the patients in this new sample were patients from the original sample. Average level of education in the new sample was 11.8 years (SD = 2.8), which was not significantly different from the control group, t(90) = .75, p<.05. The same analyses as in the dissertation study were then performed and were found to yield similar results with regard to significance and hit rates. Changes in mean scores did occur in the new sample, although no scale deviated more than 2%. Unfortunately, because of a mistake by the authors, the published article (Hammeke, Golden, & Purisch, 1978) contained the original means rather than the revised means.

In order to cross-validate the results of the initial studies, Moses and Golden (1979) compared an additional sample of 50 neurological and 50 control patients, using Form I of the LNNB. These neurological patients had confirmed neurological diagnoses made by a qualified physician, usually a neurologist or neurosurgeon employing such neurodiagnostic procedures as the CT scan, EEG, pneumoencephalogram, angiogram and skull X-rays as necessary to establish a definitive diagnosis. Of the neurological patients, there were 8 with cerebral trauma, 2 with neoplasms, 2 with infectious diseases, 29 with cerebral vascular disorders, 5 with degenerative diseases, 2 with epilepsy and 2 with metabolic or toxic disorders. The control patients were generally hospitalized on a neurological, orthopedic or internal medicine ward with disorders that did not affect brain functions. Thus, the sample included some patients with neurological disorders not involving the brain, such as spinal cord injuries.

The average age for the combined samples was 43.8 years, with an average level of education of 11.3 years. The final samples included 50 brain-injured subjects (44 males and 6 females) and 50 controls (41 males and 9 females). There were no statistically significant differences between the groups in age, education or sex distribution. The average chronicity of the brain-injured group was 7.8 months, with a standard deviation of 3 months.

The results of the study were almost identical to the results reported previously by Hammeke, Golden, and Purisch (1978). Using the cutoff scores determined by Hammeke and his associates, Moses and Golden found hit rates ranging from 62 to 80% for the brain-injured groups and from 72 to 98% for the control group. Overall hit rates for the original 14 scales did not differ by more than 6% from the results in the original study. In the case of three scales, results from the cross-validation study were superior to the results of the initial study. A discriminant analysis using all 14 scales achieved a hit rate of 96% in this sample, compared to the 93% for the original sample. A second comparison was performed by using the discriminant functions derived from the study of Hammeke et al. (1978). This discriminant function analysis yielded a hit rate of 93%, identical to that found in the Hammeke et al. study. These results clearly support the conclusions of the original study that the LNNB is an effective clinical device for making practical discriminations between organic and normal patients.

Several additional studies have generally supported these earlier results. In a dissertation, Duffala (1978/1979) compared a group of 20 head trauma patients to a younger control group, finding a hit rate exceeding 90%. This study could be criticized for a lack of age and education controls; however, even when age and education corrections (described later) are applied, the differences between the groups are still highly significant.

Golden, Purisch, and Hammeke (1980) noted the necessity of establishing formal decision rules as a further aid to discriminating between brain-damaged and non-brain-damaged individuals. In doing so, they cited the importance of a study by Marvel, Golden, Hammeke, Purisch, and Osmon (1979) which documented the extent to which age and education affect performance on the LNNB. Golden, Moses, Graber, and Berg (1981) investigated the use of objective rules for the discrimination of brain-damaged versus normal subjects. The intent was to develop an index similar to the impairment index used with the Halstead-Reitan. The authors, in an initial population of 60 normals, developed a formula for predicting LNNB scores from age and education. This prediction was then used to set a cutoff point (called the "critical level") for that individual's scores, based on the clinical observation that LNNB scores typically vary up to about 10 points above the client's age and education expected average score. Then, the number of individual scores above this cutoff point was determined. This number became the basis of classifying subjects in a second part of the study. The second part compared accuracy in 60 normal and 60 brain-injured subjects. Overall, a hit rate of 87% was obtained, just slightly below the discriminant analysis results of the earlier studies. The number of scales above the critical level was used as a criterion score in the next study reported.

Malloy and Webster (1981) replicated the initial validation studies but used neurological and control subjects with initially equivocal neurological results. The pseudoneurological group consisted of 12 subjects who presented with neurological complaints but, based on clinical and laboratory investigations, were later classified as normal; the 12 subjects in the borderline groups had normal neurological data except for the presence of abnormal EEG; and the brain-damaged group consisted of 12 additional subjects with confirmed neurological diagnoses. Using the classification rules developed by Golden, Moses, Graber, and Berg (1981), 80% of the subjects were correctly classified into the three diagnostic groups. Thus, even when confronted with the difficult task of discriminating among more ambiguous criterion groups, the LNNB performed reasonably well.

In investigating the LNNB's ability to discriminate brain damage in an elderly group, Spitzform (1982) administered the battery to 14 elderly subjects (mean age = 71.4 years). Two of these subjects had medical histories which suggested that neuropsychological dysfunction was likely. Using the objective rules for interpretation, only one of the subjects (one of the likely impaired) was misclassified, yielding a hit rate of 93%.

Noting the paucity of research designed to investigate the LNNB's ability to assess neuropsychological functioning in an elderly population, MacInnes, Gillen, Golden, Graber, Cole, Uhl, and Greenhouse (1983) compared the results of a "healthy" geriatric sample (with a mean age of 72 years) and a group of brain-damaged elderly adults (with a mean age of 68 years). Significant differences (p<.001) were found between the two groups in a multivariate analysis of covariance on 11 clinical scales, using age, sex and education as covariates. The classification rules resulted in a hit rate of 92% for the healthy group, 86% for the brain-damaged group and 88% for the total sample.

Sawicki and Golden (1984a) sought to validate two decision rules (three or more scales above the critical level and range of T-scores, both excluding the S2 and S3 scales, indicating impairment) for classification of brain function with a large, heterogeneous sample of 1,037 normal, psychiatric and brain-damaged subjects. Also, they investigated the relationship of each of these rules to demographic and treatment variables, and the amount of variance which these two classification variables accounted for in the classification of brain function, as opposed to that accounted for by the 14 original scales.

Use of the number of scales above the critical level accurately classified 73% of the normals and 80% of the brain impaired, for a total hit rate of 77%. Approximately 70% of the schizophrenic patients were classified as being impaired (when the rules for a nonschizophrenic population were used) but the pattern of scales above the critical level for this group was significantly different from that of the brain-impaired group (p<.001). A significant relationship between the number of scales above the critical level and group membership was established, and it was estimated that there was approximately 12% shared variance between this method of classification and group membership. Furthermore, the number of scales above the critical level was significantly related to peripheral auditory and motor impairment in the normal group; to marital status in the brain-impaired group; to peripheral motor impairment in the schizophrenic group; and to occupation, use of neuroleptic or anticonvulsive medications and race in both the brain-impaired and schizophrenic groups.

Although significant correlations were found between the number of scales above the critical level and age of onset of disorder, critical level, education, length of hospitalization and number of previous hospitalizations, no more than 3% of variance in the number of scales above the critical level could be explained by any of these variables. When the effects of these variables were statistically controlled, the mean number of scales above the critical level for each group changed little and significant between-group differences were still noted. When analyzed via multiple regression, a strong relationship between the scales above the critical level and overall LNNB performance was found (R=.88). The S1, C11, C2, C8 and C10 scales contributed to the majority of the shared variance between these two indices of cognitive functioning.

A significant relationship between range of T-scores and diagnostic category was also noted, with the two variables having 7% common variance. With this method, a 77% hit rate for the normals and a 74% hit rate for the brain-impaired group were achieved. Somewhat different patterns were observed for the brain-impaired and schizophrenic groups. T-score range was found to be significantly related to handedness in the normal group, to race in the brain-impaired group, to occupation and peripheral visual impairment in the schizophrenic group and to the presence of neuroleptic medication in both the brain-impaired and schizophrenic groups.

The range of scores was also significantly related to age, age of onset of disorder, critical level, education and length of hospitalization. However, taken individually, only 11% or less of the variance in range was attributable to any of these variables. Group differences were again noted when variables found to be significant were partialled out, with the normals having a significantly smaller range of scores than either of the other groups. Little change in the mean range for each group occurred as a result of partialling these variables. A multiple R of .76 was found between the range and overall LNNB performance, with the C9 and S1 scales contributing to most of the common variance.

When the number of elevated scales, the range of scores, and all LNNB original scales were submitted to stepwise multiple regression with the original diagnostic classification as the dependent variable, the number of scales above the critical level was able to predict the majority of the shared variance between the LNNB and the diagnostic criterion. A significant amount of independent variance was also contributed by both the range of scores and C6 (Expressive Speech). From the overall results, the authors concluded that both methods of classification serve as good global measures of impairment. However, in light of the potential for misclassification and the effect of several demographic and treatment variables on these measures, caution in applying these decision rules with individual cases is advised.

In response to unsubstantiated criticisms regarding the LNNB's ability to add much to determining whether cognitive impairment exists in patients with obvious sensorimotor deficits, Moses (1984f) examined the characteristics of patients with and without sensorimotor deficits. To do so, 165 brain-damaged patients (who were diagnosed on the basis of a neurological examination) were classified as either cognitively impaired or unimpaired on the basis of their performance on the LNNB. The rule of two scales above the critical level was used as the basis of this classification. Each member of the two groups was then further classified according to the presence or absence of an obvious sensorimotor (auditory, visual, or motor) deficit. This resulted in four groups: cognitively normal/sensorimotor impaired (Group 1), cognitively impaired/sensorimotor impaired (Group 2), cognitively normal/sensorimotor normal (Group 3), and cognitively impaired/sensorimotor normal (Group 4). The groups did not differ significantly from each other on any of the demographic variables investigated.

Multivariate analysis of variance for the four groups on the 14 LNNB scales revealed significant differences among the groups ($p < .001$), as did separate univariate analysis for each scale across the four groups. On all scales, both cognitively impaired groups performed worse than the cognitively impaired groups performed worse than the cognitively unimpaired groups.

Consistently, Group 2 performed worse than Group 4, Group 4 performed worse than Group 1, and Group 1 performed worse than Group 3. As indicated by Moses, the results lend support for "the inference that the LNNB is measuring cognitive and sensorimotor variables in a sensitive, consistent manner". Also of interest is the fact that the use of the objective classification rules resulted in the correct classification of 83% of the subjects (79% when those with sensorimotor deficits were eliminated and the data reanalyzed). When the results of only those who had CT scans available to confirm the diagnosis were analyzed using these same two procedures, the hit rates remained essentially unchanged.

A subsequent study by Moses (1984a) investigated the extent to which different types of sensorimotor difficulties are associated with cognitive impairments. To address this issue, 229 brain-damaged patients were classified into one of five groups: no sensorimotor impairment, auditory impairment, visual impairment, motor impairment, and mixed sensorimotor (auditory-visual, auditory-motor, visual-motor, or auditory-visual-motor). These five groups differed significantly among each other on their overall performance, based on a multivariate analysis of variance for all 14 original LNNB scales. On all but two of the scales, the worst performance was rendered by the motor-impaired groups, with the mixed sensorimotor group performing the worst on the C4 and S1 scales.

One-way analyses of variance of the five groups on each of the 14 scales indicated significant differences among the groups on only six scales (C1, C3, C5, S1, S2 and S3), all $p < .05$. Examination of each group on these six scales revealed the motor-impaired group to be significantly more impaired than the nonimpaired group on all six of these scales and significantly more impaired than the auditory and visual impairment groups on C1, S2 and S3. In addition, the mixed sensorimotor groups were also significantly more impaired that the nonimpaired group on the C1, S1 and S2 scales. The author concluded that an assumption of cognitive impairment cannot be made when sensorimotor deficits are present.

Classification Based on Scale Elevations

The accuracy of each scale was computed for cutoff scores of 60T and 70T. In using 60T as a cutoff, subjects with scores of higher than 60T were labeled as brain damaged, while subjects with scores lower than 60T were classified as normal. The data reflected evaluation of three groups, including 103 normal controls, 146 neurological patients and a heterogeneous group of 83 psychiatric patients.

The normal control group was comprised of patients who were hospitalized but had no evidence of brain injury. The majority of this group included patients with neurological disorders such as injury to the back, usually to the cervical or lumbar spine. This group also included headache patients with no known cerebral etiology (usually diagnosed as tension headaches). A small percentage of this group were patients from internal medicine wards who were hospitalized for a variety of medical ailments. The psychiatric group was comprised of 80% chronic schizophrenic patients and 29% patients with more acute psychotic disorders, as well as patients with personality disorders or neurotic disturbances. The neurological group was comprised of patients with confirmed brain injury. The patients, as a whole, did not represent acute cases of brain injury but rather more chronic cases. Patients in this group were tested an average of 8 months after the onset of their injury. The most frequent diagnoses were cerebral vascular accidents, head trauma and neoplastic disorders.

All patients included in the neurological sample were capable of cooperating with the testing procedure and understanding what was being requested of them. Patients with severe impairment in speech or motor skills that prohibited them from completing the test were not included in the sample. Patients with severe cases of brain injury that made it impossible for them to comprehend the instructions of the test were also not included in the sample, nor were neurological patients who were reluctant to cooperate with the testing procedures.

All patients in this sample were volunteers and were allowed to withdraw from testing at any time during its administration. Patients who did not complete all the testing procedures were not included in the present samples. Patients for whom a definitive diagnosis could not be established were also excluded from the sample. The effect of the selection procedures was to eliminate more severe cases of brain injury, making the sample more representative of patients actually seen for neuropsychological evaluations. As a result, hit rates have not been inflated by using patients who were clearly incapable of completing common psychological tests.

A cutoff score of 60T produces nearly optimal results for comparing the brain-damaged and the normal control groups. In all cases, the hit rate for the control group is 80% or better except for C2. In the neurological group, the hit rates are above 70% except for C3, C8, S2 and S3. Two scales, C5 and S1, demonstrated over 80% accuracy in both groups, using the cutoff of 60T. Predictably, the psychiatric group was more difficult to classify than the normal control group. Only half the scales (C7, S2, S3, C8, C4 and C3) discriminated accurately between the psychiatric and neurological patients using a cutoff of 60T.

When using a cutoff of 70T, however, the hit rates for the psychiatric group increased considerably. Less than 20% of the psychiatric patients scored above the cutoff of 70T on most of the scales: C3, C4, C8, C7, C9, S1, S2 and S3. Using a cutoff of 7-T does lower the correct classification rate in the neurological group considerably as can be seen by comparing the hit rates in the 60 and 70T columns. Note that very few control subjects scored higher than 70T on any of the scales. In general, scores above 70-T are highly indicative of brain injury. Individual cases having three or more scores above 70T were found to have a diagnosis of brain injury about 95% of the time.

Classification of Focal Brain Impairments

Validity research has also focused on studies involving patients with localized or lateralized disorders. Osmon, Golden, Purisch, Hammeke, and Blume (1979) examined the ability of the battery to discriminate among lateralized and diffusely injured patients. The study evaluated 20 patients with left hemisphere damage, 20 patients with right hemisphere damage and 20 patients with diffuse damage. The three groups were matched for age and education. Patients were assigned to each group by definitive neurological evidence that varied according to the nature of the dysfunction in each patient. The tests used to confirm localization of disorders included CT scan, surgery, EEG, angiogram, pneumoencephalogram and clinical neurological examination. These groups exhibited equally chronic histories, although they were not equivalent in terms of etiology. As might be expected, the groups with more localized lesions tended to have higher incidences of cerebral vascular accidents, neoplasms and localized head traumas. The diffuse group had more patients with degenerative diseases, diffuse head trauma and metabolic and toxic disorders.

A discriminant analysis using the original 14 scales of the LNNB correctly classified 59 to 60 patients. By simply subtracting the S2 $\underline{T}$-score from the S3 score, the authors achieved a hit rate of 75% accuracy in lateralization. In general, patients with focal left hemisphere injury performed the poorest on the test measures, while the right hemisphere group achieved the best scores. On most measures, the performance of the diffuse group fell between the two extremes.

McKay and Golden (1979b) subsequently developed a set of empirically derived lateralization scales using items which discriminated each hemisphere group from the other hemisphere group and from normals, schizophrenics and diffusely impaired individuals. $\underline{T}$-scores of 60 and 70 for the S2 and S3 scales, respectively, adequately differentiated between each hemisphere group and the normals but not between each hemisphere group and the other impaired group. A difference score (the right score minus the left score), with a positive score indicating right-side damage and a negative score indicating left-side damage, accurately classified 100% of the lateralized patients. On cross-validation, the difference-score procedure correctly classified 88% of a group of 41 left hemisphere patients and 87% of a group of 30 right hemisphere patients. The overall hit rate was 83%.

Lewis et al. (1979) examined the ability of the battery to localize brain injury to the frontal regions, sensorimotor areas, temporal lobe and occipital-parietal lobes in each hemisphere. The sample for this study consisted of 24 patients with focal right-hemisphere brain damage and 36 patients with focal left-hemisphere brain damage. In the left hemisphere group, 9 patients were found with corresponding lesions for each of the four brain areas. In the right hemisphere group, 6 patients were identified for each of the four brain areas. For a description of the group assignment methods and nature of the focal lesions in each of the eight groups created, the reader is referred to the published article.

The 60 patients for this study were selected from over 190 neurologically impaired patients who were given the LNNB. Patients for whom exact localization information was not available were immediately excluded from this study. In all selected cases, confirmation of localization was made either by surgery, angiogram, CT scan or a combination of these procedures. All patients received at least a CT scan and many had a CT scan and surgery or a CT scan and an angiogram. To be included in a particular localization group, more than 50% of the lesion had to be involved in only one of the indicated areas. In addition, there could be no substantial involvement of the lesion in any of the other areas. Operationally, "substantial involvement" was defined as having more than one-quarter of the lesion involved in any other given area. Cases for whom this criterion could not be met were excluded from the sample.

The resulting eight localization groups were then compared on a number of demographic and treatment variables including education, length of hospitalization, age at onset, chronicity, number of previous hospitalizations, number of surgeries, presence of peripheral auditory or motor impairments, evidence of hemiplegia, hemianopsia, or quadrantanopsia and age at time of testing. There were no significant differences among the patient groups on any of these variables based on multiple F tests.

The average age of the groups was 43.1 years, with an average education of 10.8 years. The average patient had been hospitalized 74.0 days and was tested an average of 210 days after the onset of the neurological condition. Overall, 30% of the patients were diagnosed as having hemiplegia and 20% were reported to have hemianopsia or quadrantanopsia. Of the 60 patients included in this sample, 20% had some peripheral auditory impairment, 10% had some peripheral visual impairment and 30% had some apparent peripheral motor impairment.

A discriminant analysis was completed using the 14 original scales to further estimate the ability of the LNNB to distinguish among these groups. Although it was recognized that an insufficient number of patients were available to legitimately conduct a discriminant analysis, it was felt that such an analysis would yield some information bearing on the effectiveness of the battery in discriminating among the various criterion groups. Overall, the discriminant analysis, using the scale raw scores alone, was able to localize 22 of the 24 right hemisphere cases and 29 of the 36 left hemisphere cases. Details on the lateralization and localization of brain deficits with the patterns found in this initial study are presented in Chapter 5.

To further determine the clinical utility of the LNNB, in addition to its statistical accuracy, classification of 78 cases was attempted on the basis of the 14 clinical and summary scales alone. Of these 78 cases, 40 were brain-injured, 20 were psychiatric cases and 18 were normal controls. In the initial test of the battery, the senior author (Golden) was able to correctly classify 70 of the 78 cases as either brain damaged or not. Errors made included four cases of chronic schizophrenia who showed extensive neuropsychological deficits on the test. (Such cases may represent brain injury even though no definitive evidence can be found.) For the brain-injured patients, 34 of the 40 patients were correctly classified as left, right or diffuse. Of 24 cases with lateralized damage, localization of injury to one of the four quadrants described above was accurate in 22 cases.

In follow-up to this study, Golden, Moses, Fishburne, et

al. (1981) compared the scores of 87 patients with localized brain damage and 30 patients who served as normal controls. Each patient with a localized lesion was classified on the basis of a CT scan if 50% or more of the lesion fell into one of eight circumscribed areas (four in each hemisphere). No attempt was made to locate cases with pure localized disorders in each of the identified areas, because of both the infrequent occurrence of such cases in actual practice and their doubtful utility to the practicing clinician.

Using the rules developed by Golden, Moses, Graber, and Berg (1981), 86% of the patients were correctly classified as being either normal or brain damaged. Using the highest localization scale to determine the side of the lesion (e.g., if L5--Right Frontal was the highest scale, then the case was classified as a right hemisphere lesion), 92% of the brain-injured cases were correctly classified as to side of lesion. Errors were made most frequently in the cases of injuries with strong subcortical localization which tend to be called right hemisphere in spite of actual lateralization (such cases were rare in this sample because of case selection procedures) and in the case of patients for whom there were two or more equally elevated localization scales which suggested different lateralizations.

For localization, using the highest localization scale as the criterion, 84% of the patients were correctly classified by quadrant and the correct hemisphere; using the CT scan as the validation criterion, 74% of the cases were assessed correctly in terms of localization. In addition, a multivariate analysis of variance showed that either the localization or clinical scales could discriminate at a high level among the localized and normal groups.

Discriminating Schizophrenia versus Brain Damage

One of the most controversial areas within clinical psychology is the relationship of schizophrenia to brain damage. As will be seen in the following studies, currently available research suggests that there is an inconsistent relationship between the LNNB and brain damage in schizophrenia, with some schizophrenics showing signs of brain damage and others not. Results across various samples have been both encouraging for the battery as well as confusing; as a result, they must be regarded as only tentative.

Purisch, Golden, and Hammeke (1978) examined the effectiveness of the LNNB in discriminating between a chronic schizophrenic population and neurological patients. This was considered an especially important study because chronic schizophrenic groups are traditionally difficult to discriminate from brain-injured patients (Golden, 1977, 1978). This study used the same neurological group described by Golden, Hammeke, and Purisch (1978).

The schizophrenic patients included a mixture of different diagnostic subtypes: catatonic (n=2); hebephrenic (n=3); paranoid (n=19); simple (n=1); undifferentiated (n=20); and schizoaffective (n=5). The schizophrenic patients had an average age of 41.3 years (SD=14.5) and an average educational level of 11.3 years (SD=2.6). At the time of testing, the schizophrenics had been hospitalized for an average of 410.4 days (SD=1,569). Their average chronicity, as measured from their first hospitalization to the time of testing, was 121 months (SD=135). Average age at the time of first hospitalization was 32.1 years (SD=12.3). At the time of testing, the schizophrenic patients averaged 4.3 (SD=3.5) separate psychiatric hospitalizations.

The patients in the brain-injured group did not differ significantly from the schizophrenics in terms of age, education or length of current hospitalization. However, the brain-injured patients were significantly less chronic than the schizophrenics, had a later onset of difficulties and had fewer previous hospitalizations. The average age of onset for the neurological group was 39.4 years (SD=22.3) and their chronicity averaged 56.2 months (SD=116.4). Thus, the schizophrenics tended to be those patients from whom one might expect poorer neuropsychological performances on the basis of longer chronicity, earlier age of onset and more frequent hospitalizations.

All individuals classified as schizophrenic in this study had normal physical neurological examinations and EEGs. In addition, none of the schizophrenic sample had a history suggestive of brain injury, such as serious head trauma, stroke or other neurological disorders. Although the selection procedures may not have eliminated all brain injury in the sample, the selection procedures made the likelihood of brain-damaged schizophrenics in the sample as low as could be expected in a practical study using these techniques.

Two-tailed t-test comparisons on 282 measures found the schizophrenics to perform significantly better on 72 items at the .05 level (see Appendix C for the data on 269 items). The brain-injured group demonstrated better mean performance on two items. A stepwise discriminant analysis of the individual items achieved 100% accuracy in classification (brain-damaged versus non-brain-damaged) with only 40 items.

Subjects in the schizophrenic sample performed significantly better (p<.01) than the brain-injured patients on 10 of the clinical and summary scales. Four scales failed to show any significant differences between the groups. Again, a cutoff point that maximized the percentage of group classification was chosen for each scale. Hit rates in the schizophrenic group ranged from 34 to 92%, while those in the brain-damaged group ranged from 38 to 78%. Four scales yielding essentially chance hit rates were C2, C10, C5 and C11. When all 14 of the original clinical and summary scales were combined in a discriminant analysis, 92% of the schizophrenic group and 84% of the neurological group were correctly classified, yielding an overall hit rate of 88%. These hit rates are significantly more accurate than other hit rates reported in the published literature with a comparable population.

Moses and Golden (1980) replicated the results of the original study that compared schizophrenic and neurological patients. Using the same neurological sample described in Moses and Golden (1979), the authors obtained a sample of 50 schizophrenic patients. Twenty were diagnosed as paranoia, 23 as undifferentiated schizophrenia, 4 as simple schizophrenia, and 3 as schizoaffective disorder. The results of this study were quite similar to the results of the original study. Using the cutoff scores determined by Purisch et al. (1978), the authors found the cross-validation results of 8 of the 14 original scales to be slightly improved over the original study, while the results of the other scales were the same or slightly reduced in differentiating the groups. These differences, however, did not exceed chance. Overall, the cross-validation study yielded a hit rate of 87%, compared to the 88% of the Purisch et al. (1978) study. As in the previous study, all schizophrenics included in the present study had normal EEGs and normal physical neurological examinations. No significant differences were obtained between the groups in age, education or sex, although the samples did differ significantly in chronicity, with the psychiatric group demonstrating significantly more chronic symptomatology (M=112 months).

Since these initial studies, there have been a number of attempted cross-validations of this work. Puente, Heidelberg-Sanders, and Lund (1982a) compared 11 brain-damaged and 15 non-brain-damaged schizophrenics, with the diagnosis of brain damage based on neurological evidence. They found that 8 of the 14 original LNNB scales discriminated between the two groups. Of the failures, four were on the same scales found in the previous studies (C2. C5, C10 and C11), whereas the remaining two scales, C8 and C6, had discriminated between the two groups previously. In the same sample, the Whitaker Index of Schizophrenic Thinking (WIST; Whitaker, 1980) failed to discriminate between the two groups.

Using a larger sample, Puente, Heidelberg-Sanders, and Lund (1982b) compared 17 non-brain-damaged and 23 brain-damaged schizophrenics on all the original scales and all the items of the battery. The authors found that 109 of the items discriminated between the groups and all 14 scales were able to significantly differentiate the two groups. While the non-brain-damaged schizophrenics performed at a level consistent with that found in normal populations, the brain-injured groups scored well into the brain-injured range. It is equally clear that a combined group of unselected schizophrenics would fall between these groups, again similar to the early findings reported above.

Moses, Cardellino, and Thompson (1983) compared 50 patients with chronic schizophrenic or schizoaffective problems to 51 brain-injured patients. While patients were not separated into brain-damaged and non-brain-damaged schizophrenics, the patients were carefully screened for brain dysfunction and not included if so diagnosed. (Many of these patients were included in other studies in which they received CT scans which were normal when using the statistical criteria described later.) The authors found the chronic schizophrenics performed similarly to the normal subjects in other studies, while the average score for the brain-damaged patients was over 60T, although they were not as severely impaired as in some other studies. The authors reported a variety of hit rates using different criteria which ranged from overall hit rates of 73% (using the discriminant formula from a sample of Nebraska patients) up to 85% using a discriminant formula derived on this sample. The S1 scale alone achieved a hit rate of 78%.

A study by Shelly and Goldstein (1983) was able to only partially replicate the results discussed above. In a study comparing 30 chronic schizophrenics and 30 brain-damaged patients matched on demographic variables, the groups differed only on S1. A discriminant analysis, however, correctly classified 90% of the cases. The authors observed that the mean profile of the schizophrenics in this study matched that of the earlier studies by Golden and his various collaborators, while the brain-injured patients performed substantially better than in those studies. This better performance accounted for the general lack of group differences.

In all these studies, it is clear that different subpopulations of schizophrenics perform differently on the LNNB, with some showing clear signs of brain damage while others appear to be normal. Golden and his associates, in a series of articles, have attempted to study these differences to see if they are predictive of CT scan variables (Golden, Graber, et al., 1980; Golden, MacInnes, et al., 1982; Golden, Moses, Zelazowski, et al., 1980). Without reviewing the methodology in great detail, the studies suggest that LNNB scores become increasingly impaired as objective measures of ventricular size expressed as a percentage of brain size (called "ventricular brain ratio") increase. It appears that schizophrenics with valid testings who fall into the brain-injured range are much more likely to show CT scan signs of brain dysfunction as measured by objective measures, although these signs must be considered, at best, mild by qualitative standards of reading the CT scan. Golden has theorized that this may reflect a developmental abnormality of the brain rather than actual damage to the brain. This research has recently been summarized in Golden, Moses, Coffman, Miller, and Strider (1983).

Using the above rules, Moses (1983c) classified the LNNB results of a group of 100 schizophrenics without evidence of neurologic impairment into three groups: no cognitive impairment, borderline impairment and cognitive impairment. The three groups did not differ significantly from each other on any of the demographic variables investigated. Multivariate analysis of variance, as well as univariate analysis for each of the 14 scales, were significant, providing additional evidence for the existence of schizophrenic subgroups. In summary, the nonimpaired group performed significantly better than the impaired group on all scales and significantly better than the borderline group on all but the two language and three academic scales. Comparison of the borderline and impaired group performances revealed the former to be significantly less impaired on only the C5, C6, C7, C8 and S3 scales.

Moses (1984e) investigated the validity of combining schizophrenic and schizoaffective patients into one group, as has been done in previous studies. He compared the scores of a group of 21 patients diagnosed as having schizoaffective disorders with those of 85 patients who had been diagnosed as having either paranoid, undifferentiated or residual schizophrenia. All patients were classified according to DSM-III. No significant differences between the two groups on demographic variables or on the 14 LNNB scales were found.

LNNB PATTERNS IN SPECIFIC GROUPS

Alcoholism

Several studies have examined the relationship between LNNB patterns and specific disorders. An initial study (Chmielewski & Golden, 1980) compared 40 male alcoholics to 40 male control subjects. In general, the degree of alcoholism was not severe; none of the subjects had well-defined neurological symptoms such as ataxia. Still, differences were found between the groups on C4, C5, C9, C10, C11 and S1. More recent (as yet unpublished data have suggested that these scales may only be the earliest to be affected. In more chronic cases, more general and severe elevations are seen.

A study by Zelazowski et al. (1981) suggests more specific relationships between the LNNB and alcoholism. Zelazowski et al. measured the size of ventricles on the CT scans of 25 alcoholics. These were then correlated with each of the original 14 LNNB scales. Significant correlations (adjusted for age and education) were found on C1, C4, C6, C10, C11 and S1. All the significant correlations were between .46 and .58. The multiple correlations between all of this set of scales and ventricular size was .70 (p<.05). The results demonstrate that LNNB scale elevations are related to at least one clearly identifiable physiological anomaly which is commonly associated with certain types of neurological dysfunction. It should be noted again that this group as a whole represented mild to moderate alcoholics. The maximum measure of ventricular size for a patient in this study was 21%, well over the 95% confidence level for normals (10%) but also well under scores of 30 to 40% or more seen in severe alcoholics with prominent neurological deficits.

De Obaldia, Leber, and Parsons (1981) found mild but consistent deficits across most of the LNNB scales in a study of 3- and 11-week abstinent alcoholics. The 3-week abstinent group differed from the 11-week group only on C2, with differences from the normal controls much larger for both groups. The results suggest a mild, generalized dysfunction which persisted at least through the eleventh week of abstinence.

Teem (1981) compared the LNNB results of a group of alcoholics with a group of patients who had suffered head trauma and a group of normal controls. Most of the alcoholics had a history of drinking for over 10 years. Except for being somewhat older, the alcoholic group did not differ significantly from the other two groups on any of the recorded demographic variables. When compared to the normals, they performed significantly worse on 7 of the original LNNB scales. The LNNB profile for this group was somewhat similar to that obtained in the De Obaldia et al. (1981) study. However, the alcoholics performed significantly better than the head trauma group on six of the scales. For the most part, their degree of impairment (as indicated by mean T-scores) fell into the mild range, with approximately one-third classified as brain impaired. The type of impairment exhibited by these individuals was characterized as diffuse.

Schizophrenia

Noting the usefulness of density numbers obtained by CT scanning as a measure of brain intactness, Wolf (1981) investigated the relationship between brain density and the LNNB in a group of 60 schizophrenic patients. All but 4 of the original 14 LNNB scales correlated significantly with the mean brain density value of the three largest CT brain slices for each subject. Also, 5 of the 8 localization scales correlated significantly with this measure. However, MacInnes (1981), using some of the same subjects from the MacInnes, Gillen, et al. (1983) study, was not as successful in his attempt to correlate the brain density value of a group of healthy elderly subjects (mean age = 70.7 years). Since only 12 of the 192 correlations between the eight localization scales and the 24 brain density values selected for the study were significant, the overall results were interpreted as nonsignificant.

Epilepsy

Berg and Golden (1981) compared the performance of a normative group of 40 nonneurological patients with that of 18 brain-damaged patients with epilepsy and 22 patients with epilepsy but for whom no specific brain injury could be documented by either history, neurological examination or radiological evaluation (idiopathic epilepsy). Significant differences were found between both epilepsy groups and the controls on all measures except C1 and C3, and the two summary scales comprised entirely of items from these scales, S2 and S3. In each case, the epileptic groups scored higher than the normative control group, suggesting impaired functioning. The only difference between the two epilepsy subgroups occurred on C1, on which patients with idiopathic seizures disorders were secondary to identified brain damage.

Multiple Sclerosis

Kaimann (1981) reported six significant and two borderline scale elevations on the mean profile of 50 multiple sclerosis patients. The results generally corroborate previous Halstead-Reitan findings with this group (i.e., findings of sensory and motor impairment in MS patients). With the addition of another subject, Kaimann, Knippa, Schima, and Golden (1983) investigated the relationship of LNNB scores with CT scan findings for a group of 51 MS patients. Eight measures derived from the CT scan investigation were used. These included the ventricular brain ratios, the mean width of the four largest sulci, the bicaudate ratio (the ratio of the width of frontal horns of the lateral ventricles in the caudate nuclei region to intracranial width on the CT slice with the largest lateral ventricle display), the bifrontal ration (the ratio of the width of the frontal horns of the lateral ventricles in the caudate nuclei region to the distance between the lateral edges of the two frontal horns) and four density readings (two contrast and two noncontrast) from the centrum semiovale. When the eight measures were factor analyzed, two factors emerged. The four density measures loaded highly on the first factor and the three distance (ratio) measures loaded highly on the second factor. It was therefore considered a third, separate measure on subsequent analyses.

The relationship between each of the clinical scales and each of the factors was investigated by computing partial correlations (controlling for age, education and sex). Twenty of the 33 correlations were significant at the .05 level. Except for C3, all the LNNB measures correlated significantly both with the distance factor and with the sulcal width index. Kaimann et al. indicated that the greater number of significant correlations between the LNNB scale scores and the various density measures (compared to the correlations with the distance and sulcal measures) is consistent with findings of density changes which are found when short-term clinical status changes occur.

With these subjects, Kaimann (1983/in press) also found that at least some of the LNNB scales were related to factors such as education, sex, length of illness, definitiveness of the presence of MS and its clinical course. Some of the scales were also significantly related to ratings on the Kurtzke Scales (Kurtzke, 1955, 1965) a frequently used tool designed to assess the degree of impairment in MS patients.

Huntington's Chorea

Moses, Golden, Berger, and Wisniewski (1981) compared 5 patients with recently diagnosed Huntington's disease with 8 patients whose onset was between 36 and 66 months prior to testing, 6 patients whose onset was greater than 72 months previous and 7 control patients equated for age and education. The results for the more chronic patient groups suggested clearly a diffuse disorder which increased in severity over time. The findings are consistent with an interpretation that the disorder develops in a progressive rather than abrupt manner.

Aging

MacInnes, Golden, Sawicki, Gillen, Quaife, Graber, Uhl, and Greenhouse (1982) correlated the LNNB and regional cerebral blood flow (rCBF) findings in healthy versus brain-damaged geriatric samples. Canonical correlations between the LNNB localization scales and the rCBF values indicated a significant amount of common variance between the gray flow measures and the localization scales. Much of this variance was accounted for by the left anterior gray flow and the right parietal-occipital, temporal and sensorimotor localization scales.

The effects of normal aging on neuropsychological functioning were investigated in two studies. Spitzform (1982) compared the mean LNNB T-scores of 13 elderly normals to those of 50 controls (mean age = 42.0 years) and the 50 brain-damaged patients (mean age = 44.3 years) reported in the LNNB manual (Golden, Purisch, & Hammeke, 1980). The elderly group had lower T-scores (i.e., performed better) than the brain-damaged group on each of the 14 LNNB scales, and lower T-scores than the Golden et al. normal group on eight of the scales. In the MacInnes et al. (1983) study, the LNNB results of a group of 29 young healthy adults (mean age = 28.0 years) and a group of 29 of the 78 healthy elderly adults (mean age = 71.4 years) were compared. Although both groups scored below their respective critical levels on all scales, the young group scored significantly better on all but three of the scales. The original 78 healthy elderly of this study were also divided into two groups: a younger geriatric group (mean age = 67.7 years) and an older geriatric group (mean age = 78.4 years). The two groups differed significantly on only two scales, with the better performance on these two being given by the <u>older</u> group.

Diabetes <u>Mellitus</u>

Strider (1982) investigated the incidence and severity of brain impairment associated with diabetes mellitus. Compared to a group of normal controls, more of the diabetics were classified as brain impaired (32% vs. 12%). Those subjects who developed the disease after the age of 25 showed a significantly greater incidence of brain damage and duration of disorder were significantly correlated, whereas history of low blood sugar and brain damage were significantly correlated in the late onset group.

Learning <u>Disabled</u>

In a study of dyslexia, Grey (1982) administered the LNNB to 21 individuals considered dyslexic and to a group of controls. The dyslexic group had previously been divided (according to their performance on the <u>Boder</u> <u>Reading</u> <u>Test</u> <u>of</u> <u>Spelling</u> <u>Patterns</u>) into three groups: dysphonetic, dyseidetic and mixed dysphonetic-dyseidetic. An analysis of variance indicated significant between-group differences on each scale. Not surprisingly, the control group showed the least impairment overall. The dyseidetic group was the least impaired of the dyslexic groups. The mixed group, on the other hand, was most impaired on all but one of the scales. Significant group differences were also noted on the lateralization and localization scales. As with the previous comparisons, significant between-group differences on all scales were noted. Again, the control group showed the least impairment and the mixed group the most. On the more specific indices, the dyslexics showed the most impairment on the left hemisphere scales, especially the left parietal-occipital and left frontal scales (L3 and L1).

Parolini (1982/1983) tested the adequacy of the LNNB in discriminating two groups of learning-disabled adolescents from each other and from a group of normal controls. Separate reading-, spelling-, and arithmetic-disabled groups were classified on the basis of discrepancies between their WRAT scores and scores on the <u>Wechsler</u> <u>Intelligence</u> <u>Scale</u> <u>for</u> <u>Children-Revised</u> (WISC-R; Wechsler, 1974) or the WAIS. The normal sample performed significantly better than one or both of the learning-disabled groups on all 11 clinical scales and the eight localization scales. In addition, the group who had difficulty with arithmetic scored significantly better than the reading- and spelling-disabled groups on five of the clinical scales and four of the localization scales. In determining the power of the clinical and localization scales to discriminate whether or not an individual was classified as learning disabled, Parolini found that the two sets of scales combined accurately classified 95% to 97% of the subjects. Hit rates of 95% and 77% were achieved when the clinical scales and localization scales, respectively, were used to predict membership in the three groups. The S1 scale also successfully discriminated among the three learning-disabled groups (p<.001). However, contrary to predictions, the two learning-disabled groups did not differ significantly in their scores on the two hemisphere scales (S2 and S3).

Assaultive Behavior

Several studies have investigated the relationship between assaultive behavior and neuropsychological functioning. Bryant (1982/1983), in evaluating a group of incarcerated criminals, found significant differences between the performance of violent and nonviolent criminals on 11 of the LNNB scales. The violent group had more deviant responses in general. More of the violent group were also classified as brain impaired by the LNNB criteria (67% vs. 37% for the nonviolent group). On 13 of the scales, the impaired group performed significantly poorer. Also, inmates less than 30 years old performed worse than the older inmates on all the scales, with their performance on eight of the scales significantly worse. Bryant noted that the violent group's performance suggested impairment of the tertiary areas of the posterior and left prefrontal portions of the brain, as well as the tracts which connect the prefrontal areas with subcortical structures.

In a similar study, Scott, Martin, and Liggett (1982) compared the LNNB results of 25 incarcerated males who had committed crimes against property (nonassaultive individuals). The mean profiles for each group were very similar to those from the Bryant study. The assaultive group's mean deviation score (obtained score minus the critical value for that individual) showed them to be significantly more impaired as a group than the nonassaultive group on all 11 clinical scales. Also, on average, the assaultive group had significantly more scales elevated above the critical level (excluding C7 and C9) than the nonassaultive group (4.59 vs. 0.31). A stepwise multiple regression indicated that the five best predictors of group membership were C11, C7, C2, C4 and the number of scales elevated above the critical level (excluding C7 and C9). The investigators interpreted the results as indicating a link between limbic system dysfunction and assaultive behavior.

The LNNB results of 110 subjects of the Bryant and Scott, Martin, and Liggett studies were combined in a subsequent study (Bryant, Scott, Golden, & Tori, 1984). The violent inmates performed significantly worse than the nonviolent inmates on all 14 scales. Also, of all the subjects classified as brain damaged by the objective criteria, 78% were classified in the violent group.

West (1981/1982) found that violent and nonviolent criminals differed significantly only on C9 and C11, possibly due to a smaller sample size and differences in classification criteria. The violent group performed better on both scales. A stepwise discriminant analysis accurately classified 72% of the total sample using only four of the scales. Also, a subgroup of rapists differed significantly from the remainder of the sample. West's violent group appeared to show frontal and temporal lobe impairment upon item analysis. McKay (1981) noted that a group of assaultive schizophrenics performed poorer than a group of nonassaultive schizophrenics on 11 of the LNNB scales though none of these differences was statistically significant.

The neuropsychological functioning of 36 males arrested for

forcible sexual assault was investigated by Scott, Cole, McKay, Leark, and Golden (1982). Subjects convicted of sexual assault performed significantly worse on the LNNB than a comparison group of nonpsychiatric, nonneurological (normal) subjects on 7 of the 14 scales. According to the LNNB criteria, 47% of the assaultive individuals scored in the brain-damaged range, while the performance of another 31% of this group was classified as borderline. The investigators then divided the experimental subjects into two groups: those who were arrested for forcibly assaulting adult victims, and those who were arrested for nonviolent assault of prepubescent children. A discriminant analysis of the LNNB, performed on the two sexual assault subgroups and a normal comparison group, correctly identified 68% of the normals, 64% of the pedophiles and 50% of the forcible sexual assaulters. As determined by the number of significant scale elevations, 36% of the pedophiles performed in the brain-damaged range and 29% fell into the borderline range. Of the group convicted of forcible sexual assault, 55% performed in the brain-damaged range and 32% were classified as borderline. The results support previous findings which suggest that forcible sexual assault may be linked to cerebral dysfunction.

Studies with some subgroups of violent psychiatric patients have resulted in unexpected findings. McKay, Golden, and Scott (1981) compared the LNNB results of small groups of auditory hallucinators, visual hallucinators, and nonhallucinators with each other. The diagnostic make-up of the groups was similar and all had histories of assaultive behavior. The visual hallucinators' mean performance was consistently lower than that of the nonhallucinators on all clinical and localization scales. In turn, the nonhallucinators showed less impairment, on average, than the auditory hallucinators on both sets of scales.

Unexpected findings were also noted by Scott, Cole, McKay, Golden, and MacInnes (1982) when the LNNB performance of schizophrenics with substance abuse histories was compared to that of nonabusing schizophrenics and normal controls. The nonabusing group scored significantly worse than the abusing and normal groups on all 14 scales. Eleven of their mean scores exceeded the critical level, while none of the scores from the other two groups did so. The normals performed better than the abusing group on all the scales. However, the difference between the two groups did not achieve significance on any of the scales. The authors explained these unusual findings as possibly indicating that the substance abusers were misdiagnosed as being schizophrenics and were instead borderline personalities or undergoing a temporary toxic psychosis at the time of diagnosis.

Using the LNNB, Rogers (1983/in press) sought to determine whether a group of 20 antisocial inmates differed significantly from a group of 20 controls in terms of their neuropsychological functioning. Subjects were included in the experimental group who met the following selection criteria: (a) met the formal diagnostic criteria for Antisocial Personality, as set forth in the DSM-III; (b) had one conviction with time served to every three arrests; and (c) had at least three charges with no violent crimes. The two groups did not differ significantly in terms of the demographic variables investigated. Although neither of the two groups' mean scores was indicative of neuropsychological dysfunction, the antisocial group performed worse than the controls on each of the 14 original scales. On six of these scales, these group differences were statistically significant.

Other Specific Disorders

Several additional studies have looked at specific disorders within single subjects. These include studies of a hyperactive adolescent with a subcortical brain pathology (Newlin & Tramontana, 1980) and a case of a temporal lobe injury in a patient with right rather than left hemisphere dominance (Larrabee & Kane, 1982). Moses and Schefft (1983) reported the LNNB results of a man with a right lateral pons infarction. In light of the patient's history and symptoms, the findings of clear motor impairment with relatively mild concomitant tactile deficits were consistent with the locus of the lesion.

Golden, Strider, Strider, Moore, and Gust (1979) used the LNNB to show the effects of secondary syphilitic infection at the beginning of and subsequent to treatment. MacInnes (1982) reported a pattern of progressive cognitive deterioration in an Alzheimer's disease patient as measured by the LNNB profiles obtained during two testings. Two cases of posterior parietal arteriovenous malformation (AVM) were studied by Conley, Moses, and Helle (1980). Both patients initially showed a similar pattern of deficits on the LNNB which was consistent with Luria's theory of cerebral organization. Noting previous findings of a relationship between aberrant sexual behavior and brain lesions, Graber, Hartman, Coffman, Huey, and Golden (1982) sought to determine the incidence of brain dysfunction in a group of six mentally disordered sex offenders. The LNNB identified three of the patients as being impaired. The results generally indicated frontal and temporal lobe deficit for these patients and subsequently supported previous assumptions of localization of dysfunction for such a group.

Webster and Scott (1983) used the LNNB along with other tests to confirm the presence of a reported concentration deficit in a 24-year-old man who had sustained a closed head injury. Bellur and Herman (1984) were able to demonstrate the effect of anticonvulsants on short-term memory, concentration and attention in a 20-year-old male whose epilepsy had resolved. The residual effects of exposure to a neurotoxic compound (trichloroethylene) or neuropsychological functioning were investigated by Steinberg (1981) using the LNNB and other measures of cognitive functioning. Sweet (1983) demonstrated the effects of depression on LNNB performance, among other neuropsychological measures. Several case investigations have also been reported in Golden, Hammeke, et al. (1982), Moses, Golden, Ariel, and Gustavson, (1983) and Moses, Golden, Wilkening, McKay, and Ariel (1983).

COMPARISONS WITH OTHER TESTS

In the development of any test, an important research aspect is the correlation of the battery with other tests. By theoretical predictions of the hypothesized relationships, construct validity may be ascertained or the data can be used to simply establish concurrent validity. To date, most of the research involving the LNNB has concentrated on its relationship to the Halstead-Reitan, the WAIS and the WAIS-R.

Halstead-Reitan Comparisons

The introduction of a new test battery generally requires comparison studies to older test batteries designed to measure the same underlying traits or abilities. Some comparisons between the LNNB and the Halstead-Reitan are clear: The LNNB takes about 2 1/2 hours to administer as compared to 6 to 8 hours for the Halstead-Reitan (including the WAIS). In general, the LNNB takes about one-third as much time as the Halstead-Reitan for the same individual. In addition, the LNNB requires much less equipment and capital investments.

Beyond the obvious comparisons lies the question of diagnostic efficiency. An initial attempt at answering this question was made by Kane, Sweet, Golden, Parsons, and Moses (1981). The authors compared diagnostic accuracy of the LNNB and Halstead-Reitan in classifying as brain-damaged or non-brain-damaged 45 difficult-to-diagnose individuals. The authors found that the batteries (interpreted by an expert at each procedure) agreed on 37 of the 45 cases. In the remaining 8 cases, the LNNB diagnosed 5 cases correctly and the Halstead-Reitan 3 cases. Clearly, under the conditions of this study, the batteries were essentially equivalent.

Studies like this, of course, can be criticized on the grounds that they are testing the "expert interpreters" rather than the test batteries themselves. One way to get around this is to rephrase the initial question about diagnostic efficiency to a question of whether the tests measure the same skills in the individual. If they do, one should be able to predict the scores of one battery from the other. If this is the case, then one in turn should be able to draw the same conclusions from the two batteries if they are properly analyzed. However, if the batteries cannot be predicted from one another, then one or both contain unique information that must be assessed for its importance.

Golden, Kane, Sweet, Moses, Cardellino, Templeton, Vicente, and Graber (1981) examined this question using 108 subjects who had taken both the LNNB and the Halstead-Reitan. The subjects ranged from intellectually superior, normal controls to patients with moderate brain damage. In some cases, diagnoses were not clearly established but diagnoses were not necessary for this study.

The 14 major LNNB scores were compared against the 15 major Halstead-Reitan scores as selected from Russell, Neuringer, and Goldstein (1970). These included the following subtests: Category Test, Tactual Performance Test (total Time, Memory, Location), Speech-Sounds, Rhythm, Trail Making Test (parts A and B), Finger Tapping (Left and Right), Aphasia (total score), Sensory-Perceptual, and the WAIS Verbal, Performance, and Full Scale IQs. Multiple correlations were then run between each test and all the tests of the other battery. The multiple Rs ranged from .67 to .95 with a median in the .80s. The lowest multiple correlation was with Finger Tapping (dominant hand). However, it was found that, using the seven LNNB speed items that are analogous to Finger Tapping, these correlations could be raised to about .85. This would make the lowest correlation 0.72. Of interest in the resulting correlation matrix is the relationship between the LNNB and obtained WAIS IQ scores: Cll correlated .84 with Verbal IQ while C4 correlated .85 with Performance IQ. The average LNNB score correlated .83 with Full Scale IQ. For a variety of reasons, the average LNNB score is the most stable estimate of current Full Scale IQ. However, the use of the Cll scale to estimate general intellectual ability has been well documented (McKay, Golden, Moses, et al., 1981; Prifitera & Ryan, 1981). Although the LNNB is more predictive of IQ than most abbreviated IQ tests now in use, IQ estimates based on the full LNNB or on Cll alone are truncated at the upper levels of intelligence. The relationship between the LNNB and the Wechsler scales is discussed in more detail below.

Vicente et al. (1980) investigated the relationship of the LNNB to the Halstead-Reitan with a group of subjects with and without brain damage, and some for whom no clear diagnosis had been established (26 in each group). All were administered the LNNB and portions of the Halstead-Reitan and the results of the subtests of both batteries were correlated. Many of the correlations were significant. Separate multiple correlations between the LNNB scales and each of the Halstead-Reitan subtests were highly significant ($p<.01$). The correlations ranged from a low of .71 (for the Categories Test) to a high of .91 (for Trail Making Test A).

Chelune (1982) felt that the overlap of the WAIS IQs with both the LNNB and the Halstead-Reitan reported by Golden, Kane, Sweet, et al. (1981) suggested that IQ contributed substantially to the relationship of the two batteries with each other in this same study. Using the same data, he partialled out the IQs and obtained partial c rrelations which were markedly lower than the correlations previously obtained. In response, Golden, Gustavson, and Ariel (1982) indicated that Chelune was correcting for a measure which is sensitive to brain damage. They suggested that correcting for premorbid IQ was more appropriate. Since education correlates considerably with premorbid IQ, this factor was subsequently partialled out of the original data. The resulting correlations were somewhat lower than the correlations reported originally but considerably higher than those obtained by Chelune after the WAIS IQs were partialled out. The authors noted that, although these correlations probably overestimate the relationship between the individual measures of both batteries, they are likely to be better estimates than those obtained by Chelune.

Kane, Parsons, and Goldstein (1983) investigated the statistical relationship of the first 12 LNNB scales and the same Halstead-Reitan subtests used in the Vicente et al. (1980) study (plus both dynamometer scores) using 46 brain-damaged and 46 control subjects. Multivariate analysis of variance of the T-scores for both sets of data revealed that the brain-damaged group was significantly more impaired than the normals on all but one of the 24 neuropsychological measures (nondominant dynamometer).

Comparison of the Halstead-Reitan mean T-scores and impairment ratings for both groups to those comparably constructed for the LNNB revealed a high level of agreement between the two batteries ($r=.78$ for the T-scores and the impairment rating). Using the combined median noninverted T-scores (for both groups) as a cutoff point, the LNNB was able to

accurately classify 87% of both groups. This compared to the
85% hit rate for both groups using the Halstead-Reitan median T-
score. The two batteries achieved the same hit rates for both
groups, respectively, when the median impairment rating for each
battery was used as a cutoff point. Separate discriminant
analysis of each battery using T-scores correctly classified 96%
of the subjects (100% of the controls and 93% of the brain-
damaged group) with the LNNB and 94% of subjects (95% of the
controls and 92% of the brain-damaged group) with the Halstead-
Reitan. When the mean T-scores and impairment ratings for the
LNNB were submitted to discriminant analysis, 86% of the
subjects (87% of the controls and 85% of the brain-damaged
group) were correctly classified. Using comparable measures
from the Halstead-Reitan data, discriminant analysis produced an
86% hit rate, with 91% of the controls and 80% of the brain-
damaged groups classified accurately.

More recently, Shelly and Goldstein (1982b) examined the
same intercorrelations in an independent sample of 125 brain-
injured patients. Their results were generally comparable to
those reported in the previous study. In addition, the authors
reported a correlation of .82 between impairment level from the
Halstead-Reitan and the LNNB average T-scores.

A more recent study (Kane, Parsons, Goldstein, & Moses,
1983) found that the two batteries were essentially identical in
their abilities to discriminate between a sample of 50 brain-
injured and 50 normal subjects. Kane et al. also found the
brain-damaged group to have significantly lower WAIS Verbal and
Performance IQs than the control group. These IQs correlated
from .64 to .78 with the summary measures of both batteries and
accurately classified approximately 85% of the sample when
entered into discriminant analysis. The authors noted that
these findings generally support Chelune's assertions (see
above) that overlap between the two batteries is largely due to
a common general intelligence factor.

Johnson, Moses, Cardellino, and Bryant (in press) also
developed a method to compute an overall LNNB impairment index
comparable to the Halstead-Reitan average impairment rating
(AIR) developed by Russell et al. (1970). This was based on
impairment ratings of 9 of the 14 original scales (excluding C7,
C8, C9, S2 and S3 scales) computed using the T-score standard
deviations of 62 controls and, subsequently, the standard
deviation of the sum of impairment ratings for an older group of
101 neurologic patients. Using a predetermined cutoff point
(based on the initial sample), the global LNNB rating produced
an overall hit rate of 90%. Using the number of scales above
critical level as the criterion, 86% of the total sample was
accurately classified compared to a classification rate of 92%
based on the discriminant function weights.

In cross validation, Johnson et al. used the LNNB results
of 34 neurologic patients and 25 significantly younger and more
educated controls. These 59 subjects represented a subset of
those used in the above Kane, Parsons, and Goldstein (1983)
study. The impairment index method was again compared to the
method using scales above critical level, as well as to the
Halstead-Reitan impairment index and AIR methods of
classification for these subjects. Neurologic, control and
total sample hit rates were 68%, 92% and 78%, respectively, for

the LNNB scales above the critical level method; 82%, 84% and 83% for the LNNB impairment index method; 85%, 88% and 86% for the Halstead-Reitan AIR method; and 79%, 84% and 81% for the Halstead-Reitan impairment index. The total hit rate using the LNNB impairment index did not differ significantly from those of the LNNB scales above the critical level or the Halstead-Reitan AIR method. Upon further investigation, the means of the LNNB impairment index and Halstead-Reitan AIR were identical and the two measures of global impairment correlated significantly with each other ($\underline{r}$=.79,$\underline{p}$<.01). Although the results are promising for the LNNB, the authors warn that the characteristics of the subjects studied warrant further investigation with samples who are older and who have disorders which might affect only small areas of the brain. The utility of the impairment index with individuals with severe psychiatric disorders also needs to be investigated.

Comparisons to the WAIS and WAIS-R

McKay, Golden, Moses, et al. (1981) compared the intercorrelations between the WAIS and LNNB in a sample of 280 mixed psychiatric, neurological and normal subjects. Correlations with the WAIS summary IQ measures were -.84 for Verbal IQ, -.74 for Performance IQ, and -.84 for Full Scale IQ for the C11 scale. (Note that since the LNNB and WAIS scores deviate in opposite directions, all correlations are in a negative direction.) IQ correlations with other scales were also high, ranging from -.81 (Verbal IQ with C9) to a low of -0.47 (Verbal IQ with C3). As expected, correlations with the individual WAIS subtests were lower. The LNNB-IQ correlations were cross-validated by Prifitera and Ryan (1981) who found correlations of -.86 for both VIQ and FSIQ, and -.76 for PIQ with scale C11.

Picker and Schlottman (1982) reported LNNB-WAIS correlations in a study employing only normal individuals. In this case, the higher correlations were somewhat lower than in the previous study, in the mid-.70s. This is due to an upper limit on the LNNB for estimating IQ in individuals with a "true" IQ of 115 or above. Above 115, there is essentially no LNNB-WAIS correlation.

Burkhart (1982) found that the WAIS Full Scale IQ significantly contributed to the variance of all 14 LNNB scales in a group of brain-damaged, psychiatric and medical control patients with below-average IQs after controlling for age, education, sex and diagnosis. However, the author did not present correlations corrected for age and educational level.

Preliminary work with the WAIS-R suggests similarly high correlations with the LNNB, with some minor differences in the correlations for specific subtests. Dill and Golden (1983) recently investigated the relationship of the original 14 LNNB scales for Form II with the 14 subtest and IQ scores for the WAIS-R. The LNNB and WAIS-R scores used in this study were those of a group of 12 brain-damaged patients, 16 psychiatric patients and 25 normals. Correlations between the LNNB and WAIS-R measures were generally higher than those found by McKay, Golden, Moses, et al. (1981) in their investigation with the WAIS. All were significant at the .01 level, and ranged from a low of -.33 between C1 and Object Assembly to a high of -.89, between C11 and Full Scale IQ. Of particular interest are the correlations between C11 and the Verbal, Performance and Full Scale IQs (-.86, -.88 and -.89, respectively). When age and education were partialled out, the correlations decreased to some extent. However, all but three of the 196 correlations remained significant (p<.05). The authors noted that, because of larger variances in the IQ scores than was found with the WAIS-R normative sample and the relative heterogeneity of the subjects used, these correlations are probably somewhat elevated. After for age and educational level, IQ accounted for about 35% of the overall variance of the LNNB scale scores.

Stepwise multiple regression analysis of the Dill and Golden data indicated that the C11 scale was the best predictor of all three IQ scores, all Verbal subtests except Digit Span and the Block Design subtest. Multiple correlations of the LNNB scales with each WAIS-R measure ranged from -.81 with Picture Completion to -.89 with Full Scale IQ. Regression equations, using C11 to predict the three IQ scores, were subsequently derived. These resulted in the correct classification of subjects into one of the four intelligence groupings used by McKay, Golden, Moses, et al. (1981) to a degree which was generally better than McKay, Golden, Moses, et al. were able to achieve (67% vs. 68% for Verbal IQ, 74% vs .65% for Performance IQ, and 74% vs. 68% for Full Scale IQ).

In an ambitious study, Shelly and Goldstein (1982a) attempted to confirm the previous findings of Prifitera and Ryan (1981) and McKay, Golden, Moses, et al. (1981) and compare the LNNB, the WAIS and the WRAT. They administered all three measures to 150 neuropsychiatric patients. Using selected T-scores for the 11 basic clinical scales of the LNNB, correlations with the WAIS and WRAT subtests were computed. Correlations with the WAIS and WRAT subtests were computed. Correlations with the WAIS subtests ranged from -.38 between C8 and Digit Symbol up to -0.73 between the two Arithmetic measures.

In general, the correlations were somewhat higher than those obtained by McKay, Golden, Moses, et al. WRAT and LNNB correlations ranged from -.33 between C4 and the Reading subtest to -.74 between C7 and Spelling. Factor analysis of the combined results of the three tests identified four factors with eigenvalues greater than 1.0. On two of the factors (one reflecting performance or nonverbal abilities, the other more verbally oriented academic abilities), measures from all three tests had high loadings. On the third factor, the C11 scale and four of the WAIS Verbal subtests loaded substantially, while only LNNB variables loaded significantly on the fourth factor. When age and education were entered into the analysis, five factors emerged. Four of the five were very similar to the four obtained from the first analysis. Only the WAIS Arithmetic and Digit Span subtests loaded significantly on the fifth factor but this factor was relatively trivial, accounting for only 3.75% of the common variance. Age was related mostly to performance or nonverbal abilities, while education was related mostly to academic and verbal abilities. The authors concluded that the three tests measured overlapping abilities through different approaches.

Comparisons With Other Tests

Ryan and Prifitera (1982), in a population of 32 psychiatric patients, found a correlation of -0.65 between the Wechsler Memory Scale (WMS; Wechsler, 1963) and the LNNB C10 scale. They also found a 72% agreement between the scales on identification of memory impairment. This is a surprisingly high relationship in light of the different contents of the two scales.

McKay and Ramsey (1983) found a similar correlation (-.60,p<.001) between the two measures of memory with a slightly older and less educated group of alcoholics. However, the correlation between the raw scores for C10 and WMS was much higher (-.82,p<.001). A regression equation to predict the WMS raw score from the LNNB C10 raw score was subsequently derived. Using this equation, the authors found an absolute mean difference of 4.3 points between the actual and predicted WMS raw scores for the sample investigated. When the five WMS subtest scores and the two predicted WMS raw scores for LNNB C10 factor scores were entered into a factor analysis, measures from both the LNNB factor scales loaded significantly on one of the two derived factors. This one factor seemed to reflect the ability to retain new information. On the other factor, two WMS measures of attention and concentration (Mental Control and Digit Span) loaded substantially, while neither of the two LNNB factors did so. This, along with the obtained correlations, led the authors to conclude that while both the LNNB C10 scale and the WMS are sensitive to the retention and attention components of memory, the WMS is more sensitive to the attentional aspect of this ability.

In addition to the concurrent validity studies reported above, preliminary correlations between the LNNB and several other measures also suggest generally high correlations of the various LNNB scales with the Peabody Individual Achievement Test (PIAT; Dunn & Markwardt, 1970), Benton Visual Retention Test (Benton, 1955), Wide Range Achievement Test (Jastak et al., 1965), Boston Aphasia Examination (Goodglass & Kaplan, 1972) and Peabody Picture Vocabulary Test (Dunn, 1970). These correlations are generally maximum in the range of .70 and .90 and follow the expected pattern of results, with PIAT and WRAT scores maximally correlated with the similar scales on the LNNB (e.g., Spelling with C7, Reading Recognition with C8, Arithmetic with C9, General Information with C11, and Reading Comprehension with C8 and C11). The Benton correlated highest with C4 and the Boston Aphasia Examination with C6 and C5.

Gillen, Ginn, Strider, Kreuch, and Golden (1983) recently investigated the relationship between the LNNB and the PIAT using brain-damaged, psychiatric and normal subjects. All the correlations between each of the LNNB's clinical, summary and localization scores and the score for the five PIAT subsections (Mathematics, Reading Recognition, Reading Comprehension, Spelling and General Information) were significant. Correlations between the LNNB's 30 factor scores and the PIAT scores ranged from .00 (between M2--Drawing Speed and the PIAT Reading Comprehension subtest) to -.86 (between RE1--Reading Complex Material and the PIAT Reading Recognition subtest). In general, the scales which correlated the highest with each of the PIAT subtests were those which would intuitively be expected to do so. Regression equations were also generated to predict raw scores for each of the five PIAT measures. The raw scores can be used, in turn, to generate age equivalents, grade equivalents and/or percentiles for the five achievement areas.

Finally, two studies (Erlandson, Osmon, & Golden, 1981; Osmon & Golden, 1981) correlated the MMPI and the LNNB. Patterns of relationships between the two tests were found. However, these patterns were complex, suggesting the absence of any simple relationship between the domains assessed by these two measures.

REFERENCES

Bach, P.J., Harowski, K., Kirby, K., Peterson, P., & Schulein, M. (1981). The interrater reliability of the Luria-Nebraska Neuropsychological Battery. Clinical Neuropsychology, 3(3), 19-21.

Bellur, S., & Herman, B.P. (1984). Emotional and cognitive effects of anticonvulsant medication. International Journal of Neuropsychology, 6, 21-23.

Benton, A.L. (1955). Benton Visual Retention Test. New York: Psychological Corporation.

Berg, R.A., & Golden, C.J. (1981). Identification of neuropsychological deficits in epilepsy using the Luria-Nebraska Neuropsychological Battery. Journal of Consulting and Clinical Psychology, 49, 745-747.

Bryant, E.T. (1983). The relationship of learning disabilities, neuropsychological deficits, and violent criminal behavior in an inmate population (Doctoral dissertation, California School of Professional Psychology, Berkeley, 1982). Dissertation Abstracts International, 43, 3182B.

Bryant, E.T., Scott, M.L., Golden, C.J., & Tori, C.D. (1984). Neuropsychological deficits, learning disability, and violent behavior. Journal of Consulting and Clinical Psychology, 52, 323-324.

Burkhart, W.A. (1982). The IQ factor in Luria-Nebraska test performance. Dissertation Abstracts International, 43, 518B. (University Microfilms No. 82-16, 115)

Cattell, R.B. (1950). Personality: A systematical theoretical and practical study. New York: McGraw-Hill.

Chelune, G.J. (1982). A reexamination of the relationship between the Luria-Nebraska and Halstead-Reitan batteries: Overlap with the WAIS. Journal of Consulting and Clinical Psychology, 50, 578-580.

Chmielewski, C., & Golden, C.J. (1980). Alcoholism and brain damage: An investigation using the Luria-Nebraska Neuropsychological Battery. International Journal of Neuroscience, 10, 99-105.

Cohen, J. (1960). A coefficient of agreement for nominal

scales. _Educational_ and _Psychological_ _Measurement_, _20_(1), 37-46.

Conley, F.K., Moses, J.A., & Helle, T.L. (1980). Deficits of higher cortical functioning in two patients with posterior parietal arteriovenous malformations. _Neurosurgery_, _7_, 230-237.

Davis, F.B. (1959). Interpretation of differences among averages and individual test scores. _Journal_ _of_ _Educational_ _Psychology_, _50_, 162-170.

De Obaldia, R., Leber, W.R., & Parsons, O.A. (1981). Assessment of neuropsychological functions in chronic alcoholics using a standardized version of Luria's neuropsychological technique. _International_ _Journal_ _of_ _Neuroscience_, _14_, 85-93.

Dill, R.A., & Golden, C.J. (1983). _WAIS-R_ and _Luria-Nebraska_ _intercorrelations_. Manuscript submitted for publication.

Duffala, D. (1979). Validity of the Luria-South Dakota Neuropsychological Battery for brain-injured persons (Doctoral dissertation, California School of Professional Psychology, Berkeley, 1978). _Dissertation_ _Abstracts_ _International_, _39_, 4439B.

Dunn, L.M. (1970). _Peabody_ _Picture_ _Vocabulary_ _Test_. Circle Pines, MN: American Guidance Service.

Dunn, L.M., & Markwardt, F.C. (1970). _Peabody_ _Individual_ _Achievement_ _Test_. Circle Pines, MN: American Guidance Service.

Erlandson, G.L., Osmon, D.C., & Golden, C.J. (1981). Minnesota Multiphasic Personality Inventory correlates of the Luria-Nebraska Neuropsychological Battery in a psychiatric population. _International_ _Journal_ _of_ _Neuroscience_, _13_, 143-154.

Gillen, R.W., Ginn, C., Strider, M.A., Dreuch, T.J., & Golden, C.J. (1983). The Luria-Nebraska Neuropsychological Battery and the Peabody Individual Achievement Test: A correlational analysis. _International_ _Journal_ _of_ _Neuroscience_, _21_, 51-62.

Golden, C.J. (1977). Validity of the Halstead-Reitan Neuropsychological Battery in a mixed psychiatric and brain-injured population. _Journal_ _of_ _Consulting_ _and_ _Clinical_ _Psychology_, _45_, 1043-1051.

Golden, C.J. (1978). _Diagnosis_ _and_ _rehabilitation_ _in_ _clinical_ _neuropsychology_. Springfield, IL: Charles C. Thomas.

Golden, C.J., & Berg, R.A. (1980a). Interpretation of the Luria-Nebraska Neuropsychological Battery by item intercorrelation: Items 1-24 for the Motor scale. _Clinical_ _Neuropsychology_, _2_(2), 66-71.

Golden, C.J., & Berg, R.A. (1980b). Interpretation of the Luria-Nebraska Neuropsychological Battery by item intercorrelation: Items 25-51 of the Motor scale. _Clinical_ _Neuropsychology_, _2_(3), 105-108.

Golden, C.J., & Berg, R.A. (1980c). Interpretation of the Luria-Nebraska Battery by item intercorrelation: The Rhythm scale. Clinical Neuropsychology, 2(4), 153-156.

Golden, C.J., & Berg, R.A. (1980d). Interpretation of the Luria-Nebraska Neuropsychological Battery: The Writing scale. Clinical Neuropsychology, 2(1), 8-12.

Golden, C.J., & Berg, R.A. (1981a). Interpretation of the Luria-Nebraska Neuropsychological Battery by item intercorrelation: The Tactile scale. Clinical Neuropsychology, 3(1), 25-29.

Golden, C.J., & Berg, R.A. (1981b). Interpretation of the Luria-Nebraska Neuropsychological Battery by item intercorrelation: VI. The Visual scale. Clinical Neuropsychology, 3(), 22-26.

Golden, C.J., & Berg, R.A. (1981c). Interpretation of the Luria-Nebraska Neuropsychological Battery by item intercorrelation: VII. Receptive Language. Clinical Neuropsychology, 3(3), 21-27.

Golden, C.J., & Berg, R.A. (1982a). Interpretation of the Luria-Nebraska Neuropsychological Battery by item intercorrelation: The Reading scale. Clinical Neuropsychology, 4(4), 176-179.

Golden, C.J., & Berg, R.A. (1982b). Item interpretation of the Luria-Nebraska Neuropsychological Battery: VIII. The Expressive Speech scale. Clinical Neuropsychology, 4(1), 8-14.

Golden, C.J., & Berg, R.A. (1983a). Interpretation of the Luria-Nebraska Neuropsychological Battery by item intercorrelation: The Arithmetic scale. Clinical Neuropsychology, 5,(3), 122-127.

Golden, C.J., & Berg, R.A. (1983b). Interpretation of the Luria-Nebraska Neuropsychological Battery by item intercorrelation: Intellectual Processes. Clinical Neuropsychology, 5(1), 23-38.

Golden, C.J., & Berg, R.A. (1983c). Interpretation of the Luria-Nebraska Neuropsychological Battery by item intercorrelation: The Memory scale. Clinical Neuropsychology, 5(2), 55-59.

Golden, C.J., Berg, R.A., & Graber, B. (1982). Test-retest reliability of the Luria-Nebraska Neuropsychological Battery in stable, chronically impaired patients. Journal of Consulting and Clinical Psychology, 50, 452-454.

Golden, C.J., Fross, K.H., & Graber, B. (1981). Split-half-reliability of the Luria-Nebraska Neuropsychology Battery. Journal of Consulting and Clinical Psychology, 49, 304-305.

Golden, C.J., Graber, B., Moses, J.A., & Zatz, L.M. (1980). Differentiation of chronic schizophrenics with and without ventricular enlargement by the Luria-Nebraska Neuropsychological Battery. International Journal of

Neuroscience, 11, 131-138.

Golden, C.J., Gustavson, J.L., & Ariel, R. (1982). Correlations between the Luria-Nebraska and Halstead-Reitan Neuropsychological Batteries: Effects of partialing out education and postmorbid intelligence. Journal of Consulting and Clinical Psychology, 50, 770-771.

Golden, C.J., Hammeke, T.A., & Purisch, A.D. (1978). Diagnostic validity of a standardized neuropsychological battery derived from Luria's neuropsychological tests. Journal of Consulting and Clinical Psychology, 46, 1258-1265.

Golden, C.J., Hammeke, T.A., Purisch, A.D., Berg, R.a., Moses, J.A., Newlin, D.B., Wilkening, G.N., & Puente, A.E. (1982). Item interpretation of the Luria-Nebraska Neuropsychological Battery. Lincoln: University of Nebraska Press.

Golden, C.J., Kane, R., Sweet, J., Moses, J.A., Cardellino, J.P., Templeton, R., Vicente, P., & Graber, B. (1981). Relationship of the Halstead-Reitan Neuropsychological Battery to the Luria- Nebraska Neuropsychological Battery. Journal of Consulting and Clinical Psychology, 49, 410-417.

Golden, C.J., MacInnes, W.D., Ariel, R.N., Ruedrich, S.L., Chu, C., Coffman, J.A., Graber, B., & Bloch, S. (1982). Cross-validation of the Luria-Nebraska Neuropsychological Battery to differentiate chronic schizophrenics with and without ventricular enlargement. Journal of Consulting and Clinical Psychology, 50, 87-95.

Golden, C.J., Moses, J.A., Jr., Coffman, J.A., Miller, W.R., & Strider, F.D. (183). Clinical neuropsychology: Interface with neurologic and psychiatric disorders. New York: Grune and Stratton.

Golden, C.J., Moses, J.A., Fishburne, F.J., Engum, E., Lewis, G.P., Wisniewski, A.M., Conley, F.K., Berg, R.A., & Graber, B. (1981). Cross-validation of the Luria-Nebraska Neuropsychological Battery for the presence, lateralization, and localization of brain damage. Journal of consulting and Clinical Psychology, 49, 491-507.

Golden, C.J., Moses, J.A., Graber, B., & Berg, R.A. (1981). Objective clinical rules for interpreting the Luria-Nebraska Neuropsychological Battery: Derivation, effectiveness, and validation. Journal of Consulting and Clinical Psychology, 49, 616-618.

Golden, C.J., Moses, J.A., Zelazowski, R., Graber, B., Zatz, L.M., Horvath, T.B., & Berger, P.A. (1980). Cerebral ventricular size and neuropsychological impairment in young chronic schizophrenics. Archives of General Psychiatry, 37, 619-623.

Golden, C.J., Purisch, A.D., & Hammeke, T.A. (1980). Luria-Nebraska Neuropsychological Battery: Manual. Los Angeles: Western Psychological Services.

Golden, C.J., Strider, F.D., Strider, M.A., Moore, G.F., & Gust, W.F. (1979). Neuropsychological effects of acute syphilitic involvement of the central nervous system: A case report. *Clinical Neuropsychology*, 1(3), 24-27.

Goodglass, H., & Kaplan, E. (1972). *Boston Diagnostic Aphasia Examination*. Philadelphia: Lea & Febiger.

Graber, B., Hartman, K., Coffman, J.A., Huey, C.J., & Golden, C.J. (1982). Brain damage among mentally disordered sex offenders. *Journal of Forensic Sciences*, 27, 135-134.

Grey, P.T. (1982). A neuropsychological study of dyslexia using the Luria-Nebraska Neuropsychological Battery. *Dissertation Abstracts International*, 34, 1236B. (University Microfilms No. 82-16,284)

Hammeke, T.A., Golden, C.J., & Purisch, A.D. (1978). A standardized, short, and comprehensive neuropsychological test battery based on the Luria neuropsychological evaluation. *International Journal of Neuroscience*, 8, 135-141.

Jastak, J.F., Jastak, S.R., & Bijou, S.W. (1965). *Wide Range Achievement Test*. Wilmington: Guidance Associates of Delaware.

Johnson, G.L., & Moses, J.A. (1984). An empirical evaluation of the decision-tree procedure for the Luria-Nebraska Neuropsychological Battery. *International Journal of Clinical Psychology*, 6, 98-102.

Johnson, G.L., Moses, J.A., Cardellino, J.P., & Bryant, E. (in press). Development of an impairment index for the Luria-Nebraska Neuropsychological Battery. *International Journal of Clinical Psychology*.

Kaimann, C. (1981). *A neuropsychological investigation of multiple sclerosis*. Paper presented at the meeting of the American Psychological Association, Los Angeles.

Kaimann, C.R. (in press). A neuropsychological investigation of multiple sclerosis (Doctoral dissertation, University of Nebraska, Lincoln, 1983). *Dissertation Abstracts International*.

Kaimann, D., Knippa, J., Schima E., & Golden, C.J. (1983). *Relationship of performance on the Luria-Nebraska Neuropsychological Battery to CT-scan findings in multiple sclerosis patients*. Manuscript submitted for publication.

Kane, R.L., Parsons, O.A., & Goldstein, G. (1983). *Statistical relationships and discriminative accuracy of the Halstead-Reitan, Luria-Nebraska and Wechsler IQ scores*. Manuscript submitted for publication.

Kane, R.L., Parsons, O.A., Goldstein, G., & Moses, J.A., Jr. (1983). *Further comparisons of the relative diagnostic accuracy of the Halstead-Reitan and Luria-Nebraska neuropsychological test batteries*. Paper presented at the meeting of the International Neuropsychological Society, Mexico City.

Kane, R.L., Sweet, J.J., Golden, C.J., Parsons, O.A., & Moses,

J.A. (1981). Comparative diagnostic accuracy of the Halstead-Reitan and standardized Luria-Nebraska Neuropsychological Batteries in a mixed psychiatric and brain-damaged population. Journal of Consulting and Clinical Psychology, 49, 484-485.

Larrabee, G.J., & Kane, R.L. (1982). Neuropsychological analysis of a case of crossed aphasia: Implications for reversed laterality. Journal of Clinical Neuropsychology, 4, 131-142.

Lewis, G.P., Golden, C.J., Moses, J.A., Osmon, D.C., Purisch, A.D., & Hammeke, T.a. (1979). Localization of cerebral dysfunction with a standardized version of Luria's neuropsychological battery. Journal of Consulting and Clinical Psychology, 47, 1003-1019.

Luria, A.R. (1980). Higher cortical functions in man (2nd ed.). York: Basic Books.

MacInnes, W.D. (1981). Aging and its relationship to neuropsychological and neurological measures. Paper presented at the meeting of the National Academy of Neuropsychologists, Orlando, FL.

MacInnes, W.D. (1982). the use of the Luria-Nebraska Neuropsychological Battery in the diagnosis of dementia. Paper presented at the meeting of the American Psychological Association, Washington, DC.

MacInnes, W.D., Gillen, R.W., Golden, C.J., Graber, B., Cole, J.K., Uhl, H.S., & Greenhouse, A.H. (1983). Aging and performance on the Luria-Nebraska Neuropsychological Battery. International Journal of Neuroscience, 19, 179-190.

MacInnes, W.D., Golden, C.J., Sawicki, R.F., Gillen, R.W., Quaife, M., Graber, B., Uhl, H.S., & Greenhouse, A.J. (1982). Aging, neuropsychological functioning, and regional cerebral blood flow: Interrelationships. Manuscript submitted for publication.

Malloy, P.F., & Webster, J.S. (1981). Detecting mild brain impairment using the Luria-Nebraska Neuropsychological Battery. Journal of Consulting and Clinical Psychology, 49, 768-770.

McKay, S. (1981). The neuropsychological test performance of an assaultive psychiatric population (Doctoral dissertation, University of Nebraska, Lincoln, 1980). Dissertation Abstracts International, 41, 4269B.

McKay, S., & Golden, C.J. (1979). Empirical derivation of neuropsychological scales for the lateralization of brain damage using the Luria-Nebraska Neuropsychological Test Battery. Clinical Neuropsychology, 1(2), 1-5.

McKay, S.E., Golden, C.J., Moses, J.A., Fishburne, F., & Wisniewski, A. (1981). Correlation of the Luria-Nebraska Neuropsychological Battery with the WAIS. Journal of Consulting and Clinical Psychology, 49, 940-946.

McKay, S.E., Golden, C.J., & Scott, M. (1981). Neuropsychological correlates of auditory and visual hallucinations. International Journal of Neuroscience, 15, 87-94.

McKay, S., & Ramsey, R. (1983). Correlation of the Wechsler Memory Scale and the Luria-Nebraska Memory scale. Clinical Neuropsychology, 5, 168-170.

Mikula, J.A. (1981). The development of a short form of the standardized version of Luria's neuropsychological assessment (Doctoral dissertation, Southern Illinois University, Carbondale, 1979). Dissertation Abstracts International, 41, 3189B.

Moses, J.A. (1983a). Revised ipsative comparison tables for the summary and localization scales of the Luria-Nebraska Neuropsychological Battery. International Journal of Neuroscience, 20, 189-192.

Moses, J.A. (1983b). Schizophrenic subgroups with normal and abnormal cognitive function on the Luria-Nebraska Neuropsychological Battery. International Journal of Neuroscience, 21, 129-136.

Moses, J.A. (1984a). Luria-Nebraska Neuropsychological Battery performance as a function of sensorimotor impairment in a brain-damaged sample. International Journal of Clinical Neuropsychology, 6, 123-126.

Moses, J.A. (1984b). Performance of schizophrenic and schizoaffective disorder patients on the Luria-Nebraska Neuropsychological Battery. International Journal of Clinical Neuropsychology, 6, 195-197.

Moses, J.A. (1984c). The relative effects of cognitive and sensorimotor deficits on the Luria-Nebraska Neuropsychological Battery performance in a brain-damaged population. International Journal of Clinical Neuropsychology, 6, 8-12.

Moses, J.A., Cardellino, J.P., & Thompson, L.L. (1983). Discrimination of brain damage from chronic psychosis by the Luria-Nebraska Neuropsychological Battery: A closer look. Journal of Consulting and Clinical Psychology, 51, 441-449.

Moses, J.A., & Golden, C.J. (1979). Cross validation of the discriminative effectiveness of the standardized Luria Neuropsychological Battery. International Journal of Neuroscience, 9, 149-155.

Moses, J.A., & Golden, C.J. (1980). Discrimination between schizophrenic and brain-damaged patients with the Luria-Nebraska Neuropsychological Test Battery. International Journal of Neuroscience, 10, 121-128.

Moses, J.A., Golden, C.J., Ariel, R., & Gustavson, J.L. (1983). Interpretation of the Luria-Nebraska Neuropsychological Battery (Vol. 1). New York: Grune and Stratton.

Moses, J.A., Golden, C.J., Berger, P.A., & Wisniewski, A.M. (1981). Neuropsychological deficits in early, middle and late stages of Huntington's disease as measured by the Luria-Nebraska Neuropsychological Battery. International Journal of

Neuroscience, 14, 95-100.

Moses, J.A., Golden, C.J., Wilkening, G.N., McKay, S.E., &
Ariel, R. (1983). Interpretation of the Luria-Nebraska
Neuropsychological Battery (Vol. 2). New York: Grune and
Stratton.

Moses, J.A., Johnson, G.L., & Lewis, G.P. (1983a). Reliability
analyses of the Luria-Nebraska Neuropsychological Battery factor
scales by diagnostic group: A follow-up study. International
Journal of Neuroscience, 21, 107-112.

Moses, J.A., Johnson, G.L., & Lewis, G.P. (1983b). Reliability
analyses of the Luria-Nebraska Neuropsychological Battery
summary and localization scales by diagnostic group: A follow-
up study. International Journal of Neuroscience, 21, 113-118.

Moses, J.A., Johnson, G.L., & Lewis, G.P. (1983c). Reliability
analyses of the Luria-Nebraska Neuropsychological Battery
summary, localization and factor scales. International Journal
of Neuroscience, 20, 149-154.

Moses, J.A., & Schefft, B.K. (1983). Report of a case of
alternating abducent hemiplegia studied with the Luria-Nebraska
Neuropsychological Battery. Clinical Neuropsychology, 5, 170-
171.

Newlin, D.B., & Tramontana, M.G. (1980). Neuropsychological
findings in a hyperactive adolescent with subcortical brain
pathology. Clinical Neuropsychology, 2(4), 178-183.

Osmon, D.C., & Golden, C.J. (1981). The relationship between
neuropsychological deficit and MMPI profile in chronic
schizophrenics. International Journal of Neuroscience, 13, 67-
74.

Osmon, D.C., Golden, C.J., Purisch, A.D., Hammeke, T.A., &
Blume, H.G. (1979). The use of a standardized battery of
Luria's tests in the diagnosis of lateralized cerebral
dysfunction. International Journal of Neuroscience, 9, 1-9.

Parolini, R. (1983). Reading, spelling, and arithmetic
disabilities: A neuropsychological investigation using Luria's
methods (Doctoral dissertation, University of Nebraska, Lincoln,
1982). Dissertation Abstracts International, 43, 1966B.

Picker, W.R., & Schlotmann, R.S. (1982). An investigation of
the Intellectual Processes scale of the Luria-Nebraska
Neuropsychological Battery. Clinical Neuropsychology, 4(3),
120- 124.

Plaisted, J.R., & Golden, C.J. (1982). Test-retest reliability
of the clinical, factor and localization scales of the Luria-
Nebraska Neuropsychological Battery. International Journal of
Neuroscience, 17, 163-167.

Prifitera, A., & Ryan, J.J. (1981). Validity of the Luria-
Nebraska Intellectual Processes scale as a measure of adult
intelligence. Journal of Consulting and Clinical Psychology,
49, 755-756.

Puente, A.E., Heidelberg-Sanders, C., & Lund, N. (1982a). Detection of brain damage in schizophrenics measured by the Whitaker Index of Schizophrenic Thinking and the Luria-Nebraska Neuropsychological Battery. Perceptual and Motor Skills, 54, 495-499.

Puente, A.E., Heidelberg-Sanders, C., & Lund, N.L. (1982b). Discrimination of schizophrenics with and without nervous system damage using the Luria-Nebraska Neuropsychological Battery. International Journal of Neuroscience, 16, 59-62.

Purisch, A.D., Golden, C.J., & Hammeke, T.A. (1978). Discrimination of schizophrenic and brain-injured patients by a standardized version of Luria's neuropsychological tests. Journal of Consulting and Clinical Psychology, 46, 1266-1273.

Reynolds, C.R. (1982). Determining statistically reliable strengths and weaknesses in the performance of single individuals on the Luria-Nebraska Neuropsychological Battery. Journal of Consulting and Clinical Psychology, 50, 525-529.

Rogers, E.B. (in press). Neuropsychological correlates of anti- social behavior (Doctoral dissertation, California School of Professional Psychology, 1983). Dissertation Abstracts International.

Russell, E.W., Neuringer, C., & Goldstein, G. (1970). Assessment of brain damage: A neuropsychological key approach. New York: Wiley-Interscience.

Ryan, J.J., & Prifitera, A. (1982). Concurrent validity of the Luria-Nebraska Memory scale. Journal of Clinical Psychology, 38, 378-379.

Sattler, J.M. (1982). Assessment of children's intelligence and special abilities (2nd ed.). Boston: Allyn & Bacon.

Sawicki, R.F. (1983). Comparative reliabilities for the Luria-Nebraska Neuropsychological Battery. Paper presented at the First Annual Conference on the Luria-Nebraska Neuropsychological Battery, Omaha, NE.

Sawicki, R.F., & Golden, C.J. (1984). Examination of two decision rules for the global interpretation of the Luria-Nebraska Neuropsychological Battery summary profile. International Journal of Neuroscience, 22, 209.

Sawicki, R.F., Maruish, M.E., & Golden, C.J. (1983). Comparison of alpha reliabilities of the Luria-Nebraska Neuropsychological Battery. Manuscript submitted for publication.

Scott, M.L., Cole, J.K., McKay, S.E., Leark, R., & Golden, C.J. (1982). Neuropsychological performance of sexual assaulters and pedophiles. In J. Cole (Chair), Psychological and neuropsychological concomitants of violent behavior. Symposium conducted at the meeting of the American Psychological Association, Washington, DC.

Scott, M.L., Martin, R.L., & Liggett, K.R. (1982). Neuropsychological performance of persons with histories of assaultive behavior. In J. Cole (Chair), Psychological and neuropsychological concomitants of violent behavior. Symposium conducted at the meeting of the American Psychological Association, Washington DC.

Shelly, C., & Goldstein, G. (1982a). Intelligence, achievement, and the Luria-Nebraska Battery in a neuropsychiatric population: A factor analytic study. Clinical Neuropsychology, 4(4), 164-169.

Shelly, C., & Goldstein, G. (1982b). Psychometric relations between the Luria-Nebraska and Halstead-Reitan Neuropsychological Test Batteries in a neuropsychiatric setting. Clinical Neuropsychology, 4(3), 128-133.

Shelly, C., & Goldstein, G. (1983). Discrimination of chronic schizophrenia and brain damage with the Luria-Nebraska Battery: A partially successful replication. Clinical Neuropsychology, 5(2), 82-85.

Spitzform, M. (1982). Normative data in the elderly on the Luria-Nebraska Neuropsychological Battery. Clinical Neuropsychology, 4(3), 103-105.

Steinberg, W. (1981). Residual neuropsychological effects following exposure to trichloroethylene (TCE): A case study. Clinical Neuropsychology, 3(3), 1-4.

Strider, M.A. (1982). Neuropsychological concomitants of diabetes mellitus (Doctoral dissertation, University of Nebraska, Lincoln, 1982). Dissertation Abstracts International, 43, 888B.

Sweet, J.J. (1983). Confounding effects of depression on neuropsychological testing: Five illustrative cases. Clinical Neuropsychology, 5(3), 103-109.

Teem, C.L. (1981). Neuropsychological functions in chronic alcoholism. Dissertation Abstracts International, 42, 791B. (University Microfilms No. 81-14,380)

Vicente, P., Kennelly, M.A., Golden, C.J., Kane, R., Sweet, J., Moses, J.A., Cardellino, J.P., Templeton, R., & Graber, B. (1980). The relationship of the Halstead-Reitan Neuropsychological Battery to the Luria-Nebraska Neuropsychological Battery: Preliminary report. Clinical Neuropsychology, 2(3), 140-141.

Webster, J.S., & Dostrow, V. (1982). Efficacy of a decision-tree approach to the Luria-Nebraska Neuropsychological Battery. Journal of Consulting and Clinical Psychology, 50, 313-315.

Webster, J.S., Dostrow, V., & Scott, R.R. (1984). A decision-tree approach to the Luria-Nebraska Neuropsychological Battery. International Journal of Clinical Neuropsychology, 6, 17-21.

Webster, J.S., & Scott, R.R. (1983). The effects of self-instructional training on attentional deficits following head injury. Clinical Neuropsychology, 5(2), 69-74.

Wechsler, D. (1974). Wechsler Intelligence Scale for Children-

Revised. New York: Psychological Corporation.

West, C.Y. (1982). Discrimination of violent and nonviolent inmates with the standardized Luria-Nebraska Neuropsychological Test Battery (Doctoral dissertation, California School of Professional Psychology, Berkeley, 1981). Dissertation Abstracts International, 42, 4218B.

Whitaker, L.C. (1980). Whitaker Index of Schizophrenic Thinking. Los Angeles: Western Psychological Services.

Wolf, B. (1981). Prediction of the Luria-Nebraska by changes in brain density. Paper presented to the meeting of the American Psychological Association, Los Angeles.

Zelazowski, R., Golden, C.J., Graber, B., Blose, I.L., Bloch, S., Moses, J.A., Zatz, L.M., Stahl, S.M., Osmon, D.C., & Pfefferbaum, A. (1981). Relationship of cerebral ventricular size to alcoholics' performance of the Luria-Nebraska Neuropsychological Battery. Journal of Studies on Alcohol, 42, 749-756.

BRIEF REVIEW OF THE NEBRASKA

NEUROPSYCHOLOGICAL EVALUATION (NENE)

Charles J. Golden

Department of Psychiatry
University of Nebraska Medical Center
Omaha, Nebraska

In any book using extensive case examples, there is the
issue of whether all readers are familiar with all the tests
employed, especially in an area like neuropsychology where there
are thousands of tests to choose from. The following is a short
description of the Nebraska Neuropsychological Examination
(NENE) since it is a very new test although based on the earlier
work with the Luria-Nebraska Neuropsychological Battery (LNNB).
Since the LNNB is better known and covered in the preceding
paper, it will not be covered here.

NEBRASKA NEUROPSYCHOLOGICAL EXAMINATION (NENE)

The Nebraska Neuropsychological Examination (NENE) is an
expansion of the original Luria-Nebraska Neuropsychological
Battery. The test contains 37 scales which represent expansion
of the factor scales on the LNNB plus additional areas of
testing not included in the original version. The test items
also cover a wider age range (from about age 4 or so upward),
thus effectively combining the childrens and adult version of
the LNNB. The test consists of considerably more items, but not
all items are administered to all patients. The test allows the
administrator to set ceiling and floor levels to avoid
unnecessary testing which is either too easy or to hard.

The 37 scales are augmented by five factor scales (scales
38 through 42, sometimes abbreviated as scales F1 through F5)
which represent scales derived from the factor analysis of the
original 37 scales. Unlike the original LNNB scales, the scales
of the NENE are much more factorially "pure" from a face
validity perspective. However, the need to be aware that any
scale can be missed for a variety of reasons must not be
forgotten in this or any other test.

Users familiar with the LNNB factor scales will recognize
many of the NENE scales. They will find additional scales that
expand the coverage of the test, adding capabilities to the
test. The following is a summary of the scales and factors:

The Scales

Scale 1. Bilateral Motor Coordination. This scale examines a variety of items requiring coordinated and speeded activity of the two hands or two feet. Scoring is dependent both on accuracy and speed.

Scale 2: Right Sided Motor Movement. This scale examines speed of the right hand.

Scale 3: Left Sided Motor Movement. This scale examines speed of the left hand.

Scale 4: Purposeful Motor Movement (Imitation). This scale examines the ability to do motor movements from imitation or verbal instruction. Accuracy rather than speed is emphasized in scoring.

Scale 5: Oral Motor Movement. This scale examines speed and accuracy of mouth movements.

Scale 6: Drawing. This scale evaluates drawing accuracy and speed, with a greater emphasis on accuracy.

Scale 7: Non-Verbal Auditory Processing (Tones and Patterns). This scale examines the ability to process rhythmic patterns and to discriminate tones. It is nearly identical to the LNNB Rhythm Scale.

Scale 8: Non-Verbal Sound Interpretation. This scale examines the ability to discriminate and identify complex sounds such as a whistle or a door closing.

Scale 9: Right Tactile Discrimination. Similar to the LNNB Tactile Scale, this subtest examines the ability to discriminate objects with the right hand as well as the ability to discriminate site and type of touch with single stimuli (such as the difference between up and down or strong and weak.)

Scale 10: Left Tactile Discrimination. This is identical to scale 9 but with the left hand.

Scale 11: Right Tactile Complex Pattern Discrimination. This scale evaluates the ability of the right hand to discriminate shapes, numbers and letters written on the back of the wrist.

Scale 12: Left Tactile Discrimination. Same as Scale 11 with the left hand.

Scale 13: Double Tactile Discrimination. This scale evaluates accuracy when two touches are involved either in different body parts (double simultaneous discrimination) or on the same part (two point discrimination.)

Scale 14: Visual Identification. This subtest involves the ability to decode pictures of varying difficulty and to identify the objects in the picture. Items vary from highly representational pictures to pictures which are overlapping or distorted.

Scale 15: Visual Spatial Analysis. This subtest involves
items which require analysis of a visual-spatial relationship
and angle discrimination.

Scale 16: Complex Visual Analysis. This scale requires
active manipulation of a spatial relationship which requires
intellectual analysis.

Scale 17: Connecting the Circles. This scale is similar to
the Trail Making Test, presenting somewhat abbreviated versions
of the test with performance limited to 60 seconds.

Scale 18: Phonemic Discrimination. This assesses the basic
ability to discriminate phonemes from one another. Patients may
respond by repetition, writing, or pointing.

Scale 19: Auditory Comprehension. This scale evaluates the
ability to understand and follow basic commands.

Scale 20: Complex Auditory Comprehension. This scale
involves the understanding of more complex grammatical
structures than Scale 19. These can include compound
statements, inverted grammatical structures, sequential
comparisons, and complex sentence structures.

Scale 21: Repetition. This is the first of the Expressive
Language scales, examining the ability to correctly repeat words
and sounds.

Scale 22: Expressive Naming. This scale examines the
ability to correctly name objects from pictures or descriptions.

Scale 23: Speeded Repetition. This subtest involves the
rapid pronounciation of words like "mustache" and sentences like
"Sandy seldom saw the sun."

Scale 24: Patterned Expressive Speech. The subtest
examines the patient when speaking patterned material such as
the alphabet.

Scale 25: Generation of Complex Expression. This scale
examines the ability to generate speech in response to a
picture, story, sentence, or other ambiguous source.

Scale 26: Motor Writing. This is the first of the
achievement subtests. This examines the act of motor writing of
words, phrases, and letters.

Scale 27: Spelling. This scale examines the ability to
spell independent of writing skills.

Scale 28: Reading Recognition. This scale examines the
ability to pronounce words properly from written material.

Scale 29: Reading Comprehension. A wholly new scale, this
subtest examines the ability to understand sentences of various
complexity.

Scale 30: Arithmetic. Similar to the LNNB Arithmetic
scale, this subtest evaluates arithmetic skills from simple
counting and number recognition to fractions and square roots.
The items involve written and mental calculations.

Scale 31: Non-Verbal Memory. This scale examines the ability to remember non-verbal patterns with and without interference.

Scale 32: Verbal Memory. This scale examines the ability to remember words and sentences with and without interference.

Scale 33: Stroop Color and Word Test. This is a direct adaptation of the Stroop, whose main task is naming the color of a ink that a word (RED, GREEN, or BLUE) is printed in. The test evaluates the degree to which the word interferes with the naming of the color.

Scale 34: Intellectual Analysis and Integration. This scale includes the patients ability to interpret pictures, organize scenes into a correct order, and find inconsistencies in pictures.

Scale 35: General Intelligence and Orientation. This scale examines basic vocabulary, orientation, proverb interpretation, category similarities and differences, and word arithmetic problems. The scale has much in common with general tests of intelligence.

Scale 36: Analogies and Comparisons. This scale examines the ability of the patient to understand analogies and comparisons such as opposites and categories.

Scale 37: Visual Intellectual Analysis. This scale is a more difficult version of Scale 16 which requires more active intellectual analysis of the spatial relationships which are seen on the pictures.

Scale 38 (F1): Basic Identification and Analysis. This factor involves scales which measure the ability to make simple recognitions and show basic understanding of speech and instructions.

Scale 39 (F2): Academic Achievement. This factor is analogous to an overall measure of academic achievement.

Scale 40 (F3): Visual/Motor Performance Skills. This factor represents a measure of spatial analysis and motor skills such as seen in drawing.

Scale 41 (F4): Complex Verbal Analysis. This factor involves higher level analysis and understanding of verbal material.

Scale 42 (F5): Kinesthetic Feedback / Integration. The final factor involves the ability to use tactile feedback for understanding of complex somatosensory stimuli.

coring the NENE

All scales of the NENE are assigned scores on the basis of the performance of 50 brain damaged and 50 intact individuals in the age range of 5-75. About one-third of the group was under age 16. Mean scores of this group were assigned an arbitrary value of 100. This score thus represents the midpoint between

the means of the brain damaged and the normal group. The
standard deviation of all scales was arbitrarily set at 10, so
that a score of 110 represents a performance one standard
deviation worse than the mean of the 100 reference patients.
High scores represent worse scores on all scales. All scales
also yield raw scores except for the factor scales.

Interpretation

All scores are compared to the patients critical level.
This represents the highest score the person should receive if
they are normally functioning for a given age and level of
education. This score is used in the same way and with the same
limitations as the critical level for the LNNB. Six or more
scales above the critical level is considered indicative of
brain dysfunction.

INDEX

Aging, 161
Alcoholism, 159
Alzheimer's disorder, 43
Assualtive behavior, 163-165

Brain, 40-42
  damage, 155-158
  function, 20

Children, 19-20
  brain injured, 41-42
Cognitive problems, 57-58
Credentials, 19
Criminal law
  neuropsychological testing,
    45
  neuropsychological defense,
    46
Court testimony, 18-19
Cut-off points, 10

Developmental sequencing,
  28-30
Diabetes Mellitus, 162
Deposition, 17-18, 105-138
Developmental issues, 92-93
Developmental stages, 30-33

Emotional problems, 57-58
Epilepsy, 160
Equipotentially approach,
  20-21
Etiology, 42
  Alzheimer's disorder, 43
  Frontal lobe damage, 43,
    45-46

Forensic issues, 66-68
Forensic neuropsychology, 1

Forensic reports, 15
  children, 19-20
  credentials, 19
  testimony, 17-18
Frontal lobe
  damage 43, 45-46
  prefrontal lobes, 27
  tertiary frontal lobes, 28
Functional systems, 22-28
Halstead-Reitan
  compared to Luria Nebraska
    Neuropsychological
    Battery, 166-169
Halstead-Reitan Neuropsycho-
    logical Battery, 12
Head trauma
  behavioral observations, 58,
    95
  cognitive and emotional pro-
    blems, 57-58
  developmental issues, 92-93
  forensic issues, 66-68
  Huntington's Chorea, 161
  interview and observation
    results, 50-51
  medical findings, 72
  medical treatment, 76-79,
    93-94
  neurological findings,
    71-72
  neuropsychological evalua-
    tion, 58-63
  pre-existing alcoholism, 65
  premorbid disabilities, 49
  referral and legal consider-
    ations, 79-80
  subtle residual symptoms, 75
  test results, 52-56, 68-71,
    82-85, 95-99